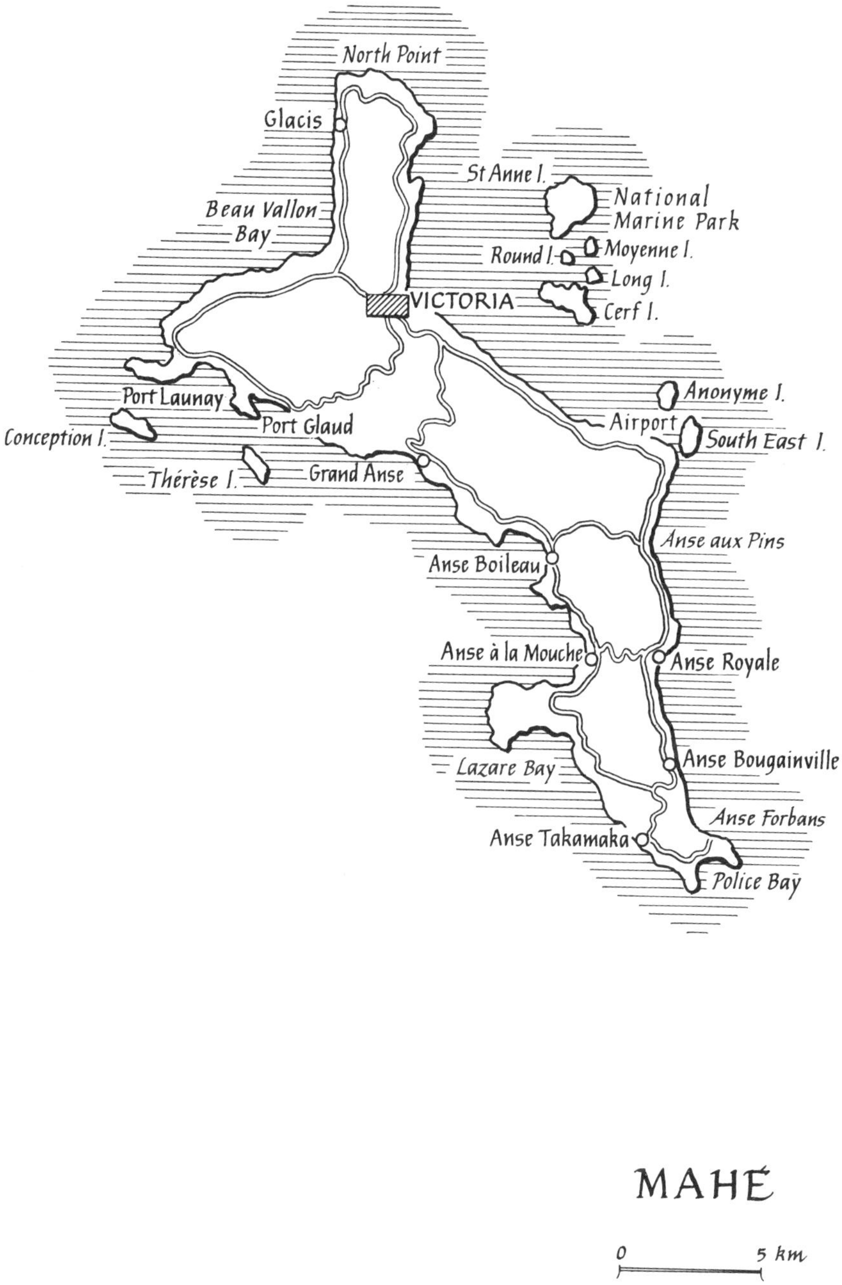
North Point
Glacis
St Anne I.
National Marine Park
Beau Vallon Bay
Round I.
Moyenne I.
Long I.
VICTORIA
Cerf I.
Anonyme I.
Port Launay
Airport
Port Glaud
South East I.
Conception I.
Grand Anse
Thérèse I.
Anse aux Pins
Anse Boileau
Anse à la Mouche
Anse Royale
Anse Bougainville
Lazare Bay
Anse Forbans
Anse Takamaka
Police Bay
MAHÉ
0
5 km

Paradise Raped

BY THE SAME AUTHOR

*Reflections and Echoes from Seychelles
Island Splendour*

James R. Mancham

Paradise Raped

LIFE, LOVE AND POWER IN THE SEYCHELLES

METHUEN

To my father Richard, my brothers Mickey and Philip, and my grandmother Roselmie – all too long departed.

First published in Great Britain 1983 by
Methuen London Ltd
11 New Fetter Lane, London EC4P 4EE

Copyright © 1983 James R. Mancham

ISBN 0 413 52900 2

British Library Cataloguing in Publication data
Mancham, James R.
    Paradise raped.
    I. Mancham, James R.   II. Statesman—Seychelles
    —Biography
    I. Title
    969'.6'0924   DT469.S4
    ISBN 0-413-52900-2

Printed in Great Britain by
Butler & Tanner Ltd,
Frome and London

Though nothing can bring back the hour
Of splendour in the grass, of glory in the flower;
We will grieve not, rather find
Strength in what remains behind;

Thanks to the human heart by which we live,
Thanks to its tenderness, its joys, and fears,
To me the meanest flower that blows can give
Thoughts that do often lie too deep for tears.

WILLIAM WORDSWORTH

List of Illustrations

between *pages* 128 *and* 129

1. Called to the Bar, Middle Temple, 1961
2. With my wife on our wedding day
3. Leading a demonstration against independence
4. Discussing the Indian Ocean's strategic importance with Senator Tower
5. Sir Bruce Greatbatch and I escort the Queen and Prince Philip
6. On the beach at Beauvallon, Mahé, with Olga Bisera
7. At State House, Mombasa, meeting Mzee Jomo Kenyatta
8. Sir Seewoosagur Ramgoolam provides a head of state's welcome
9. I become the Seychelles' first Prime Minister
10. Minister for External Affairs Chevan greeting me on arrival in Delhi with Helga Wagner
11. Meeting Indira Gandhi
12. With Adnan Khashoggi and his brother Essam
13. Attending the Non-aligned Conference, Sri Lanka, in 1976
14. Joachim Hasse introduces his Seychelles Brew to the Duchess of Gloucester
15. Independence: Albert René swears allegiance to the constitution
16. Dancing with the Duchess of Gloucester
17. At the Franco-African summit in 1977

18. President of the Malagasy Republic, Didier Ratsiraka, and I
19. Meeting President Marcos of the Philippines
20. Addressing a press conference after the coup
21. René poses with his guerrillas
22. Victoria on the first day of René's rule
23. My children, Richard and Caroline
24. With Catherine Olsen

Prologue

THREE FORTY-FIVE in the morning is a bad time for telephones to ring. Unless the caller is a beautiful woman or a close friend, and preferably both, telephones should be silent after eight in the evening. In the middle of the night it's usually trouble.

I was in a deep sleep, a heavy contented slumber in a suite in the Savoy Hotel, the guest of Her Majesty's Government, invited in my capacity as President of the new Republic of Seychelles to take part in the Queen's twenty-fifth Jubilee celebrations. It was 5 June 1977. In two days' time I was due to address the Commonwealth Heads of Government Conference, honoured to be chosen to answer Prime Minister Callaghan's speech of welcome. In addition I had my own guest beside me, sleeping prettily.

I reached for the phone, idly wondering who was calling, aware that hotel operators, especially such guardians of privacy as those at the Savoy, are reluctant to disturb their guests.

'President Mancham?' The tone of voice was apologetic. 'Mr Adnan Khashoggi has been trying to get in touch with you. Would you please call him urgently at his Paris number?'

Khashoggi? What on earth did he want? I had known him for several years and we had become the best of friends. I knew him as an astonishing character, one of the world's richest and most successful businessmen, and supposedly the model for and inspiration of Harold Robbins' book *The Pirate*. I gave the operator his number and as I waited for the call to come through I felt the first shiver of apprehension. Khashoggi was a busy man. He worked eighteen-hour days and did not waste much time sleeping, but he was not in the habit of phoning his friends in the middle of the night.

I was wide awake by the time the call came through and I snatched at the receiver. Adnan came straight to the point. He was sorry to wake me but there had been a coup in my country.

For a moment I said nothing, just blinked and shook my head, like a fighter who has taken a surprise punch. I think I said something like, 'This is no time for a joke.' Something like that, but my voice did not sound convincing even to myself. Adnan does not make such jokes.

Slowly and precisely he told me that he had been talking to the captain of his yacht, the *Khalidia*, which was moored in Port Victoria in Seychelles. The man had heard on his radio that shots had been fired and a curfew imposed. Adnan said that he would get back to me as soon as he heard anything more. I thanked him and hung up.

Shock has varying effects. Some people are anaesthetised and forget what has happened. Others think with unusual clarity. I remember staring for some time at a moth which was fluttering on the bedroom table. Then I slipped out of bed, pulled on a dressing-gown and padded out of the room, conscious of the pile of the carpet and the heavy silence of the night. Three sheets of paper lay on the drawing-room floor. It was my speech which I had worked on the previous afternoon. I picked it up and moved to the window, opened it and gazed out.

London was grey. The Thames moved sluggishly. The buildings on the south bank were a formless mass. The occasional taxi gurgled past beneath me. Everything seemed lifeless. I thought of home. It would be almost eight o'clock. The sun would have risen over the hills of Mahé, the main island. In the capital, Victoria, on a normal day, the shops and offices would already be opening, the town coming slowly and lazily to life.

I shivered, thinking of Adnan's words. They did not fit. Gunfire and curfew were words that applied to other places, troubled countries with crime statistics and dictators. The Seychelles were not like that. They were paradise islands. Some travellers had seriously suggested that the Garden of Eden was situated there. It was the land of song and laughter, islands in the sun, a place of *joie de vivre* and *plaisir d'amour*, of *laissez-faire* and *laisser-vivre*, of *coco-de-mer* and the giant tortoise. The Seychelles had always been described in the warm phraseology of the tourist brochure, not that of gunfire and curfews.

I glanced at my speech, at a passage I had underlined, something I had planned to emphasise to the Heads of the Commonwealth.

'It is really important,' I had written, 'for us to exchange views and learn from each other, to share our common experience, to examine present and future problems, to profit by the wise advice of one and constructive criticism of another. It's imperative that we find acceptable solutions by making use of the aims and quality of knowledge and reason in order to reach a higher level of communication, of co-operation, of trust...'

Trust! The word stuck in my throat. I screwed up the paper and threw it at the waste basket, thinking of Albert René, my Prime Minister. We were both Seychellois and both lawyers, but that is where the similarity ended. René is an introvert, quiet and steady, a man who works at a set pace, a methodical man. He had always advocated independence from Britain and thought that violence was a legitimate political weapon. For many years I had opposed him, firmly believing that a perpetuation of our links with Britain was the best way to keep our people free and our islands stable. His party had been funded by leftists in the Organisation of African Unity, but despite that, I had always beaten him at the polls. When independence was eventually pressed upon us, however, I formed a coalition government with him, believing that it would be in the best interests of our country for us to settle our differences and work together.

Only three nights earlier we had dined together at State House. He had brought his wife and we had discussed the approaching first anniversary of Seychelles as a sovereign republic. We talked about the plans for the celebration and went over the list of famous and interesting people whom we were to invite for the occasion. It included Adnan Khashoggi, Kirk Korkorian of MGM, Giano Agnelli of Fiat, Prince Talal of Saudi Arabia, Gunther Sachs, Peter Sellers, George Harrison and many others. They were all people whose arrival would confirm that the Seychelles had become the place for the jet set to indulge themselves.

It had been a pleasant evening. A boy with a guitar had serenaded us with my favourite song, 'La Paloma Blanca'.

The next day René had come to see me off at the airport. He had taken my arm, kissed me on both cheeks, wished me *au revoir* and *bon voyage*. As I recalled his embrace, I thought of Judas Iscariot. It would be René now, with his gun, in charge, pulling triggers and imposing curfews.

'Trust,' I said aloud. 'There should be a saying, "A fool and his trust are soon parted."'

I felt sick and began to blame myself. It was not as if I had not been warned. The American Chargé d'Affaires, Greg Matson, had warned me that René was plotting with Tanzania. Others had told me to watch out for him, but I had dismissed their warnings as paranoia.

Then there was Bruce McKenzie, the big South African who was Jomo Kenyatta's Ambassador at Large. He had come to visit me in April following a cable from Kenyatta and I had invited him to dinner at State House. Bruce was an adventurer, a burly man with a large handlebar moustache and a taste for the good life. A former fighter pilot, he had become a farmer in Kenya and the only white minister in Kenya's first independent government, earning himself the title of 'the white Kikuyu'. And he had made this trip especially to warn me about René.

He wasted no time coming to the point. 'This man,' he said, waving his fork at me. 'I must tell you, Jimmy, you will have to do him before he does you.'

I blinked at him, thinking that perhaps he had had too much wine, but he was deadly serious.

'What I am saying,' he continued, 'is that at two in the morning you must send someone to shoot the bastard.'

I blinked. 'Then what?' I asked incredulously.

'At four, you must get some of your most trusted police officers to plant some guns on his colleagues. Then, after all the bastards have been arrested, you appoint one of your favourite lawyers as magistrate to try the case.' He leant back in his chair and grinned. 'And you make sure that your magistrate is Mr Maximum.'

He left soon afterwards, leaving me a worried man. No-one had ever suggested such a short-cut solution to our problems. My immediate reaction was simply to dismiss his advice as melodrama, but that night I found that I could not sleep. Kenya was a thousand miles of ocean from the islands but nonetheless it was our most friendly neighbouring country. We shared a philosophy of free enterprise and were collaborating on a tourism package, something which had put me in the bad books of Nyerere of Tanzania and which had strengthened the link between René and the Tanzanians.

Now Kenya was giving me a warning. Neither Jomo Kenyatta nor Bruce McKenzie was a fool. They were not likely to give such a warning without good reason. They had shown me the way but I did not know if I could take it. For three nights I hardly slept. How could I possibly order the execution of a man who, to all outward appearances, was energetically collaborating towards the success of the coalition government? I could not do it. Such a thing was anathema to me. I am by nature a romantic who detests violence. I did not believe in it, nor had I any experience of it. I had never seen a shot fired. Like most of my people I am peaceful and happy-go-lucky. It was impossible for me to order someone's death.

I finally came to the only conclusion possible, that McKenzie's suggestion was a typically African solution to a typically African problem and that the thousand miles of ocean covered a million miles in attitudes. I had forgotten far too soon the bomb explosions, the arsons and general violence which had characterised René's party before the coalition.

And so I did nothing, and now I was suffering for it. My dream for Seychelles was a place of smiles and laughter with, under each coconut tree, a young man with a guitar. That dream had turned into a nightmare. The young men were under the trees all right, but with Russian-made machine-guns instead of guitars.

(A year later I heard that Bruce McKenzie had been assassinated on the orders of Idi Amin and, while I was saddened by his death, I realised the truth of the saying, 'He who lives by the sword, perishes by the sword', and I found a certain consolation in the thought that perhaps if I had ordered René's execution I would have started out on a bloody road which would have ended in my own *cul-de-sac*, a violent dead end.)

I turned away from the window and looked at my speech of optimism lying crumpled and irrelevant in the basket and the face of Taferi Bante came to my mind. Bante had become President of Ethiopia following the fall of Haile Selassie and I had met him at a conference in Sri Lanka. He had heard that soon I was to attend another conference in Rwanda and that I would be passing through Addis, and so he had invited me to a reception in his capital while I was *en route* to Rwanda. I had accepted but later, on the day I was driving to the airport, I heard on the radio that he had been assassinated. There was nothing for it but to continue with my plans and when my aircraft landed at Addis the flags were out for my welcome. But it was not Bante who welcomed me. It was his killers. There was no choice. I had to shake those hands.

Now, in the Savoy, with Adnan's words finally sinking in, I thought of the cold reality of twentieth-century politics and thanked God that I was still alive.

Just then, my guest appeared in the doorway, yawning, her hair tousled. Only a couple of hours earlier I had been idly contemplating the question of why English women tanned so seductively, a pleasant inconsequential line of thought.

She asked me what was wrong.

'Nothing,' I said.

She went back to bed and I watched her go, feeling completely alone for the first time in twenty years. Nothing she could do could help. I glanced at the clock. I had been standing at the window for twenty minutes but it felt like hours. I had gone to bed as James Mancham, President of Seychelles, and awakened a displaced person with no fixed abode. But there was no value in feeling sorry for myself. I had to think positively.

I may have been the victim of a treacherous, backstabbing coup but I still had powerful friends. The British would surely help. After all, we had become independent just a year earlier following a constitutional agreement to which this government was an essential party, an agreement which had passed through Parliament and which had received the royal assent. The Foreign Office had undertaken to provide funds to modernise our police force and build an intelligence network. I had been made Honorary Knight Commander of the Most Excellent Order of the British Empire and only the day before I had lunched in a fashionable Knightsbridge restaurant with Dennis Greenam, who had been my political adviser for two years and was Prime Minister Callaghan's adviser on African affairs. Surely, the British would help...

Then there were the French. I was the first man to re-establish official contact between France and Seychelles when I had met President de Gaulle at Versailles in 1968. I had pleased them by opting for a policy of balanced bilingualism on the islands and they had rewarded me with a medal of Officier de la Légion d'Honneur. The French were my friends.

So too were the Americans. I had established friendly contact with them in 1963 when they built a satellite tracking station on Mahé. On the eve of independence I had signed a document under which the CIA was to help us in different ways. Although this help never materialised because of the way bureaucracy works in that democratic country, I knew that the Americans would still be interested. They were after all building the largest naval base since Pearl Harbor in nearby Diego Garcia and they knew that René was anti-American. They would not like the idea of him being in charge, backed by his Marxist friends.

As I stared again at my crumpled speech I recalled the slogan which I had announced on Independence as symbolising our foreign policy. 'Seychelles', I had said, 'would be a friend to all and an enemy to none.' It was a lovely idea that had been forced by the pressure of circumstances upon a romantic island man but how far removed from the hypocrisy and turmoil behind today's geo-politics....

PART I

Chapter One

I WAS BORN on 11 August 1939. Soon after, all the bells on every populated island of Seychelles rang out. For some time my parents mischievously led me to believe that there was a connection, before eventually deflating me with the news that the bells had not tolled for me but for the outbreak of something called the Second World War. The effects of that terrible conflict reached out as far as our islands when two British troopships arrived and took away two thousand young Seychellois to fight for King and Country in the Egyptian desert, seducing them with the offer of bully beef and a pair of Army boots. Even as the islanders sampled the new culinary delights and squeezed previously unshod feet into the boots, they had no inkling that the nights in the desert would be cold and that camels were no substitute for women. The result was that many returned with two previously unknown afflictions – tuberculosis and homosexuality. The lesson was not lost on us. Contact with the world outside could be dangerous. It was a lesson that was to be taught again and again over the years.

Another result of the war was that my father Richard Mancham became prosperous. He had a provisions business in Victoria on the main island of Mahé and a ship-chandler's licence, and with the increased naval activity he was constantly busy. Like most Seychellois, he was of mixed blood, his mother French and his father Chinese. He was eight when his father died and he was sent to relatives in South China. There was a war on and by the time he returned to the islands at the age of thirteen he had matured into an adult with a clear sense of values.

My mother Evelyn is French Seychellois. Orphaned at six, she was brought up in a convent by French and Irish nuns. She met my father when she was fifteen and they married in 1935. She was sixteen, he was twenty-one. I was their first child and my early memories were of the regular arrival of brothers. First there was Thomas who, for some reason, was always known as Billy; then Francis, known as Babi; then Michael and Frank and finally a sister, Anne Marie. In addition there was Philip, our half-brother, the result of a pre-marital relationship of my father's. Philip lived with our paternal grandmother but spent most of his time with us.

No-one could have asked for a better start to life. Our house was large and comfortable, a wooden building of several bedrooms. From my room I could see below the rooftops of Victoria, the only town on the islands. The garden was surrounded by a tropical orchard of mango groves and apples, and the sun shone continually.

At that time few people had heard of Seychelles. Mahé was accessible only by the passenger ships which called every six or seven weeks on the run between Mombasa and Bombay. The islands were beautiful, tranquil and poor. In Victoria, magnificent *sang-dragon* trees (so called because when scratched they drip red sap which looks like blood) stood like a guard of honour above the road to Government House. Fish, eggs and rice were cheap but wages were correspondingly low, and there were more rickshaws than bicycles in the streets, and few cars. Nevertheless, with war raging outside, Seychelles seemed more like the world as God intended it to be. Each morning was fresh and new, and evenings brought peace and companionship.

I knew that other islands were often hit by cyclones and that in other countries the seasons could be described in terms of weather but I did not know what they meant by cold or fog or snow. There are no seasons in Seychelles. The temperature rarely drops below 75° F or rises above 85°. When the rains come, they come down fast and furious and usually leave quickly.

Mother had her own philosophical outlook on life. I particularly remember her happy vitality; she gave much of her time to church and parish activities as well as caring for her large and growing family. She had a fine voice and would sing the children to sleep from her extensive repertoire of romantic French songs.

Naturally, knowing nothing different, I took the beauty of my surroundings for granted. The water was warm and clear. The sand was white, the vegetation lush. It was not until I had travelled that I realised that, by comparison, the Seychelles were indeed paradise islands, that I had been brought up in technicolour while much of the rest of the world was painted in greys.

I took for granted the fact that my friends came in all shapes and colours, that a Seychellois could be blond with blue eyes or as black as night, or any shade in between. It was not until I had travelled that I discovered something called racial prejudice, although I was conscious of a certain aloofness from those who called themselves the *grand blancs* and who claimed to be directly descended from the original French settlers.

In Victoria I would meet my friends under the Clock Tower, which is a replica of the clock in front of Victoria Station in London, and I thought nothing of the fact that the clock of the Roman Catholic cathedral always chimed twice: the first time on the hour, then three minutes later, in case you hadn't heard it the first time. I learnt that a man could be fined for taking a coconut out of a plantation but I knew nothing of crime. There was some petty larceny on the islands and occasionally we heard terrible stories of years ago when a murder had been committed. I knew the policemen in Victoria and the fact that they had very little to do.

And I knew why some of the coconut palms were numbered and known as toddy trees. Their sap produced a potent drink called *calou* which could make the adults sing and dance and sometimes fall down, to such an extent that the government was compelled to control their tapping by licensing the trees. It seemed that everything we needed was close at hand.

At weekends we would go to our beach house at Glacis where we would swim and fish. During the week, when I was not studying, I would play football with my brothers and the boys who came to our garden. We were fortunate in having proper footballs. There were others who had to make do with kicking breadfruits around.

It was a good life, the highlights being the arrival of a boat from overseas. We had no television or newspapers, only the radio which occasionally received the BBC World Service, and so the boat was our only physical link with the outside world. I remember the excitement caused when the harbour siren would blast after a ship had been sighted from Signal Hill. The whole town would gaze out to sea, each one trying to be the first to catch a glimpse of the approaching vessel; then we would run to the pier to wait for her to come in. There would be friends on board and strangers from distant corners of the world.

Memory can be a faulty indicator and in my case it conjures up only the good things. If there were times of pain and tears, then they have been forgotten. If there were teenage tantrums or adolescent rebellion, then they must have passed in the night, because I have no recollection of them.

Each day I cycled two miles to the Seychelles College which was run by missionaries of the Order of Christian Instruction, most of whom came from Quebec. They were dedicated and strict but I enjoyed the work. I did not need to be dragged to school. From the first day my father encouraged me to study. Like many successful self-made men, he was conscious of the fact that he had never gone to university and he was determined that his children should not lack the opportunity; and like most islanders he looked up to doctors and lawyers as men of unfathomable knowledge.

'Study well,' he would tell me in a serious voice, 'and when you leave school I will send you to Europe to become a lawyer. I want you to be a man of letters and culture.'

There was no question about it. He wanted me to be a lawyer and so a lawyer I would be, if I could.

At school I learned about the islands, their geography and history. I learned that Mahé is situated just south of the equator, that the group comprises ninety-two islands spread over 200,000 square miles. Some were granite mountain peaks of a sunken continent; others were of coral formation with their attendant reefs, all uninhabited until French pirates discovered them two hundred years before. The buccaneers were followed by French settlers, refugees from the revolutionary fervour of France or the collapse of the French Empire in India. They were wealthy and brought slaves with them. At the time of the French Revolution, someone conducted a head-count and wrote that the population of the Seychelles – which had been named after a Controller-General of Finance, Vicomte Moreau de Séchelles – consisted of '69 persons of French blood, three soldiers of the garrison, 32 coloured persons and 487 slaves'.

It might have been idyllic had not the islands already become a victim of their geographic position. The British were engaged in naval rivalry with the French for control of the sea routes to the East Indies and piracy in the area was also becoming rampant, with the British merchant fleet suffering colossal losses. Thus it was that in 1794 a British frigate sailed in and demanded the unconditional surrender of the islands. Twenty years later the French ceded sovereignty to the British who remained in charge till 1976, although the French influence is still strongly apparent, in religion, language and law.

Britain ruled, or rather neglected to rule, the islands as a dependency of Mauritius until 1903 when Seychelles became a Crown Colony, complete with a cast list of Governors which might have been invented by Noël Coward. There was Sir Bickham Sweet-Escott, followed later by Lt. Col. the Hon. Sir E. E. Twistleton-Fiennes, grandfather of Ranulph Fiennes who recently crossed the North and South Poles. Still later came Sir De S. M. G. Honey; compared with them, the first Governor I became friends with had the almost commonplace name of Sir Selwyn Selwyn-Clarke.

My teachers took their work seriously, yet ironically it was two of them who unwittingly furthered my less formal education. The first turned up one evening with her young man in a quiet spot frequented by lovers and proceeded to enjoy themselves, unaware that a friend and I were watching from behind a tree. To us, the sound and the sight of love-making was absurd and hilarious. We could not contain our laughter and when we ran away we were recognised. Next morning our teacher had reported us to the headmaster, the Rev. Brother Norbert, saying that we had been shouting names at her. The punishment was ten cuts of the heavy wooden ruler and as I stretched out my hands, I closed my eyes and saw again in my imagination my teacher's wonderful legs thrashing around in the moonlight.

Not long afterwards, another teacher took us on a nature ramble to the Botanical Gardens. When we arrived, we were met by a young agricultural officer who lived in a timber cottage among the tropical flowers.

'Children,' said our teacher. 'I want you to collect butterflies this afternoon. Catch as many as you can. At the end of the day, the gentleman here ...' (pointing to the young man) 'will give each one of you a mango. Now, all of you disappear and let me see who will bring back the most butterflies.'

We all ran off. Looking back I saw the teacher and the agricultural officer sneak into his cottage. Wise now to the ways of the world, I decided to forget about butterflies and crept back to the cottage where I saw my teacher in all kinds of positions. It was the most instructive hour of nature study I ever had.

Seychelles was an ideal place for budding peeping Toms. With no distractions like television (which still has not been introduced to the islands) and no commercial cinema, except for an irregular showing of outdated British newsreels by the Government

Information Unit, the islanders enjoyed themselves as nature intended, and much of the activity took place out of doors. In other parts of the world a married man on the loose traditionally needs to check his collar or handkerchiefs for lipstick. In Seychelles, he was given away either by grass stains or adhesive grains of sand.

Although I knew the facts of life before I was ten, it was five years later before I took an active part in these mysteries. As a practising Roman Catholic I had been taught that to have carnal knowledge of a girl outside marriage is a mortal sin, and I always dreaded the idea of having to tell my confessor about such a terrible thing.

One evening I had been doing some extra work in the school library and was walking back home, some two miles away. The moon was half full and the atmosphere balmy and sensuous. As I approached the Botanical Gardens, with visions of my teacher's and the agricultural officer's performance flooding my mind, I saw walking alone towards me a maid from a nearby village, about twenty and very attractive. In Creole the words appropriate to such occasions are 'Donne moi un petit coup', meaning 'Give me a little kick', and sure enough the lady was ready and willing to do so and knew the right spot for it, a mango tree behind the enclosure where some giant tortoises were kept. But as we walked, she leading the way, I started to think about the serious sin I was about to commit and became suddenly engulfed by a strong feeling of guilt. When we got to the mango tree my friend took off her knickers, lay down on the grass, lifted her skirt and revealed to me, for the first time at close quarters, a woman's private parts. I do not think I much liked what I saw, but in no time my mating chemistry acted prematurely and soon I was fleeing the scene, feeling more guilty than ever before and leaving a confused girl wondering what had caused me to desert her.

Back home I realised it was Friday night. Had I to go to confession? Had I committed a mortal sin? When did I commit it? Was it when the thought of having sex first came to mind? Was it when I made the suggestion to the girl, or was it when nature did its work? I was, to say the least, confused in my mind and decided that for the sake of inner peace I had to face my confessor. Father Eustace was an elderly priest in charge of the parish of Plaisance.

On Saturday afternoon I went to confession.

'Forgive me, Father, because I have sinned. I accuse myself of having done bad things.'

'The bad things you did, son, was it with a boy or a girl?'

'With a girl, Father.'

'What about boys, have you ever done any bad things with them?'

'I do not know what you mean, Father.'

'Have you ever played with your body?'

'Not deliberately, Father.'

'Tell me, my son, this woman you did bad things with, was she married or single?'

'I do not know, Father.'

'All right, my son, you will recite ten Our Fathers and six Hail Marys. Your sin is forgiven. You can go in peace.'

Another lesson had been learned. Absolution, it seemed, can come easily.

In early 1947 father made plans to take my mother, my brother Billy and me on a three-month holiday to Kenya. It was to be the first time that I had left the islands and my excitement was tempered by doubt that we would get a passage, since there was always a long waiting list and the British India Company's official policy was 'first come, first served'. But father had his ship-chandler's connections and at the eleventh hour it was confirmed that we had secured passages. We were to travel in the ship's hospital, on the pretext that Billy and I were in need of 'urgent specialist attention in Nairobi'.

Father was a man of tremendous *joie de vivre* and every evening for the three days of the voyage the hospital of the SS *Aronda* saw some lively drinking. Each morning it fell to Billy and me to tidy up and remove the empty beer and whisky bottles in time for the captain's inspection. When the uniformed captain and his entourage arrived, Billy and I would try to look ill and father would put on his most lugubrious face, which after the previous night's party was not all artifice. The inspection party included the English purser and the Indian doctor, father's accomplices and drinking companions.

In Kenya we stayed with my mother's cousin, Mr Michel Hoareau, an official of the East African Railways and Harbours, and even then it was obvious that trouble was brewing in that most beautiful of African countries. People were classified by race, European, Asian or African, each with a corresponding pay scale. The injustices and pressures which this system created were nowhere more apparent than among the multiracial Seychellois who had found jobs in East Africa. Because Uncle Hoareau was classed as a European he had a large home and a much higher salary than Mr Dagama, a Seychellois of Asian extraction who was three times more competent. No one could blame Mr Hoareau for taking advantage of the situation, but it caused severe social strains which divided the Seychellois community in Kenya.

I worked happily through my years of secondary education, fit and strong and without a care in the world. Jacques Yves Cousteau, the French underwater pioneer and inventor of the aqualung, came to Mahé to make his famous film, *The Silent World*. As a member of the Seychelles Sea Scouts I visited his ship-cum laboratory, the *Calypso*, and went away, like most of the islanders, with a new enthusiasm for underwater exploration. After Cousteau's visit, I spent most of my weekends spear-fishing, unconcerned about any danger. There were plenty of sharks around the Seychelles but they had never been known to attack anyone. They did not bother us and we, in turn, did not worry about them. In a paradise island you can coexist quite happily with almost any living creature.

At school I became friendly with Robin Crawford, the son of Sir Frederick, who became Governor in 1951. Robin became my classmate and close friend for two years and I was often a guest at Government House. I had no idea, of course, that years later I would occupy the house as President, nor, looking at the dignified figure of the Governor, so apparently secure in his position, that he would be so shabbily treated by his colleagues in Whitehall. (Sir Frederick's passport was confiscated in 1967 by the British Government because he had appeared in public places with members of the Ian Smith government. He died in Cape Town in South Africa in 1978, a bitter man, sacrificed on the altar of political convenience and the shabby diplomacy which often surrounds it.)

I also became fascinated with another visitor to the islands. Archbishop Makarios of Cyprus was sent into exile by the British Government and lived for a year in Sans Souci, a magnificent house which commanded one of the most beautiful views on earth. Occasionally I saw him walking in Victoria, wearing his heavy black cassock and black hat, his beard and hair immaculately groomed. To a schoolboy he looked impressive and dignified. I think I was slightly in awe of the man with his vaguely sinister smile and I could never have imagined that only a few years later he would be coming to me in my position as Chief Minister asking to revisit the islands.

At that time I was busy working under the progressive tutelage of a kind British teacher called Brother Austin O'Donnell. I spent the last three years at college under his instruction and it was through his efforts and encouragement that I passed my exams. I became captain of the football XI, then house captain and finally head prefect. At Speech Day in my final year I addressed the annual gathering of parents and students. I was seventeen and had been accepted as a law student by the Middle Temple in London. I had my father's blessing to go abroad and a testimonial from Brother Austin that I was 'full of initiative' and that I had 'on several occasions displayed leadership qualities'.

A few weeks later I packed my bags and made my way to the pier, waved my parents, family and friends goodbye and climbed aboard the SS *Amra* bound for Mombasa. I was on my way to London with an imagination filled with preconceptions and bolstered by the blind confidence and enthusiasm of youth. I stood motionless on deck for what seemed like hours, watching Mahé becoming smaller as the vessel steamed across a featureless ocean.

Suddenly the ship's radio blasted out a message for me from a girl-friend, followed by a song request. It was Harry Belafonte singing about leaving a little girl in Kingston Town.

> 'Cause I'm sad to say
> I'm on my way.
> Won't be back
> For many a day ...

I cried, laughed, was excited ... a new dawn was before me.

Chapter Two

A YOUNG MAN'S first trip away from home and family inevitably leads to an assault on his innocence. As I changed ships at Mombasa, boarding the British ship MV *Braemar Castle*, I felt ready for anything, eager to gobble up the fruits of experience. Soon I made friends with a young Rhodesian of my own age. Peter Kilief was the son of a wealthy tobacco grower and as enthusiastic about his journey as I was. We swapped stories and boasted about the things we would do together when we reached our first port.

All through the trip and particularly as we approached Egypt, the main conversation was about the Anglo-French-Israeli invasion of Suez. It was also questionable whether we were going to be allowed to pass through the canal. It was only when we reached Port Said that the dimension and consequences of the conflict was brought home to us by the sight of the damage done by the bombs and the sullen stares of the Egyptians as they watched the British ship dock.

Nevertheless we were the first down the gangplank, feeling grown-up, like sailors on leave, sniffing the air like puppies, wanting to make friends with the world.

Our first friend was a skinny young Egyptian dressed in a *dhoti*. He must have been lying in wait for likely-looking passengers because, as we came through the dock gates, he jumped out at us, tugged our sleeves and asked in English whether we wanted 'lady company'.

He didn't need to ask twice and we followed him through the busy streets into the centre of the town. It was hot and dusty, a dry heat that grabbed at your throat, a different climate from home. The people were bustling around, going about their business as if the world was coming to an end. In the Seychelles, people move slowly. There's plenty of time for everything. We scampered after the boy feeling important, men of the world, ready for anything.

The bar was called Cecile, dimly lit and cosy. We tipped the boy, watched him go and settled ourselves at a table. No sooner had we ordered a couple of beers than two women had joined us, fondling us and asking in English if we wanted to buy them a drink.

By all means. What would they have?

Champagne.

Well, of course. What else would a young lady expect from a man of the world?

The longer we sat with them, the more excited we became, so that we could hardly contain ourselves, but they seemed in no hurry to take us upstairs with them. A second bottle of champagne arrived. Then a third. It was beginning to get late. Surreptitiously, with Peter distracting the girls, I sipped from one of their glasses. It was cold tea.

Affronted, I called for the bill. It was enormous. We paid and left the place in dignified silence, aware that we had been taken for a ride, but still too young to know that we had fallen into the oldest of all tourist traps.

The young Egyptian was waiting for us. Far from being ashamed of himself, he sympathised with us, saying that the girls were no good and to make up for it he would take us to a sex show which apparently featured a donkey in a starring role.

Again we followed him, this time down a meandering lane. It was pitch black. The bombers had knocked out the electricity. Eventually we stopped outside a massive door. The boy told us that the show would start in half an hour and would cost several piastres. We paid, he went inside and disappeared. For a while we stood in the lane, wondering what we were going to see; then the memory of the champagne-tea returned and I pushed open the door. There was nothing inside, just rubble and a shattered roof. It was a bomb site.

Slowly we began to wander back up the lane, two disillusioned young men. We could hear the ship's siren calling the passengers back on board and suddenly our anger turned to fear. We were lost in the dark. Luckily we soon found a man with a horse and cart who said in English that he would take us to the ship. The cost of the ride was several more piastres. Again we paid up and climbed in. Ten minutes later we stopped at another bomb site. The wail of the siren was further away than before and the man was demanding another four hundred piastres before he would go any further. Now we were angry again and in a panic. We argued with him, seeing a group of soldiers watching us. The man pulled out a flick knife and snapped it open in front of us. We looked at the soldiers who were laughing at us. There would be no help from them. There was only one thing to do. Again we reached into our wallets.

Twenty minutes later he dropped us within sight of the ship and as I ran towards it, sadder but wiser and certainly poorer, I realised that the acquisition of experience was no cheap business.

After that, the rest of the voyage was plain sailing. As we entered the Mediterranean, the *Braemar Castle* wrote itself into the history books as the last vessel to go through the Suez Canal before Nasser closed it. In Genoa I discovered the delights of Italian ice-cream and the same evening what remained of my innocence finally evaporated in an encounter with a beautiful young woman. She was a professional but this time there was no confidence trick and I returned to the ship a happy young man.

Three weeks after leaving Mahé, the ship entered the Thames estuary. Although it was a July morning at the height of an English summer, I was shivering. It was cold and windy, conditions I had never experienced, but I was too excited to worry about the weather. Alone on deck I peered upriver for historic buildings and bright lights, searching for the London I had read about, the London of St Paul's Cathedral, Westminster Abbey, Hyde Park Corner and Big Ben. But there was nothing to see except the flat Kent coast on one bank and the damp Essex marshes on the other. I rushed down to my cabin to finish packing, determined to look my best when I disembarked, to make a grand entrance on the London scene. I put on my suit, the first I had owned, made by a local tailor in Mahé. It was grey with bell bottoms.

I checked my appearance in the mirror, straightened my tie and stepped onto the deck, straight-backed and proud, looking for signs of approval from the other passengers. Their reaction was not what I had expected. Nobody complimented me on my attire. Finally we docked at Tilbury and I was met by a young man from the British Council. He took one look at my suit and, to give him his due, he fought hard to swallow a grin. To him I must have appeared as something out of a time machine. By the time we reached the Council's hostel near Harrods I had made myself a promise that I would find a good tailor so that never again would anyone have the chance to laugh at my appearance. No sooner had I unpacked at the hostel, 1 Hans Crescent, than I went exploring. I discovered dance halls in Piccadilly. Inside, men in strange jackets and wearing odd haircuts were jerking around: Teddy Boys. I gazed at them in disbelief. Outside, in the bustle of the city, there seemed to be prostitutes everywhere, openly on offer. Even outside the hostel I was propositioned. It was the year before the Street Offences Act drove them into more discreet corners.

I discovered that they would take their clients in a taxi by night round the quiet streets of the City of London and was told why the taxis in those days had no driving mirrors, and that for a percentage of the girl's earnings the driver kept his eyes fixed firmly on the road ahead.

For the first few days I wandered around open-mouthed as if I were on another planet. I went into Burtons, bought myself a suit and merged with the crowds, less conspicuous now with my Mahé suit hung in a cupboard, never to be worn again. I looked up two friends from the islands, George Rassool and Edi Camille, who had arrived in England some years before. George later became the first Seychelles High Commissioner in London with Edi his deputy. Then, when I felt a little bit more at home and had stopped tripping over the kerbs, I packed my bags again and moved to a college in Blackheath, a suburb in south-east London where I was to study for three months before starting law at the Middle Temple in October.

Wilson's College catered mainly for European students and in those three months I made a number of discoveries. As summer turned to autumn I learnt that in my digs the nights were cold. I learnt about sixpences in gas meters, about sharing a bath tub with strangers and the meaning of central heating, or rather the lack of it. More importantly, I learnt that I could get on with most people. I had wondered on the voyage whether I might be shy and tongue-tied with new people, but luckily this was not the case. The conventions of London life were new to me. Ideas and attitudes often seemed strange, but I did not make the mistake of mocking the conventions. I simply transferred my inborn sense of fun to others when they seemed to be taking themselves too seriously. I discovered that I had a certain talent to amuse and to be amused, a characteristic which has served me well over the years.

After Wilson's, I moved nearer to George and Edi, taking a

room at 9 Frognal, Hampstead, determined to respect the theory that all work and no play makes Jack a dull boy. After studying all day and early evening at the Middle Temple, I went off with a pound in my pocket to a club called Moulin Rouge in Finchley Road. It was a friendly place, owned by a Czech, and it attracted students and *au pairs*. There was a band which played Latin American music and we could dance most of the night away, the pound note being good enough for the entrance fee and three or four lagers and lime. During my student days I slept just enough as was necessary. Sleep was time wasted and I didn't want to waste any time.

From the beginning I discovered that girls were fascinated by the idea of the Seychelles. Invariably when I met a new girl I would be asked where the Seychelles were. Not one of them knew, nor did they have any knowledge that the Seychelles was British. It surprised me that they were so ignorant about my country but on the other hand their interest gave me something to talk about and there were very few who would become bored with the conversation; as often as not, one thing would lead to another.

I remember an attractive Jewish girl whom I met in the library and who invited me back to her house. When I turned up I discovered one of the most impressive mansions in north London. Rachel's father, it seemed, was a very successful businessman. He also, that night, came home earlier than expected and I found myself hiding naked in his library waiting for him to say goodnight to Rachel. At that time visions of headlines appearing at home in the local paper came to my mind. However, there is a God who looks after young lovers and later that night I tiptoed safely out onto the gravel clutching my clothes like some extra from a Whitehall farce.

Then there was the older woman I invited back from the Moulin Rouge to the flat I shared with my brother Billy and two Seychellois friends. I was excited. She must have been ten years older than me. On the way home I saw something sticking out of her handbag.

'It's my nightie,' she said, patronisingly stating the obvious.

I lasted with her until three that morning and could take no more. I heard one of my flat-mates coming home on his own and he took over. Then at eight another flat-mate turned up. He had been working all night and took over the sexual baton. It was evening before the lady left with a smile on her face and three young Seychellois happily asleep.

Yet during all this time the realisation that people knew nothing about my islands began to irritate me. It was brought to a head one morning when I visited the Colonial Office in Great Smith Street to discuss a seminar to which I had been invited by the University of Manchester. I was met by a walking caricature of the British colonial breed. He wore a superior expression and a pin-striped suit, a club tie, a stiff collar and an even stiffer upper lip.

'Where is it you're from again?' he asked.

I told him.

'The Seychelles?' he sniffed. 'Is it one of ours?'

Everyone has a personal road to Damascus when something happens or is said to illuminate aspirations. This, I believe, was mine. Faced by this man's arrogant ignorance, I made up my mind there and then to do everything I could to put my little country on the map.

Shortly afterwards I realised how I might begin to achieve this ambition.

In order to qualify for admission to the English Bar it is necessary to eat a prescribed number of dinners at the Inns of Court, and it was at one of these dinners that I made acquaintance with the politics of emergent Africa. I found myself seated next to an African gentleman, immaculately clad in a Savile Row suit.

'I say, old boy, what do you think of West African politics?' he enquired, as we sipped our wine. My response seemed to impress him, and he invited me back to his house in St John's Wood for a drink after dinner and gave me his card, which read 'Kwasi Armah, Deputy High Commissioner for Ghana'. Outside the Middle Temple we climbed into a Rolls-Royce driven by an Irish chauffeur, and I learned that Kwasi Armah had been reading law in England for several years, that he was finding real property a tough subject because his mind was more attuned to politics, that he had been President of the Ghanaian Students' Union in London, and that he owed his present appointment to his steadfast loyalty to President Kwame Nkrumah. I decided there and then to profit from his example by organising the dozen or so Seychelles students into a union, and it was as its president that I made a base for entry into Seychelles politics before returning to the colony.

Some time later the Ghanaian High Commissioner, at that

time fell out with President Nkrumah and Kwasi Armah actually became Ambassador to the Court of St James while still a law student. I saw him again, an imposing figure in traditional robes, as leader of the Ghana delegation to the Kenya independence celebrations. But the last time we met was by chance in Edgware Road. He was a political exile, dressed again in a western suit, and this time more interested in real property than African politics.

As President of the Seychelles Students Union I organised regular social gatherings for Seychellois students and their friends in London. On one occasion we gave a cocktail party in honour of Sir John Thorpe, who was visiting London before taking up his new appointment as Governor of Seychelles, and also invited Monseigneur Oliver Maradan, Roman Catholic Bishop of Seychelles, who happened to be in London on holiday. The temptation to strike a blow for progress was irresistible. In my speech I told Sir John that one of his first tasks should be to repeal the law, one of those passed to protect the almost feudal privileges of the planters, which made it an offence for an ordinary Seychellois citizen to be in possession of a coconut without a written permit. To the Bishop, I addressed the message that several of the practices of the Church under his administration were long overdue for reform. One of these was the conduct of funerals. For fifteen rupees a first-class service was provided, with choir, organ and all the cathedral bells. A second-class funeral cost seven rupees, which covered a choir but no organ and only half the bells. A burial of the third class was free, but there was no choir, no organ, no priest at the cemetery and only one small bell. I questioned whether this and similar practices were really in accordance with Christian principle and social justice. Sir John took it all in good part but the Bishop was not amused, as I was later to discover.

It was this action which signalled my entry into Seychelles politics. My speech was reproduced as a newsletter and posted to several people on the islands. The planters and some of the priests were furious. I also received a letter from my father who, far from approving my boldness and initiative, was severely critical. 'I am spending money for you to become a lawyer,' he wrote. 'Politics is a cheap and dirty occupation. In this day and age it is best left to opportunists, rogues and vagabonds.' Who will say that he was not right?

But my mind was set on politics. Around this time, Prime

Minister Harold Macmillan had visited the Republic of South Africa where he had delivered his famous 'wind of change' speech which committed the British Government to an overt policy of decolonisation, of dismantling the empire and getting rid, as much as possible, of their colonial responsibilities. There was no doubt that one topic of conversation which dominated all others within the corridors of the Middle Temple and other educational institutions which I frequented was the question of independence for the long list of British colonies.

Already at that time I spent long hours reflecting on the effect of this new policy on Seychelles. I truly could not conceive how a group of ninety-two small islands spread over 200,000 square miles of ocean, without an airport or a viable economy, could really secure for itself a meaningful independence in what was becoming an increasingly troublesome world. Despite the fact that Britain had in many respects neglected us I became convinced that the devil you know is better than the one you don't know.

I took to politics with the zeal of the newly converted. I was lucky enough to be invited regularly to tea by an ex-Governor of the islands, Sir Selwyn Selwyn-Clarke, and spent many hours at his home in Hampstead listening to his stories and discussing his political experience. Sir Selwyn was a man of great humanity who had been Director of Medical Services in Hong Kong and had suffered terribly as a prisoner of war of the Japanese.

I read the daily papers from cover to cover and one day had a letter published in the *Evening Standard*, in which I agreed with the Bishop of Southwark's view that it should be possible for us to go back to school for a period when we are half way through life, concluding, 'The Bishop's emphasis on the importance of culture shows that he is aware what the basic elements are that makes a nation great.'

The publication of that letter gave me great satisfaction. I was still a very young man, conscious of my background, and it meant a lot to me that my opinion had been found worthy of publication in the letters' column of a London paper. Meanwhile I had been sending articles home, accounts of my holidays in various countries. Many of these articles were printed in the *Seychellois*, the mouthpiece of the Planters Association. They were well received at first until they began to acquire a political flavour. Once I wrote an article comparing Catholicism in England, where the adherents were in a minority, to Seychelles where they were a vast majority. I also took the liberty of giving my opinion that age-old religious attitudes were holding back progress on the islands. This resulted in a fierce attack from a leading spokesman of the planters who had noticed that my ideas had become a talking point among the locals.

A few weeks later, the editor of the *Seychellois* was severely criticised for publishing an article from the Students' Union leaflet, *SSU Calling*. It was written by a medical student, Guy Ah Moye, and attacked labourers' conditions and the limited franchise which gave the vote only to a small percentage of the adult population.

The result was immediate. The planters attacked us in print and refused to publish anything more from us. It was then that I learned an early lesson about politics. Soon afterwards I received a letter from the islands' British administrative body offering the union a grant of 2,000 rupees and asking permission to print the minutes of the union's meetings.

Needless to say the British administration could see what was on the political horizon. They realised that the Planters Association was marred by a semi-feudal attitude and they were quick to make use of us, applying that important ploy of British diplomacy – divide and rule.

And so, as the fifties became the sixties, I became politically aware. As I mentioned earlier, I was invited to attend a seminar on adult education in Bangor, North Wales, organised by the University of Manchester. I joined the Allied Circle Education Trust, a social club in Park Lane, then, in May 1961, the Colonial Office selected me to represent the Seychelles at a lunch in the Guildhall to open a Commonwealth Technical Training Week. Dressed in a hired morning suit, I was presented to the Duke of Edinburgh. It was one of the proudest moments of my life and as I shook the Duke's hand, I could not help thinking of the native youth in his island suit on the *Braemar Castle* a few short years ago, and what a difference London had made to him.

Five months later I passed my finals and my father cabled me sixty pounds with the family's congratulations. And on 21 November, dressed in my wig which cost me £26 5s. and my gown (£11 5s. 7d), I was called to the Bar.

One of my guests at the ceremony was a girl I had met at the Moulin Rouge. Heather Evans was a classic English rose, slim, blonde, delicately featured and from a wealthy family. Her grandfather had founded the Anchor dairy company in New Zealand and when I met her she was living with her mother and sister in Richmond, her father having died ten years earlier. Neither Heather's mother and sister, nor her friends with whom we spent weekends, were particularly impressed by my colonial background. To them, someone who was not a certain type of Englishman and did not speak in a certain way was, by definition, somewhat inferior. Their attitude, however, did not worry me. I accepted them as a challenge to get to know the English better and I grew to like them.

That day Heather was proud of me and I knew that leaving her would be painful. What I did not know was that our separation would prove impossible and that a year later she would leave home in comfortable Richmond to travel out to the middle of nowhere to be my wife.

I have always loved London, which has given me a professional education, many memorable experiences and much hospitality and understanding. When in 1974 the Lord Mayor, Sir Hugh Wontner, was kind enough to give a luncheon in my honour at the Guildhall, I tried in the course of my speech to give expression to those feelings.

'Since I first came to London as a student of law, this greatest of all cities has been my second home. Never have I found it friendless or lonely. To me it has always been a place brimming with opportunity and rich in reward for those who are bold and adventurous whether in love or in commerce, in scholarship or politics:

> London is a female city
> Pert, and fickle, gay and witty.
> If you chat her up with fervour
> She will take you for her lover.

'So she has, and this occasion, one of the proudest of my life, makes the relationship almost respectable.'

After three months post-final work in London my father agreed that I should spend six months in Paris as an *auditeur libre* at the Law Faculty of the University of Paris. At that time two features, one the war in Algeria and the other Jean-Paul Sartre's philosophy of existentialism, dominated Paris life. I was staying on the Left Bank in a small hotel not far from the Sorbonne, and it was not unusual to be awakened three or four times a night by the blast of exploding bombs and accompanying police and ambulance sirens. It was rumoured that de Gaulle was about to abandon the settlers' cause in Algeria and make peace with the FLN over their heads, and the French capital was full of sectional tension, the political right against the political left and the *pied noirs* against the North Africans. It somewhat resembled the French Revolution except that the prevailing 'live and let live' philosophy of Sartre influenced many to face the crisis calmly.

Personally, I found the atmosphere exhilarating and the experience rewarding. Sometimes I would sit on the banks of the Seine listening to a lone guitarist echoing the aches in his broken heart, or I might wander in the streets, where prostitutes of all shapes, sizes and colours displayed themselves, and once I saw a drunken *clochard* jump into the river shouting, 'Après moi le deluge.' Paris was paradise and purgatory rolled into one. In this environment I felt more like a young poet than a staid lawyer and soon I was sleeping most of the day and moving around at night, more interested in the human comedy than in the codes which Napoleon had enacted for the better government of his subjects and empire. When I had a few extra francs I would go to one of the *boîtes* where one could buy a bottle of *vin de famille* and add one's voice to the communal singing. Paris was gay and lively and I was glad to be young and full of vigour.

One day the proprietor of the hotel asked me to take charge of it for a few hours while he took his wife to visit her relations in the country. The hotel was full and I merely had to act as *concierge* until he returned. He had scarcely left when a tubby little man of about sixty came to the desk, accompanied by a girl a third of his age. At first I took them for a company director and his secretary, but he asked if there was a room available. I pointed to the sign which announced that the hotel was full. 'But monsieur,' he pleaded, 'this is the third hotel I have tried and all are full. We have not much time. Can't you help? We only want a room for two hours.'

I recalled a similar predicament when a landlady had barred a girl-friend from my room and we had ended up on Hampstead Heath, and my sympathies were aroused.

'Well, monsieur, I can lend you my own room if that would suit you,' I offered.

'Thank you, monsieur, you are most understanding,' the gentleman murmured as I handed him the key to my eight francs a day room. Later, when they were about to leave the hotel, looking relaxed and happy, the man handed me a hundred franc note. I was on the point of handing it back when the thought occurred to me, who will benefit from this gesture? Not the gentleman, who would be embarrassed, and certainly not I, who have only a thousand francs a month with which to enjoy the delights of Paris.

In Paris I reviewed my future prospects. Now equipped with professional status, I felt confident, but looked forward with mixed feelings to returning home. I knew that I would miss the sophistication and culture of Britain and Europe. Beautiful Seychelles certainly was, but it was also remote and inaccessible – 'a thousand miles from anywhere', without a single modern hotel and with only a handful of visitors each year. But I knew that go back I must. I was the eldest child and could not desert the parents who had made my education in London and Paris possible. And I could not suppress the thought that the islands would remain isolated from the modern world unless educated Seychellois returned to them to work for progress.

I decided to take the leisurely route home, seeing as much of the world as I could, and so I bought a ticket that would allow me to stop at Geneva, Rome, Athens, Istanbul, Beirut, Tehran, New Delhi and Bombay. I wanted to see as much as I could. To this day, I am a fanatic for travel. As far as I am concerned, the cliché of travel broadening the mind is quite legitimate. It means new friendships, a better understanding of people and their cultures and problems, the chance to accept and emulate that which is good and to reject that which by my standards is wrong.

Two impressions of the journey home have stayed with me.

My arrival in Turkey coincided with a visit to this NATO ally by Lyndon Johnson, then Vice-President of the United States. At that time thousands of people from Turkestan had sought refuge in Turkey because of Soviet penetration, and a delegation of them had gathered outside the Istanbul Hilton, where Johnson and his entourage were staying, to deliver a message for President Kennedy. I joined the crowd of colourfully dressed Turkestan people. At last there was a bustle and out came a group of US military and diplomatic officials, led by a black man who turned out to be Charles Rowan, then head of the US Information Service and now one of America's leading political columnists. After the leader of the Turkestan delegation had delivered his message through an interpreter, Rowan replied in these words:

'People of Turkestan, on behalf of the President of the United States of America, on behalf of the Vice-President, Lyndon Johnson, who has delegated me this morning to address you, and on my personal behalf, I wish to thank you for coming in such great numbers and to assure you that as long as you, like the people of Turkey, provide us with the moral support which we deem important and necessary, the forces of aggression in this part of the world will *not* prevail. Indeed we once again make it clear that any aggression directed against the soil of Turkey will be deemed aggression against the United States herself.'

The crowd responded to this brief but forceful statement with a great emotional shout of 'Long Live President Kennedy. God bless America.' I remember being profoundly moved by the United States of America's clearly expressed resolve to champion the cause of freedom. Sadly, this faith was not to survive later experience.

In Bombay I found awaiting me a letter from my father. 'If you are short of money,' it said, 'please call on my friends, Superb Traders Ltd, who are our regular onion suppliers. You will find their business card attached to this letter. Meanwhile I am making arrangements with the Mercantile Bank of India to send a cheque for 5,000 rupees.'

The business card was impressive. Against the outline of a ship resembling the *Queen Mary* was inscribed, 'Superb Traders Ltd., Great Patel Building, Chakla, Bombay.' At the bottom of the card, bold red letters proclaimed that 'Honesty is our Best Policy' and 'We cover the World for Export'.

I summoned a taxi. 'Please take me to Superb Traders in Great Patel Building,' I said.

'Great Patel Building? Where is that, sir?' the driver enquired.

'In Chakla,' I replied, astonished that he did not know the location of a company which covered the world for export.

After driving around Chakla for what seemed like hours, he stopped with a cry of triumph. 'Great Patel Building, sir,' he announced. It was a dilapidated old warehouse with a huge signboard carrying well over a hundred trading addresses. Superb Traders was listed among the occupants of the fifth floor, to which I climbed.

Three Indians were sitting at rickety tables surrounded by piles of onions, ginger, garlic, potatoes, chillies and oriental spices. Behind each man was a large safe.

'Welcome to the Gateway of India,' said one of them. 'What can I do for the son of my friend, Richard Mancham?'

I explained that I needed a small loan while awaiting the arrival of my father's cheque.

'No problem, Mr Mancham, no problem at all. How much do you need? Ten, fifteen, twenty thousand?'

I had never before met an Indian trader so willing to part with his money. 'Three thousand rupees will do,' I said.

'Let us make it a round five thousand,' he insisted.

'All right,' I agreed, 'I'll endorse my father's cheque to you when it arrives.'

'Oh no, Mr Mancham, oh no, there's no need for that,' he protested. 'When you get home ask your father to send the equivalent amount to this account in London.' He handed me the address. 'Now let's have an Alphonso mango juice together.'

Outside Great Patel Building, and many times after that, I was accosted by people offering double the official rate of exchange for dollars, sterling or Swiss francs, and I realised why Superb Traders were so keen to lend me money. Honesty is indeed a superb policy, I mused.

The last stage of the journey was a six-day voyage from Bombay on the SS *Kampala*. On the final day I rose with the dawn and stood at the rail, gazing at the outline of Mahé on the horizon. As we steamed closer, the first light of day picked out the *sang-dragon* trees on the slopes of Morne Seychellois, while below the palm trees stood as motionless as the great granite boulders. The sand was whiter than anywhere else on earth, the sea bluer. As I heard the waves ripple on the reefs, I realised more than ever before what a spectacular sight lay before me, that this indeed was a paradise island, a natural playground for fun and relaxation ... if only visitors could find their way.

I had had a hard enough time getting home. At one point I had been told by a London travel agent that there was a twelve-month waiting list for a berth on the *Kampala* and I had managed to get on board only because of a cancellation. I took my father's latest letter from my pocket and looked at the envelope. The government had stamped a message across it: 'For your next holiday visit Seychelles. Isles of unsurpassed beauty 1,000 miles from anywhere where a friendly welcome awaits you.'

A reasonable sentiment, I thought, but they had forgotten to add that you needed your own ocean-going yacht to get there. The attraction of the Seychelles lay in an essential contradiction: our geographical isolation was our greatest asset and our greatest drawback. If we were to join the twentieth century, an airport was the first essential.

Then I heard the siren blow and I could see the small boat coming out to meet us with my family on board. The next half hour was lost in tears and handshakes and welcoming hugs, and when I heard the clock chime twice, I realised that I was finally home.

Chapter Three

THE WELCOME HOME party was a typically Seychelles affair. It went on and on. At one point it seemed that the whole island had turned up. Day lurched into night and blearily back into day and it was a decidedly weary young lawyer who presented himself before Chief Justice Sir Nicholas Patrick France Bonnetard, QC, to take his place at the Seychelles Bar. With my London wig and gown and my certificate I was well set up to become a respected member of the community.

If, as my father suggested, I could forget about politics, then my secure and comfortable existence was guaranteed because legal practice was lucrative. There was no separate profession of barrister and solicitor and only a handful of us to represent an assortment of clients in their encounters with the law. Nor were there any real estate agents, and we attorneys tended to fill the gap, not altogether ethically but often quite profitably.

When acting as an estate agent in property deals, a lawyer took on the guise of 'legal adviser' and usually received 5 per cent of an agreed price and 50 per cent of any additional amount which he managed to obtain. Even before the airport and tourism sent land values soaring, and town planning cast its shadow over the scene, there was an active market in real estate offered for sale by members of Seychellois landowning families who wished to emigrate, often to Australia.

One such deal concerned Cousine, a beautiful little island, which, with its neighbour Cousin, later a bird sanctuary, lies close to Praslin, about twenty miles from Victoria.

A young Italian man had been living an idyllic existence there with a Seychellois woman, but the idyll had been shattered by the return of the lady's husband, a merchant seaman. The husband demanded moral damages from him for seducing his wife and the Italian settled out of court, by handing over his boat, which was worth some £5,000. He returned broken-hearted to Rome while the happy husband sold the boat and went off to Australia with his faithless wife. I thought that I had seen the last of the Italian, but six months later he cabled me saying that he wanted to buy Cousine. The owner was willing to sell for 100,000 rupees and agreed on the usual terms with me. I cabled back saying that the Italian could have the island for 135,000 rupees and the young man accepted.

Since I was heading for London I arranged to stop off in Rome to hand over the title deeds.

It was a changed man who met me at Leonardo da Vinci airport. Dressed in typical *dolce vita* style, with Gucci boots and Valentino tie, he drove me into the city in his smart Maserati, and on the way he explained that he had gone to Seychelles originally to nurse a broken heart after quarrelling with and parting from his wife. Since returning to Rome he had fallen madly in love with an Italian blonde and wanted to marry her and take her back to Cousine as soon as he could arrange his divorce with the Vatican.

Money was no problem. His father was a wealthy stamp dealer, and when I visited his offices I was shown a stamp worth £15,000. It made me think what a crazy world we live in. There was a scrap of printed paper valued at nearly twice the price which the young man had paid for a hundred acres of unique, unspoilt, natural beauty.

But the price went up later on. The Italian sold the island for £50,000 to a group of German industrialists, who just before the coup refused £400,000 for it.

Court work was monotonous in one way – we always appeared before the same judge or magistrates – but stimulating in others, because of the variety of cases and the large crowd of interested or idle onlookers who packed the court each day and later used what they had heard and frequently misunderstood to fuel the fires of gossip throughout the islands. With the temperature in the eighties and humidity to match, we sweltered in our black gowns and white wigs to uphold the dignity of justice.

Most of the cases were larceny, petty and grand. One morning a washerwoman turned up asking me to represent her husband, who had been charged with stealing the safe of a Chinese merchant. The safe had contained 30,000 rupees.

'I'll pay you anything,' she said, 'if you can get him out of this mess.' To prove her point she plunged her hand down the front of her dress and drew from an enormous bosom a wad of notes that would have choked a horse. I counted out 5,000 rupees. There was no doubt where the money had come from. The husband was unemployed and she earned a pittance. However, I took the case, pocketed the fee and tried my best. I lost. My client got three years, which was not bad since the money was never recovered.

In another criminal case a certain Mr Joseph, who owned cinnamon bushes capable of producing about a ton of bark annually, was found in possession of twenty-five tons of it, packed in gunny bags and covered with coconut leaves. He was consequently charged with stealing or receiving the commodity, which had rocketed in value because the Vietnam war had stopped that source of supply and cinnamon is an essential ingredient of both Coca and Pepsi Cola.

Two days earlier a man had been sentenced to six months imprisonment for a similar offence, and Mr Joseph was a very worried man.

'Sir,' he said, handing me a brand new Barclays Bank savings book, 'I will pay whatever fees you ask.'

I looked at the book. Mr Joseph had opened the account two days earlier with a deposit of Rs 50,000, somewhat out of proportion to his monthly wage of Rs 800 as a carpenter.

I said that my fee would be Rs 7,000. 'Mr Mancham,' he replied, 'I'll pay you Rs 15,000 but please get me out of this mess.'

As sometimes happened, the police evidence was muddled and contradictory, one witness saying that Mr Joseph had denied knowledge of the cinnamon and the other that he had claimed it as his own property. I managed to convince the magistrate that my client had no case to answer, and he not only agreed but ordered that the cinnamon be returned to him.

That night Mr Joseph arrived at my house in a lorry. 'Sir,' he said, 'I've brought you half of the bark. I feel you deserve it.'

Meanwhile an important question was hanging in the air. Heather had written to say that she was missing me. She wanted to know what would become of our relationship now that we were separated by 10,000 miles. The fact was that I had started an association with the girl next-door. It was a problem. Heather, by island standards, had a certain sophistication and was certainly not provincial in outlook. She had been a faithful and loyal friend throughout three long years which had included many bitter cold winter nights. I had to face the situation realistically. Either I got her to join me on the island or our relationship would wither away.

My mother put pressure on me to decide. She was particularly fond of Heather and not very happy with my island love affair. Eventually I made my decision and cabled Heather about marrying me. This was done more out of a desire not to lose her love rather than a readiness to put an end to my bachelor life. It was a selfish attitude, but I was still a young man; too young, I suppose.

Heather accepted and for her it was a brave decision. To leave the comforts and the culture of England to join me on a remote island which time had passed by was, I thought, an act of true love. She managed to find herself a berth and within a few months she was with me.

In the Roman Catholic cathedral on 22 February 1963 Heather Jean Evans was given away by the head of the civil service and about seven hundred guests, including the Governor, Lord Oxford and Asquith, attended the reception. Of the many telegrams from friends overseas the one I liked best was from a wealthy American couple, Carl and Eleanor Heintz, on whose yacht I had spent a memorable few days visiting some of the outer islands. It said with typical courtesy and charm, 'Farewell to a wonderful bachelor.'

We went to live in a house at Glacis, at the northern end of Mahé, which had been in my mother's family for years and which looked across ten miles of ocean to the enigmatic island of Silhouette, its steep slopes covered by the last indigenous forest to be found in Seychelles and its summit usually capped by a puff of cloud even in clear weather. In the evening we sat quietly, awed into silence by sunsets of indescribable beauty, as the mynah birds chattered and fluttered among the bushes. Or we took the boat out and went fishing, cut off by a few hundred yards of water from insistent callers and the clamorous telephone. Often I reflected with Herbert Hoover that 'no one can catch fish in anger or malice' and pondered on the fisherman's unquenchable optimism that his luck will soon change for the better.

I was twenty-three. I had a beautiful wife and a secure future. I was living on a tropical paradise surrounded by friends and family. What more could any young man want? But every Garden of Eden has its serpent and mine was this constant itch of ambition, not only for myself, but for the improvement of the lot of the Seychellois. I had seen things that they had not and I wanted them to have a similar chance. I was blessed – some might say cursed – by the nagging need to do something more. I was unable just to lie back and enjoy myself. My work seemed little more than cosy retirement on a good pension. It did not stir the blood. And I could see complacency all around me.

The islands were run by a Governor appointed by the Colonial Office in London and in this man was vested all executive powers. He received advice from an Executive Council made up mostly of people he had nominated himself. Then there was the Legislative Council which passed laws but whose members were elected on a basis of limited franchise.

Unless you owned land or were receiving a minimum salary of some thousand rupees you had no right to vote. It is not surprising, therefore, that the only active political or quasi-political body in the country was the Seychelles Taxpayers and Producers Association which was made up of leading farmers and representatives of the mercantile community. It did not take me long to realise that *laissez-faire* and complacency was rampant throughout the whole administration.

Something needed to be done. For the first time in living memory the island was experiencing an element of political turmoil. As always the problem was money. A Seychellois surgeon, Tony D'Offay, had returned home after years working in England. He was in his fifties, a Fellow of the Royal College of Surgeons. It did not take him long to realise, however, that he was receiving a salary of something like 30 per cent less than expatriate colleagues, including some trained in Bombay and Madras, where they had been jobless. This anomaly was the result of the British Government's policy of paying an inducement allowance to expatriate civil servants. The idea was to encourage professional people to work in inhospitable climates, in deserts or malaria-ridden territories. This was all very well in theory, argued D'Offay, but you should not need an inducement to come and work in 'paradise' and he considered it unfair for Seychelles professionals to earn less than outsiders.

The government, in reply, argued that it could not induce people to work in their own country. It was a neat little argument, something that could have been dreamed up by Evelyn Waugh, and at first I found myself agreeing with D'Offay. Then, however, backed by the Taxpayers Association, he came to an absurd conclusion. In his irritation with the government, he decided that the Seychelles should go for immediate self-government.

In effect the Taxpayers Association was clamouring for an Ian Smith type of self-government, a split from Britain with the privileged few in control. This, to me, was ridiculous. The country was not ready for independence and I said so to anyone who would listen. I wrote to the *Seychellois* but my letter was not printed. The editor, Gustave de Commarmond, wrote back to me, saying that my article was contrary to editorial policy. This made me angry and when Tony D'Offay was put forward by the Planters Association for the vacant seat of Victoria and the Outlying Islands in a by-election, caused by the death of Major Ernest de Coulhac Mazerieux, I decided to stand against him and fight his self-government policy.

I made my first speech in a church hall. At first I was nervous, looking down at the expectant faces. There were teachers and civil servants watching me curiously, men and women who earned enough to vote. There were also the disenfranchised, the barefooted from the plantations, waiting for me to say something to them. They were not particularly interested because nothing any politician or would-be politician had said had ever affected their lives.

'While I was in London,' I began, 'I followed events in Africa with great interest and formed an opinion that the word "colonialism" had become synonymous with oppression, injustice and brutal exploitation. Yet this could not be said of Britain's role in these islands.'

They looked at me blankly. Some shuffled their feet. Others yawned.

'It is true that Britain has been apathetic towards social reform and economic progress but British administration still signifies the freedom of speech and the rule of law which for citizens of newly independent countries is rapidly becoming a distant memory.

'The term "wind of change" was a timely expression once but has become overworked, mistakenly applied to the huffing and puffing of self-seeking and vainglorious demagogues. Let us not be afraid to change and to change drastically, but let us do it because we want to do it and because it is good for us, not because others have decreed it or because it is fashionable elsewhere.'

There was a smattering of applause at this and I continued. 'This whole expatriate business is a complex one. There are one or two expatriate heads of department in this town who walk about with an air of United Kingdom Secretaries of State, sometimes carrying a Bible in one hand and a bottle of whisky in the other, and they are as much to blame for the confusion as those planters who sit under coconut palms criticising government and talking about the terrible things the British did to Joan of Arc.'

This drew a few chuckles, especially from the barefoot brigade.

'Right in the middle of those two extremes stands the government of the Seychelles who, through its own lack of wisdom and forethought, created the very problem it was its sacred duty to avoid, namely a rift between two important factions of the community, the officials from abroad and the local-born élite. How can you call a place "paradise" but yet have to induce people to come and work in it? The officials from abroad should be given as much as they deserve on the basis of qualification, experience, and market values, but this inducement allowance business must be sent to hell never to return.'

A few people clapped but others looked confused. What was I doing agreeing with my opponent? But I noticed a few others who nodded and grinned. They knew that I had taken the wind out of D'Offay's sails. But what next? they were wondering.

I said that self-government under the taxpayers was a crazy notion. The cure would prove more fatal than the disease. Those who were seeking the privilege to govern were not entirely interested in the welfare of the mass of the people.

'Despite the history of benevolent neglect,' I shouted, 'we need the British link.'

Then I produced my trump card. I said that I was standing for an election on a ticket for introduction of universal suffrage – one man, one vote. Admittedly I was playing the game of political opportunism. To me it was incomprehensible how my vote – with my experience and qualifications – could be counterbalanced by that of a fellow islander who had spent his entire life on a far-away atoll doing nothing more than picking coconuts. True, the average person has a basic commonsense but I knew it was always dangerous to 'give a man a gun without first teaching him how to handle it'.

'Long live Mr Mancham,' they roared.

'Long live Seychelles!' I roared back at them. It was a good start.

During the campaign I discovered that the articles I had written from London had given me a political base. The voters had been faced with the same policy – or lack of policy – for years and they felt in need of a change. I spoke about the need for an airport to break our isolation and they began to take notice. I spoke about the potential for economic growth if we came into contact with the outside world. And while the voters were giving me a sympathetic hearing, the underdogs, those on the edge of the crowd without a voice, listened in awe.

I felt for the first time the extraordinary exhilaration of feedback from a receptive and enthusiastic audience. I felt that there was good vibration in the air. I felt that the people were ready for change. I felt like a prophet.

Meanwhile my father was watching from the sidelines with mixed emotions. One part of him was proud of me, but at the same time he was anxious. My political opponents were his friends and drinking partners. He had to sell to them to prosper and he was worried in case my political activities would harm his business.

On the day before the election, Tony D'Offay made his final speech. Standing in the same church hall, a tall, white-haired and distinguished man, one of the island's leading citizens, he described me as an inflated balloon from which all the air would soon escape when pricked.

However, to his amazement, the voters were in no mood for pricking and the 'balloon' won. It was on 12 August 1963, the day after my twenty-fourth birthday, that I was formally announced as the elected Member of the Legislative Council.

The planters could hardly believe it. For the first time someone had challenged their way of life and threatened their privileged existence. As I was sworn in, I felt proud. But truly I did not realise what I had taken on.

Chapter Four

THE MOST COMMON plea from outsiders who come to the islands can be summed up as, 'This is Paradise. Please leave it alone.' They see the beauty of the place and the friendliness of the people and they argue that any change can only be for the worse. Anything that interferes with their concept of paradise can only be wrong. The fundamental ecological law that interference with nature destroys the natural balance of things applies also to people, they will argue. And of course they have a point, which was illustrated one morning to me when a banker on holiday on Mahé came into my office. He was shaking his head and grinning to himself.

'I've just been talking to a fisherman a few miles from here,' he said. 'I'd been watching him from my room. Each morning he takes two hours to row slowly out to his one-basket trap. It seemed to me such a waste of effort that I suggested to him that he get a bank loan and buy an outboard motor, which would save time so that he could make six trips in the two hours. He looked at me as if I was crazy.

'"Six traps?" he said. "What would I do with all the fish?"'

'"Money," I said. "With all those fish you'll get more money."'

'"But what will I do with it?" he asked.'

'"Well, once you've paid your loan off," I explained, "you will be able to save until you have enough to relax and take life leisurely."

'He shrugged. "I'm doing that already," he said.'

The banker chuckled to himself. There was no answer to the fisherman's logic. It was a typical Seychellois attitude which went hand in hand with a gentle quality of life that over the years had caused visitors to describe the Seychellois as inhabitants of the last lost paradise, a place where paradoxically you can be poor but rich and happy, a land of little yet of plenty.

Others argued against any form of change by quoting the story of owls which had been imported from Mauritius to reduce the rat population, which was damaging the coconut plantations. Unfortunately the rats were too smart for the owls which turned instead on the beautiful sooty terns which were a feature of the islands. The government, which had previously paid a bounty for dead rats, now offered money for every owl shot, but despite all attempts the owls continued to multiply along with the rats while the sooty terns became almost extinct.

The moral must be, 'Don't import owls; don't import anything; leave the last lost paradise alone.'

It is an understandable romantic notion but, as I argued to the banker, 'This may seem like heaven to you, and your fisherman might seem content with his lot, but there are others who don't want to remain like museum pieces, frozen in time and space. They also want to travel and find out what the world is all about.'

I have seen groups of Seychellois cluster round a postcard from New York. To them it was amazing. To live fifty floors up must be next to heaven, they said. They did not know that it took an elevator to get there, that sometimes elevators get stuck, that the air was polluted and there was nowhere for children to play. But they were curious.

Whether the outsider, hunting for Nirvana in our islands, liked it or not, the problem of rising expectations had arrived and now, having tasted the first fruits of political success, it was my duty to do something about these great expectations and to loosen the shackles of isolation.

Social reforms in several areas were long overdue. The country was being run on a subsistence economy, balancing its budget on taxes raised locally with no surplus for capital development. The only aid from Britain was a road network that was being built on a labour-intensive basis. With no organisation of labour, there was a need for a minimum salary bill to protect the average working man. There was considerable unemployment. There was no maternity leave for expectant mothers and no paid annual leave for anyone.

It was obvious that the preoccupation of the taxpayers and producers was to get the best price for their copra and to pay as little tax as possible. It was also clear that the limited franchise meant that there could be little popular involvement in any possible progress. There was so much to be said and done but with *Le Seychellois* closed to me I had nowhere to write what I wanted. Then one morning I met Joseph Stravens in the street. He was about to retire as head printer for the government and he asked why I was no longer writing for the *Seychellois*.

I told him, 'Every time I write they refuse to publish.'

He frowned. He had enjoyed my articles. Then he smiled.

'Why don't you start your own newspaper?' he said. 'I inherited an old clam shell printing machine years ago. You can have it.'

And so, out of that brief encounter, the *Seychelles Weekly* was born, the first edition printed in October, a month after the election.

It was while working on the paper that I began to come into regular contact with an old friend. David Joubert was headmaster of St Paul's School in Victoria. A short, muscular black man and a little wild with a drink in him, Joubert is a born entertainer, intelligent and ambitious.

I had first got to know him in London. He had joined the British Army to find out what the outside world looked like and had quickly risen to the rank of sergeant. He then applied for a commission and was turned down. At that time the British Army was not ready for black officers. Furious, he had come to my Hampstead flat looking for advice. Together we drafted a letter to his commanding officer criticising the prevailing prejudice and seeking the right to opt out. The Army had been only too willing to agree and Joubert returned home.

Now with the paper launched, I found that we were meeting nearly every day in my office in Progress House where Joseph Stravens had sent the press. We found that we were in almost total agreement about the way forward for the islands and it was out of our continuing discussion that the Seychelles Democratic Party would be born.

But in the meantime I discovered that the outside world was taking an interest in what I was doing.

Three months after the election I received a call from the Governor, the Earl of Oxford and Asquith, suggesting that I should represent Seychelles at the Kenya and Zanzibar independence celebrations.

I was flattered. The trip would cost me a year's savings but the money would be well spent making contacts and so, for the first time as a politician, I left the islands, my wife beside me, on the SS *Karanja* bound for Mombasa.

The Zanzibar Government put on an elaborate programme of celebration. The highlight was the independence ceremony which began late in the evening of 9 December with HMS *Ark Royal* and her escort HMS *Eskimo* putting on a naval display in the port watched by all the guests of the Sultan, including Prince Philip who was representing the Queen.

The next day the Sultan gave a lunch party at the palace where I met Prince Philip, Mr Ralph Bunche, of the United Nations Organisation, and dozens of politicians. One of them was a short man in the uniform of the Chinese Communist Party, introduced as Ho Ying, the Chinese Ambassador to Tanganyika. He drew me aside and spoke through an interpreter. I knew that he spoke good English but he made use of the interpreter so that he had more time to weigh up questions and answers. After exchanging pleasantries, he took my arm and moved closer.

'Mr Mancham,' he said. 'If you are interested in getting rid of the British, come and see us in Dar es Salaam after you've been to Nairobi.'

I think I just blinked, said something inoffensive and moved away. I was quite shocked but the irony of the situation was quite apparent. Here was I, a young inexperienced lawyer, hardly elected and paying my own fare, mingling with high-ranking politicians and being approached by a representative of the greatest population on earth.

Those were the days when the Red Chinese were very active in African politics, trying to win support in the United Nations against Taiwan.

As I backed away from Mr Ying, the RAF planes swept over the palace in close formation and I remember thinking, 'Zanzibar may be gone but the RAF is still braving the skies.' Prince Philip looked up and smiled while Mr Ying stood, looking suitably inscrutable.

A few days later Heather and I boarded a BEA Fokker Friendship bound for Nairobi. Among the passengers were the Rt. Hon. Duncan Sandys, Britain's Secretary of State for the Colonies, and Mrs Indira Gandhi with her two sons. She was representing her father, Prime Minister Nehru.

Kenya's independence celebrations were a great success. African dancers from all over the country performed masterpieces to the applause of the throng who had packed Uhuru Stadium.

The most grandiose event of the celebrations was undoubtedly the State Ball which took place in City Hall on 12 December. For the first time Kenya showed an atmosphere of racial harmony. Kenyatta was the first on the floor with Miss Sandys, daughter of the British Secretary of State and a grandchild of Sir Winston Churchill. Next was Prince Philip with Mrs Milton Obote, wife of the Uganda President, and, to crown all this, a grand cabaret with special guest Harry Belafonte and other stars performed in an ambiance of colour, joy and extreme gaiety.

It had been an impressive trip for Heather and me but its true significance did not hit me until later. Not long after I had got back home came the news of the coup that deposed the Sultan.

The Tanzanian Government had involved itself in the violent overthrow of the new island nation twenty-three miles off the coast of Tanganyika, a revolution which resulted in the slaughter of thousands of Arabs. A few months later Nyerere was to forge a federation of the two countries into the new state of Tanzania. Zanzibar, once known as the Isle of Cloves, ceased to exist as a nation. Western diplomats and businessmen were expelled, an American satellite tracking station was closed and all the farms were nationalised.

I remember seeing the big delegation Nyerere had sent to the celebrations even as he was planning the violent overthrow on the island. So much, I thought, for the Organisation of African Unity and its sacred tenet of good neighbourliness. I remembered Mr Ying, the Ambassador to Tanganyika. The coup was a clear indication to me, if one was needed, that we would be better to stick close to Britain. Without them we would be defenceless and liable to be swallowed up like Zanzibar and its sister island Pemba.

Meanwhile Joubert and I were organising the formation of the islands' first political party. We decided to call it the Seychelles Democratic Party, committed to universal adult suffrage and integration with Britain. Its office was my office and the office of the *Weekly* – Progress House, Victoria. It seemed a good address and a good omen.

The party was born that December with the motto, 'Democracy and progress through moderation and stability'. I was leader with Joubert as my deputy and for sixteen years we worked well together despite the occasional disagreement over policy and timing.

Joubert set about organising trades unions, the first time such a thing had been attempted, and I helped him with the first strike, in which the dockworkers finally gained a respectable rate of pay for off-loading and loading the ships. We also managed to raise maternity benefits and gained two weeks annual paid holiday for the workers.

Yet I was still very much my father's son and whenever I wrote anything in the *Weekly* which I thought might annoy him, I made sure that on the day the paper came out I would be on another island, well removed from his anger.

We had our party and we had our newspaper. Now we needed something to publicise ourselves beyond our shores. Seychelles was hardly ever mentioned in the international press. There had been only two occasions when we had made the front page, when Makarios was exiled to Mahé and when Governor Sir John Thorpe drowned. We were not exactly big news.

I thought back to the voyage to Zanzibar when news of the death of President John F. Kennedy was announced on the radio. Passengers of different races and religions spontaneously burst into tears. His aura had been built up in such a short time, a glamour which was a natural phenomenon but intentionally built up by the painstaking work of a team of highly competent experts. Public relations was of immense value to politicians but, as I could not afford to hire people to blow my trumpet for me, I decided I would have to do it myself.

And so the Seychelles News Service was born. Neither Reuters nor Associated Press had a stringer in Seychelles and they were each glad to accept the service. I gave them priority for news items in strict rotation and every now and then I filed a story about myself and the SDP.

When an oil tanker hit an uncharted rock off Mahé and sank, it was AP's turn to receive priority. I filed the story, waited three hours, reworded it and filed to Reuters, who promptly cabled back, 'You must have been out fishing when the tanker went down. AP filed hours before.'

The news service was not designed solely for the aggrandisement of Jimmy Mancham, however. It was also set up to put Seychelles on the map and it was surprising how often opportunities came along for free publicity. A new fifty rupee note appeared with an illustration of a group of coconut palms, the branches quite clearly spelling out the letters *SEX*. This admirably suited the island of love image which Seychelles had acquired during the Second World War when travellers turned up to find that much of the male population was absent and the women friendly. When I drew the note to the attention of the press, I was flooded with calls. Pictures of the note appeared all over the world along with stories of the premium it was fetching from collectors. I was never able to discover whether the artist had done it intentionally.

Another publicity scheme which paid off handsomely was based on Shell Oil's slogan 'C'est Shell que j'aime'. I had seen it in France and persuaded the company to print stickers 'Seychelles que j'aime', the words framed in the company's clam shell emblem. The stickers were an instant success on the island and it became *très snob* for visitors to have one on their cars when they returned home. Once in Switzerland I met an old monk who had retired after years of working in Seychelles and who became deeply nostalgic when he saw the sticker on a Rolls-Royce parked in Montreux.

We also made headlines in Britain when the Labour MP for Pontypool, Leo Absé, returned home after visiting the islands and criticised the Governor in Parliament for closing down a proposed birth control advice bureau. The Governor, himself a fervent Catholic with five children, had taken this step in order not to offend the Church, which was all powerful and firmly in charge of the emotions of the islanders, 90 per cent of whom were Catholic. Mr Absé pointed out that the illegitimacy rate was 44 per cent and that he had seen hospitals crowded with children suffering from malnutrition.

The reaction of successive British governments was that if we wanted aid we would need to do something about birth control. Eventually the Governor got round the problem by introducing an advice centre funded by the International Planned Parenthood Federation which, as it was not government-sponsored, did not offend the Church.

But my father grinned when he read about Absé's protest. Through his ship-chandler's business he was the sole agent for and distributor of Durex contraceptives. Every time a warship arrived at Port Victoria, the captain would buy his entire stock for free distribution among the sailors. This practice annoyed the parish priest of Victoria, the Reverend Angelin, and one Sunday he denounced my father from the pulpit as 'a Catholic who is distributing a product aimed at interfering with the course of nature and the will of God'.

That evening, at a party hosted by the French Consul, Monsieur André Delhomme, my father cornered the priest. Father was always frank, especially after a few whiskies, and he told the priest a home truth – that the sailors and the locals did not buy the contraceptives as a birth control measure but as protection against venereal disease.

'And another thing,' he said. 'Promiscuity is rampant and it is the Church, not Richard Mancham, which is responsible for the moral well-being of the community.'

Reverend Angelin's sermon turned out to be the best advertisement Durex could have had. From that day on, more and more people came to my father's shop and those who did not know how to describe what they wanted asked for an 'Angelin'. To this day, the priest's name is synonymous with Durex in the islands.

Everything seemed to be going well until one day in May when we read an article from the East African newspaper *Daily Nation* in which Albert René, on his way back to Seychelles after two and a half years in London, announced that he had formed a political party whilst in England. Under the headline 'Independence or Else', we read:

> The president of the Seychelles People's United Party, 29-year-old Mr F. A. René, has spent the last two weeks in East Africa seeking support from leaders for his party's demand of Independence from Britain next year. Said Mr René in Nairobi yesterday, 'The situation in the Seychelles is getting more and more tense. People are impatient with the British rule. At present only a small minority of the population has the right to vote. The Legislative Council members are the puppets of the rich planters.' Mr René added that if the British Government did not accede to the wishes of the people, the party might declare 'positive action' as well as appealing to the United Nations. 'We won't reveal the details now because of the security position at home. But it is for this reason that we have sought help from all socialists and co-operative movements in the world before we embark on the actual struggle. No matter what methods we use, we must achieve independence next year,' he concluded.

The article was accompanied by a serious, almost angry-looking René in the company of an angrier looking Philibert Loizeau. René was keeping strange company. Loizeau had, to say the least, a worrying background. He had been convicted for the murder of a sailor and sentenced to be hanged but on appeal the sentence was quashed and he was jailed on a lesser charge. We had not seen or heard of him for years, only that he had been living in East Africa following his release from prison.

I reread the article. In theory there was nothing wrong with two political parties operating democratically and the formation of the SPUP would probably accelerate progress towards a one-man, one-vote system, but what worried me was the idea of independence next week and the implicit threat of violence in René's words.

Again I looked at René's serious face. He was four years older than I, small like Joubert but white; a hard-working, serious-minded lawyer. He had first left Seychelles to train for the priesthood in Switzerland but soon abandoned the idea and went to London – to Middle Temple – where he studied hard and was soon called to the Bar. He returned to the islands as I was following his footsteps to London. While I was away, he had practised law for two years but without apparent success. Again he travelled to England where no one had heard of him until now.

What we did not know was that he had been taking his holidays in Russia and that he had marched in London during the Cuban missile crisis, shouting 'Kennedy No: Castro Si', or that his party was supported by the international communist movements and that in the pursuit of his objective he was determined to be both ruthless and violent.

Blissfully ignorant of this, I invited a group of sympathisers to a meeting to discuss this new development. It was obvious to all of us that despite the 'winds of change' speech, the Conservative Government, under Sir Alec Douglas-Home, had not made up its mind what it wanted to do with us. We were geographically isolated, economically grant-aided and socially neglected. More worrying still, the Labour Opposition had stated that it wanted to liquidate its colonial responsibilities as fast as possible.

'Think of Zanzibar,' I said. 'Like other territories, independence has resulted in the loss, not a gain, of individual liberty. Dictators come in and the people have become prisoners with no rights and no defence. We don't want to let petty feelings of nationalism blind us from realities. The average Seychellois is looking for a better life in a framework of democratic freedom, not just a flag and our own stamps.'

After talking for hours we came to the conclusion that we

should accept the challenge of going all out for integration with Britain. We knew that Britain would quite probably give us independence tomorrow but integration, despite Colonial Office utterances about the wishes of the people being paramount, would be a different matter. It would be tough, but as I suggested, 'We lose nothing by aiming for the sky. We can at least hope to get over the trees.'

After agreeing on that policy that night, as President of the SDP, I sent a telegram to the late R. A. Butler, then Minister of State for Foreign and Commonwealth Affairs, stating that the party dissociated itself from René's demand for independence and that we wanted integration with Britain.

'And as a point of emphasis and example,' the telegram continued, 'if the USA can incorporate Hawaii as a state and France can consider Tahiti as a department, there is no reason why Britain cannot keep Seychelles.'

A few days later the Governor acknowledged the cable but within a couple of weeks Prime Minister Douglas-Home announced the date of an autumn general election – an election which would see the Labour Party returned to power.

Chapter Five

AS SEYCHELLES WAS losing its political innocence, a group of strangers arrived. There was a collection of them, all US Air Force personnel who had arrived following an agreement between Britain and America to build and maintain a satellite tracking station on Mahé.

The first I had heard of it was when the Governor called me to his office and presented it to me as a *fait accompli*. Mahé, it seemed, was exactly half way around the globe from the Philco Ford-operated tracking station in Palo Alto in California and therefore an ideal – and necessary – spot for monitoring orbits in space. My first reaction was indignation that the islanders had not been consulted but when I complained, the Governor pointed out that our request for integration was being taken seriously and any controversy over the station could only harm our case. If we wanted the privilege of integration, then we must accept the burden, he said. And so I merely registered my protest and did nothing further. I did not realise at the time the weight of the burden: Americans in Mahé meant automatic interest from Moscow.

The station was built quickly, in a matter of a few months, and we watched with growing curiosity as a strange shape took form on the top of the mountain called La Misère, four miles from Victoria. Soon the white dome dominated the area and was christened the Golf Ball. Inside was housed some of the most sophisticated electronic equipment in the world, tracking satellites which moved unseen miles above us. At a stroke the Seychelles had gone from the eighteenth to the twenty-first century.

We were on the map at last. I soon got over my irritation at not being consulted and got on with making the best of it. Soon after the station was built, representatives of Pan Am and the Philco Ford Corporation called on me to look after their legal interests. The retainer was $300 a month from each of them. I accepted and began making new friends. René, on the other hand, was committed to make enemies out of them. From the start he saw the tracking station as something he could attack and make use of. It had soon become obvious that René's party, unlike our home-grown variety, had not only been organised from abroad but was also funded from abroad. He set up his headquarters in Victoria Road and had the building painted bright red. From there he launched a newspaper with a rising sun as a symbol, called the *People*.

From the very beginning the paper carried articles deliberately calculated to disparage the USA and to lower the esteem of the American people in the eyes of the Seychellois. They were painted as villains in Vietnam and racialists at home.

The Americans bent over backwards to be accepted. They made it clear that if any of their people got in an argument with a Seychellois, he would be sent straight home. Here was the greatest democracy on earth expressly presuming its sons to be guilty and denying them the right of defence in order that peace could be bought in paradise. The trouble was that their wealth made them obvious targets for anyone who wanted to stir up trouble. No matter what they did, they were wrong.

They had the only modern refrigerator system on the island and began by buying stocks of lobsters. René accused them of depriving the locals of food. They took the point and imported their lobsters from Kenya. René then accused them of failing to support the local fishermen.

The same logic might have applied to fraternising with the girls. Ignore them and you discriminate. Don't ignore them and, with your money and sports cars and offers of US passports, you inspire jealousy. However, there was no way the Americans were going to ignore our women, and a number of them told me happily that it was a relief to find such friendly company after the rigours of feminism back home.

One of the conditions of the agreement between London and Washington was that the Americans could import food and provisions into the island free of duty. René attacked them. Here was the richest nation on earth, he said, depriving a poor island of much-needed revenue. The Americans reacted quickly. Through the auspices of the Catholic Relief Service Agency they imported tons of bulgar wheat in sacks as a substitute for the rice which was the islanders' staple diet. The trouble was that the Seychellois hated the stuff and René attacked them for dumping on us leftovers that their cattle and pigs had not consumed.

(Recently I saw that the lessons still had not been learned. Travelling in Micronesia in the Pacific, I saw a number of islands under American trusteeship. Behind most of the thatched houses stood beautifully mounted fifty-horse-power Johnson outboard-motors, monuments to American generosity but of no practical benefit since the islanders had no idea how to replace a simple spare.)

While attacking the Americans, René was also putting his case for independence.

It was a seductive case, especially to the poor and illiterate, and I realised that I had a hard job on my hands to convince them of the dangers that I saw in his policy. To begin the job it was decided that the SDP would be holding a meeting in Garden Square on a Sunday in July.

Joubert and I drove down in the van that afternoon, wondering if anyone would bother to turn up. We were amazed at the sight which greeted us. There must have been 5,000 people crammed into the square. They had come from the seaside resorts and mountain tops, coconut plantations and tea estates, slum areas and fishing villages. There were the old and the young, black and white and all shades in between and from all walks of life. It was an astonishing turn-out. Now I had my audience and it was up to me to try to convince them. As I stood on the roof of the van listening to Joubert introducing me, a group of René's supporters turned up. The *Seychelles Weekly* later described their attempt to wreck the meeting:

> Frustrated-looking Serge Pothin, man-about-town Harold Underwood and never-satisfied, Zanzibar-born Harry Payet with a small group of Victoria's detested hooligans walked in the field carrying banners with such slogans as 'Down with Mancham' and 'Up with the SPUP' and inviting the people to listen to them.
>
> Despite all their calls for an audience, not one adult left the crowd to follow them, not one person offered a word of support as they marched on the northern side of the square in fascist style pursued by a small group of innocent young children. They were finally chased off the field by Chief Police Officer Hook to the satisfaction of everyone except themselves.

The interruption over, I addressed the crowd. I told them that we needed economic development and a policy of friendliness to all. I explained my fear of communism, the threat of class warfare having no relevance to the islands. I outlined my fears of independence and finally challenged them to say whether they wanted it. They roared back 'NO' at me, a vast bellow of agreement which echoed in the distant hills of Trois Frères.

'Long live the Seychelles Democratic Party,' they roared.

'Long live the Seychelles,' I roared back, as the van drove off.

It was one of the most satisfying days of my life. And so began the first skirmishes of a battle between the two parties which led up to a general election in 1970.

One Sunday, the main square would be filled with people dressed in red for an SPUP rally; the next, it would be awash with the blue of the SDP. It was an exciting time, the first time the islanders had played political rock'n'roll, but eventually it led to a terrible rivalry with families split and fathers at the throats of their sons.

One day Victoria would wake up to find the shops and buildings covered in red-painted slogans, 'Yankees Go Home'. The next the whole island would wake up to see the entire road network splashed with blue, 'Yankees Yes, Communists No'.

The Governor at that time of growing political turmoil was a gentle character. The Earl of Oxford and Asquith was the grandson of the British Liberal Prime Minister, Asquith. Tall and white-haired with black bushy eyebrows, he liked nothing better than to search the reefs for coral shells. He was a likable Governor, not aloof like some of them, and everyone, even René, found it easy to get on with him.

One morning his secretary rang and asked me to come and see him in Government House. He had another *fait accompli* for me. Britain was about to annex three of our islands, Aldabra, Desroches and Farquhar which, with Diego Garcia 600 miles to the east, were to be known as the British Indian Ocean Territory. The idea was that Britain would then lease Aldabra to the Americans who wanted to build a military base.

I blinked at him. Visions of the tracking station returned. We had not been consulted about that. We were not about to be consulted about this either.

I asked him why the feelings of the Seychellois had not been canvassed and he shrugged. Britain and America, he said, were getting sick of blackmailing pressure exerted by governments in whose countries they had built military or naval bases. The concept now was to have a chain of bases around the world on uninhabited islands. It all added up. The British policy of withdrawal east of Suez coincided with Russian reaction to the Cuban missile crisis. At the same time as the Russians were taking an interest in the Indian Ocean, the socialist government in Britain was committed to working hand in hand with the Americans although they themselves were pulling out.

Since the closure of the Suez Canal, the super-tankers took their oil from the Gulf States to the West via the Cape. Aldabra was close to the sea lanes and it only needed a penny atlas to see its strategic value.

I huffed and puffed for a while, but the Governor reminded me again that I was pressing for integration and that with the privilege came certain responsibilities. And then he played his trump card. The price of the islands was to be an airport built with Anglo-American funds.

I had to agree. It was like putting a piece of cake in front of a starving child. But it would have been nice to have been asked.

It was obvious that BIOT was being born under a veil of secrecy.

The Americans were quick to recognise my potential value to them as a rising politician who was essentially on their side. I was invited to the States for two and a half months under their Leader Grant programme which was designed to enable them to meet the cost of educating leaders from the Third World as to what America was all about.

I saw for myself how this modern democracy worked – and, in some cases, did not work. If there were ghettoes to be seen, then I was taken to them. If people were poor, then we did not just drive by. If there was fairness then I discovered how fair and for whom it was fair. If there was something to learn then I learned. From government to administration, to bureaucracy, to legislation. It was all there.

Right upon arrival it was carefully explained that the United States was a free and open society and that it was for me to decide how best to make use of the government's hospitality. I said that in view of the SDP's policy of integration with Britain I would like to visit the US island dependencies of Hawaii, Puerto Rico and the Virgin Islands, and also some of the slum areas in order to understand better the problem of ghettoes. A programme was arranged which met these wishes and included a tour of Harlem.

But the greatest insight came from a part of my visit that was never intended to be on any State Department tour – and was not.

A few months before leaving the islands, I had met Carl and Eleanor Heintz aboard their yacht *Wanderlure* and when they heard I was visiting the States they insisted I should come their way and relax. It did not exactly turn out that way. The Heintzes eldest son, Carl Jnr., and his partner Peter Malatesta, who was a nephew of Bob Hope (and who recently started a controversy by claiming in a book that Frank Sinatra once worked for the CIA), took me on a weekend of parties in Beverly Hills and Palm Springs. We then headed for the Balboa Yacht Club in Newport and a gentle cruise around the island of Catalina. The company was agreeable and uncomplicated. Apart from my hosts, we were joined by two of Barry Goldwater's children, an assistant to Senator John Tower of Texas and a clutch (if that is the correct collective noun) of starlets from the Hollywood lots. Imagine the scene: young, easy-going people. Republicans in the traditional sense, confident and, in their case, rich. It was a frame from the Good Life, yet the Technicolor was turning to sepia.

As we sailed off the coast, Watts burned.

When we arrived back at the pier, the whole group was ushered into a line of Cadillacs. The tans were still even, the eyes were heavier. Within minutes, the cars pulled up outside the gunsmith and we all went inside. Within minutes, we were out again, back into the cars, each with a handgun 'to protect us on our ways home'.

The yacht, the starlets, the rich style. All these things I could cope with. But this was something beyond me. I sat in the car with its air-conditioning protecting me from the outside, but the atmosphere was right there in my hand. It was the first and only time that I have ever handled a gun, yet I have never forgotten its terrible touch, nor that day. It was the day that I learned that children of democracy could and would fight each other for the right to live their version of what I, as an island boy, thought was everybody's equal right – self-determination. That day, democracy let me down and I returned to Washington and stood for a long time with my back to the Lincoln Memorial and wondered how many Americans were also questioning the values of their society.

But was I really to reject this system? Had there not been a strength in Watts that was disturbing, but at the same time comforting? What about the other things I had seen and heard? What about Archibald MacLeish and Dean Rusk? I had listened to them talking during the memorial service for Adlai Stevenson. These were great men, bred by a system and ready to defend it against all who would destroy it without showing it could be replaced with anything better. There were the Webbs. I had spent six days in Vermont with Derrick Webb and his wife, both staunch Republicans. His grandfather had been a hard railroad man and had pushed the spikes and whistles of his form of democracy across the Union. The Webbs in the comfort, but not the smugness, of their home were willing to face any challenge to defend the system. It was a feeling of belonging, not simply to a system, but to a country that lived by and not just with that system. It must be remembered that in spite of my education in London and Paris and having been called to the Bar of the revered Middle Temple of Law in England, I was miles away from this American society of the early sixties.

But then one day in a bar in San Francisco (this was after Watts) somebody asked me which state I was from. To an American, this might seem an innocent incident, but to me, it was a question that made me realise the strength I felt in the system I was trying to understand. If I had replied New York, New Mexico, Arizona or Florida, he would have had no reason to doubt me. What he did not realise was that with my accent, my culture and my background, I could never *feel* like an Englishman. I could never *feel* like a Frenchman. Yet I knew I *could* become to feel like an American.

It was a feeling that has remained with me. Yet it was also a feeling that was to be tested during the coming years as time and time again I found myself having to defend my affection and trust in the West against those who would destroy it, given the slightest chance.

Before leaving the USA I returned for a final meeting with my host. Mennen Williams, better known as Soapy for his familiar association with the Mennen cosmetic empire, had been six times Governor of Michigan before Kennedy had appointed him Secretary for African Affairs, in which capacity he had been slapped on arrival in Salisbury by a white man for having once made a statement in favour of majority rule. He received me graciously and listened to my comments on the fact that the islands' social stability and price structures were being profoundly disturbed by the sudden advent of 200 highly paid American technicians, separated from their wives and competing for the best accommodation in which to instal the island's prettiest girls, and addicted to driving fast cars while under the influence of strong drink.

I also said that they had dragged Seychelles into the arena of international power politics which tracking stations signified, however innocent their purpose was claimed to be. In the circumstances I felt it was my duty to make a plea for some American financial support for the development of the islands.

Secretary Williams expressed sympathy but declared that congressional laws prevented the USA from giving aid to a territory that was dependent on another country. Here was another example of bureaucratic rigidity. I left the US feeling rebuffed and disappointed, and conscious of the difficulty I would have in explaining to an unsophisticated electorate that the richest nation on earth would give nothing to our islands in return for the use of our land and the problems that were caused. Here was another godsend for René's propaganda machine.

Those ten weeks had proved fascinating but they had taken their toll. Standing in line at Washington International Airport waiting for my flight to London, I felt unusually depressed. According to the news the Vietcong had massacred another hundred South Vietnamese. The world was a dreadful place and politics the worst profession. Only an encounter with a beautiful and intelligent woman would restore my normal optimism.

Then I saw one. She was elegant, sophisticated, unmistakably wealthy and she was definitely on my flight. I edged into the line of boarding passengers and dropped into the seat beside her. She was reading a copy of French *Vogue*.

'Excuse me, madame,' I said in French after a respectable interval, as the plane levelled off at 33,000 feet, 'I beg of you to enable me to settle a bet with myself.'

'And what could your bet have to do with me?' she replied with a slight twitch of her delicate lips.

'It is that I can identify the perfume you are wearing. If I lose the bet, or if you decline to answer the question, I shall have to impose on myself a penance of frightful severity.'

'Then you had better guess right,' she invited.

'Well, then, chère madame, it has to be one which parallels your elegance, which matches your style, which complements your beauty. It could not be Joy, which Patou vulgarly advertises as the world's most expensive to attract Americans. It must be one of those subtle fragrances which appeal to discriminating tastes. Would I be wrong in saying that the only scent which meets the qualifications you required of it today is Calèche?'

'You must be an expert, monsieur,' she said, plainly surprised. I shrugged modestly, forbearing to mention that my wife owned a shop which sold perfume and that I had made use of occasional visits there to educate my nose.

Once the ice has melted it is a matter of time until the water gets warm, and soon I learned that Isabelle was the wife of a wealthy Swiss banker, who valued her as a social and domestic asset but was unresponsive to her yearning for personal fulfilment. She was bored with the mixture of money politics and village gossip which characterises Lausanne society and was looking forward eagerly to two days alone in London, which a friend, the wife of a retired industrialist, and whose amorous intrigue with an Italian waiter she was facilitating by regular invitations to afternoon tea, had assured her was now the centre of gaiety and permissiveness.

We dined at Annabel's and spent Sunday in bed, wrapped in each other and the illusion of immortality peculiar to such moments, and not until late that night did we give a thought to the future.

'My darling,' said Isabelle, 'I think it must end here. You are a well-known person and my children are growing up. I cannot afford scandal. It is best that I do not give you my address.' Then remembering some lines from Shakespeare's *Julius Caesar*, when Mark Antony bad farewell to Brutus, I said, 'I understand how it is,' and I added manfully, 'If we ever meet again we shall smile indeed. If not, well, this parting is well made.'

People working under pressure often need an opening valve to let off steam. Some go for alcohol. Others smoke heavily. A few become the unfortunate victims of drugs. I discovered with Isabelle that my strong – or maybe weak – point was that I found great solace in the company of women, particularly those who were both intelligent and beautiful. A *tête-à-tête* by candlelight would normally provide temporary and useful respite from whatever political problems and frustrations that beset me.

Leaving Isabelle, I took a taxi to the Colonial Office in Great Smith Street, the place where only a few years before I had met the man who did not know whether Seychelles was British. But now I was returning as the leader of a political party to meet Anthony Greenwood, Secretary of State for Colonial Affairs. I was slightly apprehensive about meeting a member of the victorious Labour Party which had declared a policy of relinquishing the colonies. But Greenwood lost no time in assuring me that the British Government remained committed to respect the wishes of the people, which wishes would always be regarded as paramount. I was happy with this. The next question was about the construction of the proposed airport. I had not started my plea when Greenwood asked whether I had heard the dreadful news.

'What dreadful news?' I asked.

'Whilst you were in the USA a bomb exploded at the Seychelles Club,' he told me.

It had been placed under a table where three visiting British MPs had been sitting. Fortunately everyone was dancing when it exploded and no-one was seriously hurt.

I could hardly believe the news. A bomb in Seychelles? It was unthinkable, a contradiction in terms, and I realised that with the explosion the islands had lost their political virginity. No more would the *Weekly* be able to write light-heartedly about Police Officer Hook chasing a group of demonstrators. It had suddenly become serious.

I flew straight back to Mombasa where the Americans gave me a seat on their seaplane to Mahé. It was a privilege because civilians were not normally permitted on board an Air Force plane. As it splashed down in the harbour at Port Victoria, I realised that perhaps I was the first Seychellois to come home by air, but whatever little pleasure I felt was soon dispelled when I met the SDP's welcoming party.

'You heard about the bomb?' Joubert asked, adding, 'The place is still in a state of shock ...'

'Was it the SPUP?'

Again he shrugged. The police had been unable to find the bomber and no-one had claimed responsibility, but everyone was convinced that René was behind it.

Later with hindsight we realised that those who funded liberation movements had been appalled at the squandering of funds by so-called leaders who preferred the salons of London and the gaiety of Paris to the dangers of physical revolution. It appeared that a COD system had been established. 'Show us some positive action and you will get your cheque.'

The Seychelles Club bomb was the first in a series of invoices . . .

Chapter Six

FOUR MONTHS LATER René's party was given another target to attack when in the House of Commons Anthony Greenwood announced the formation of the British Indian Ocean Territory. Greenwood said that the islands of the new colony would be available for the construction of defence facilities by the British and Americans. Appropriate compensation would be provided. Mauritius was to get £3 million for the Chagos group which included Diego Garcia, while we got our airport.

It was the sort of target which René could not miss. Immediately alongside the banners about independence were hoisted others proclaiming 'No to Base'.

Now more than ever before, outside finance was being poured into his kitty to stir up trouble and create maximum opposition to the continuation of British rule. From that moment onwards, his philosophy of positive action started to take concrete shape. Paid propagandists were recruited to penetrate the most distant households, to spread anti-West, anti-SDP and anti-Mancham feelings.

Three months later when the British Government's emissary, Sir Colville Montgomery Deverell, arrived in Seychelles to investigate the constitution, internal politics had reached a feverish pitch and the SPUP were more than ever committed to a policy of disturbing the peace.

I could have been the first victim when someone placed a bomb beneath the floor of my office in Progress House. Luckily I was home at Glacis when it exploded. It was an amateurish device and went off at the wrong time, in the middle of the night. Instead of blasting the building, the thing exploded downwards, gouging out a large crater. I was, to say the least, shocked by this unexpected violent development.

The following Sunday, after a public meeting in Takamaka,

west of Mahé, David Joubert and his wife were on their way to evening service at St Paul's Cathedral when they were manhandled by a group of eighteen. Joubert was thrown over a bridge into the river, then stabbed in the throat with a broken bottle. The wound required several stitches but he was lucky that the glass just missed his jugular vein, or he would have been killed. Today he still bears the mark of that vicious attack.

The bomb and the attack on Joubert showed how far the islands had come. They were now a long way from being the most peaceful group of islands in the world.

Our party responded to the SPUP political violence with restraint. I knew that the great majority, brought up under Christian ethics, abhorred violence and I knew that the way to the hearts of the people was through song and laughter.

My brother Mickey, perhaps the best vocalist the islands had produced, became a great asset to our campaign bandwagon. He wrote over fifty songs which on the whole popularised the theme of non-violence, said 'No' to independence and called for fraternal understanding.

We were now fighting a real election. Sir Colville Deverell's visit had resulted in the introduction of adult suffrage, which saw the electorate expand from 2,500 to almost 20,000. These new electors were to vote for a new Governing Council with eight members, the Council to be a legislative and executive body.

We fought the election with Mickey's songs and a carnival atmosphere. The songs attracted big crowds who, in between the singing, were being educated about what we saw as the social and political consequences of breaking our links with Britain. The lesson of Zanzibar was regularly recalled. 'Think of all the dozens of political leaders who made use of emotional issues to seek popular support for independence,' we said. The result was the most gruesome type of dictatorship and the denial of human rights.

For five months before the December 1967 election political skirmishes were fought throughout the islands with meetings now almost daily. The debates became fiercer and families more divided, yet we still tried to keep it lighthearted. On one occasion a group of us disrupted one of René's meetings by reciting Hail Marys as he tried to speak. He was not amused.

By the time the elections came round, we had done just enough to convince the majority of our case, winning four seats to three with one going to an independent. The result was a blow to René who had continually proclaimed that the majority supported his policy. As always he had an explanation for his defeat.

In an editorial typical of many, he wrote,

> We are all aware that as a people we are very fond of music. We like fun and we never miss an opportunity to be gay. We enjoy entertaining and being entertained. It is this very love of amusement that in the past made us lose our sense of balance with Mancham. He would go into Seychelles history not for what he will or will not do for the Seychelles people. He would be remembered for having realised that thousands of Seychelles people shut their minds to reason and logic when fed with fun, music and beer.

(This was another way of confusing the people, most of whom could not anticipate that the fun, music and beer they were enjoying were far tastier than the bombs, machine-guns and rifles that were to come.)

So the new Council was set up, but the problem was that the Deverell constitution was an experiment that was untried elsewhere in the empire. René and I and the independent elected member, Dr Hilda Stevenson Delhomme, were each made chairman of one of the committees, the objective being to advise the Governor on the formulation of policy, but it soon became obvious that the polarisation of politics made the constitution unworkable.

If I made the proposal, for example, for an increase of fifty rupees on holiday allowance, the SPUP would move an amendment for seventy-five rupees – all for partisan advantage *vis-à-vis* an illiterate mass which tomorrow would have a vital vote to decide the future.

Whether we were for integration or independence, it became obvious that the only system around which we could agree had to be based on a Westminster style of government.

It was important to try to get some answers from Britain. The new constitution was unworkable and the people were worried about the BIOT agreement, wondering whether Britain was taking a piece of strategic territory with one hand while trying to get rid of her responsibility towards us with the other.

On top of that, a local court case had confused people about the intention of the British administration. A leading trades unionist, named Finley Roselie, had resigned from the SPUP when he had discovered the party's links with the communists. Out of the SPUP files he had stolen a letter from Philibert Loizeau to René which proved that they were plotting something with the Russians. Roselie published the letter in the *Seychelles Weekly* and was promptly charged with theft. Poor Roselie. Under the Russian system he would have won a medal for his bravery. In Seychelles, under the British administration, he was heavily fined by Chief Magistrate Eric Bossy, MBE. The result of the case demoralised many SDP supporters who wondered what game the administration was playing.

And so again I packed my bags and headed for London. Again I walked through Whitehall and through the portico of the Foreign and Commonwealth Office. Again the civil servant who met me was polite and evasive, and it was obvious that I would get no positive response to my queries about our future status. It was the old noncommittal story of wait and see.

There was only one thing to do. I met the press. Next day the Seychelles' plea for integration was all over the national papers. The reporters noted that investment was being held up because of uncertainty over our status. They wrote about my fear of a possible take-over and they posed the question, what was wrong with giving us similar status to the Channel Islands? One writer speculated that the government was worried about setting a precedent. Give the Seychellois the right of unrestricted entry and perhaps 3.75 million in Hong Kong would immediately agitate for the same privilege.

Thomas Hughes of the *Daily Telegraph* was particularly astute.

'Their needs are clear,' he wrote. 'What cannot be foreseen is Britain's need of them in a space age. In a world of changing political patterns, it would be foolhardy to spurn their advances.'

He might have added that few in Britain could have foreseen the future strategic importance of our islands.

Despite this press coverage, the trip had not been reassuring, so I decided to go to Gibraltar on my way home to assess possible support for an idea that had been developing in the back of my mind. I thought it would be a good thing to form an anti-independence front with Gibraltar and Fiji, to present a united case to influence Britain into maintaining links with each of us. The Gibraltarians did not want independence because of their fear of Spain; the Fijians were worried because their Indian immigrant population had exploded to an extent that it formed the majority on the islands.

I landed at Gibraltar and met Chief Minister Sir Joshua Hassan and the Leader of the Opposition, Peter Isola. They were both responsive to the idea and for a while it seemed as if it might work. I was also getting positive replies from Fiji. Unfortunately the whole idea came to nothing because Britain, anxious to dismantle the empire, soon bought off the Fijians by offering them a constitution which assured the native minority the government mantle over the Indian immigrants. Naturally they took up the offer and became independent.

The trip had proved to be of little use and I had returned to the islands with no promises and no further clarification about our future. However, one thing I had been assured of. Construction of the airport was definitely on.

It was my custom, for the *Seychelles Weekly*, to check the incoming passenger list on the *Kampala* and *Karanja* to see if there was anyone who might make a good interview. One day I saw the name Sara Leighton. I knew only that she was a painter from London and that she had been described by her mentor, Pietro Annigoni, as 'probably the most perfect example of an English Rose'.

That was enough for me. When the siren sounded announcing the sighting of the *Kampala* I jumped into the launch and set out for the five-mile trip off the reef where the ship normally anchored. When I saw Sara, I knew exactly what Annigoni meant.

In her book, Sara describes our meeting:

The launch arrived but instead of our host and hostess, a young journalist had audaciously pirated the craft in order to get an immediate interview and I had no choice but to let him take us to the mainland. I was somewhat rattled at these Gordion Knot tactics. The man was young with black hair and his blue eyes were at variance with the slight Oriental cast of his features. He was well-built and attractive but I was in no mood for his dynamic strategy, as he tried to interview me over the roar of the engine.

'Young man,' I said, trying to make myself heard as I turned my face from the rising spray, 'If you want to interview me, would you kindly do it up at the house – not here where I can't hear myself think.' I had, I felt, put him firmly in his place. It was as well that there was not a shred of malice in his make-up. For the next time we met, not only did he own the newspaper – he was the Prime Minister as well!

Not quite Prime Minister, Sara – not at that time. As far as I was concerned she was sophisticated, attractive and appealing, and I was determined that she should not leave the Islands of Love without sampling their delights.

Within a few days I was driving her around the beauty spots. She told me that she had been asked to come to Seychelles by a man called Rex King who was one of the first businessmen to recognise the potential of the islands. He had set up a company in London called the Seychelles Development Corporation and bought a prime site at Beau Vallon and an estate at Anse à la Mouche, the latter to be divided into high-class residential plots. Sara was the darling of the London gossip columnists and King wanted her to visit Seychelles in order to attract publicity for his scheme. She had thought it over and told him she would do it – for one of the plots.

Sara and I had become very close and would spend time together whenever she was visiting Seychelles or I was passing through London. A wonderful woman, in more ways than one. Despite the years and the different stories which revolved around our lives, we remain special friends sharing a common philosophy about the mysteries of life and love.

And I shall remain eternally grateful to her. On one occasion during a later visit to the islands I told her a sad story. A nun and her Mother Superior had come to see me. The nun was in tears. The Mother Superior had just discovered that the girl was pregnant. In a small country with a majority of Catholics, any news of this would be a disgrace not only to the nun, but to the Mother Superior, the religious order and indeed the whole Church.

The Mother Superior had pleaded with me. 'What can you do to help? We have prayed all week and last night I dreamt that I should come and see you.'

I did not know what to do but immediately Sara came up with the solution. She would take the nun to London where she would quietly have her baby. And that is exactly what happened. Today the girl is back in Seychelles. No longer a nun, she is now married to the father of her child.

The girl's plight highlighted the power of the Church and I knew as an aspiring politician that it was important not to overlook that power, especially in a country where 90 per cent of the population is Roman Catholic.

Soon, people were identifying the priests with one or other of the parties and after each Sunday service the faithful were putting their own political interpretation on the sermons.

The priests were powerful and I had made some enemies close to the Bishop because of my father's controversial contraceptive sales and I also knew that some priests were trying to steal our thunder by demanding that we find overnight solutions to problems which had existed for as long as the Church had. If only, I thought, I could arrange a private audience with the Pope. That would show my commitment to the teaching of the Church.

My chance came early that year when I was invited to attend a study course in Geneva run by the International Labour Organisation. Maybe, I thought, on my way I could stop off in Rome. I dictated a cable to my secretary addressed to the Minister of Foreign Affairs of the Vatican, saying that James R. Mancham, the President of the majority party of Seychelles, would be visiting Rome and requesting an audience with His Holiness the Pope. It was signed by Frankie Grandcourt as First Secretary to the leader of the majority party. We did not add that he was the *only* secretary.

Within a few weeks I received a reply saying that the Pope would be happy to see me. There and then I decided to keep the matter to myself and not make any announcement until after the event.

And so I broke my journey to Geneva at Rome and one morning, dressed soberly in black suit, white shirt and tie, I was led awestruck by two Swiss Guards to the Pontiff's audience. The building was as I had imagined, grand and dignified, but I was surprised that I was not searched and as the door opened and I saw before me the frail little figure of Giovanni Battista Montini, Pope Paul VI, I was even more surprised that I was to be left alone with him.

For twenty minutes, the leader of 900,000,000 Catholics talked to me in French. I was astonished by the trust and confidence of the Vatican and impressed by the modesty of the Holy Father, who held my hands in the manner of a grandfather with a child. He had obviously been well briefed. Although he seemed to know nothing of the emerging politics on the islands, he knew that we had Swiss Franciscan priests and French religious brothers teaching at the school, and Irish nuns looking after the hospital. I remember answering his questions but I don't remember doing anything to lead the conversation.

At the end of the audience he gave me a book on the Vatican and his medal depicting him as an apostle of peace. I realised that the audience was over when a photographer appeared. I was pleased to have the occasion on record – for me, for Seychelles and for posterity, and at the time I thought nothing of the rather exorbitant fee charged by the photographer for his portrait of the Pope and me.

As soon as I left, I cabled the *Weekly*, making sure I was first with the news before the Vatican Radio announced it.

My cable took the country by surprise. René was angry and it took a long time before the Bishop forgave me for by-passing him. But my supporters thought it was a miracle and there was no doubt that I had considerably enhanced my standing among the people of the islands.

Chapter Seven

AS THE BATTLE between our two parties continued, it was announced in the international press that Tanzania was sponsoring the admission and recognition of the SPUP as a liberation movement, something that was to be discussed at the summit conference of the Organisation of African Unity in Algiers. Such recognition in essence meant that regular financial and material support would be given to René's party. They would also receive training in subversive activities through the Liberation Committee of the OAU.

The OAU was committed to the total decolonisation of Africa including what were described as the offshore islands. With Seychelles more than a thousand miles off the African mainland it was difficult to see where Africa started and ended. However the Prime Minister of Mauritius, Sir Seewoosagur Ramgoolam, had taken his country into the OAU and it seemed that there was no way out for us. We felt that as we could not fight such an organisation, the best policy was to join it.

The SPUP had in addition opened an office in Nyerere's capital, disseminating propaganda, and it became urgent for us to explain to our African neighbours that our policy of integration with Britain did not mean that we were, in consequence, anti-African. We were ready to argue that since Africa was denouncing the Ian Smith government in Rhodesia as representing a minority, they could not flout the wishes of the majority in Seychelles by subsidising a minority party. With these objectives in mind, the party decided that Joubert and I should go to Algiers to make ourselves heard.

Just as I was preparing to go, my father went into hospital with a liver complaint. Two days later, on 28 August 1968, with all the family at his bedside, he died.

On hearing the news, all the shops and offices in Victoria

closed spontaneously and his funeral attracted the biggest crowd ever seen in Seychelles.

As I said my last farewell to him, unconnected memories flashed through my mind. I remembered the straight-faced expression of a wireless officer on our second day out on the voyage to England when I first left home. The man handed me a cable from my father which read, 'Your future lies before you like a sheet of virgin snow. Take care how you tread on it for every step will show.' I remember being embarrassed in front of the wireless operator and now I felt ashamed of my embarrassment.

I recalled a letter he wrote to me when I arrived in London. 'Now you are in England, 10,000 miles from home. Give praise to God for all your blessings and do not forget to honour and respect the Queen. In this way you will show your appreciation for the country which is providing you with the opportunity for further advancement.' He followed this with a piece of advice. 'When you buy a suit, buy it a size too large. This will save you money as you will grow into it.'

Richard Mancham would have been a notable character in any community and in Seychelles he stood out prominently. Left poor and fatherless, he had worked his way up to become one of the island's most successful traders, yet money was not his god. He had a prodigious appetite for knowledge and his opinions were widely respected. He loved life and laughter, and could not bear to see a melancholy face at the club where he drank. Soon he would have everyone singing and depression would vanish like a morning mist. Yet he took parenthood seriously. He was a great man.

It was suggested that I cancel the trip but I decided to carry on. Father would not have wanted it otherwise. For him, if duty and affection were in conflict, then duty had to prevail. Members of the party had collected several thousand rupees and so we went, Joubert and I.

At that time we were relatively inexperienced about international conferences and it appeared that the new military government of President Boumédienne also had very little knowledge and information about what was happening in Seychelles. I had cabled the Algerians about our coming and on arrival we made the big mistake of 'playing the game' when our host mistook us for representatives of the Seychelles Liberation Movement. We were given a car with a chauffeur, constant military escort and a villa in a prestigious village some seventy kilometres from the Algerian capital, which had been specially built for the summit. Our villa was between that of the Mozambique Liberation Movement headed by Samora Machel, who is now President of the Independent Republic of Mozambique, and that of Joshua Nkomo and his delegates of the Zimbabwe African People's Union.

We were able to attend all the secret sessions of the Liberation Committee and to learn a few things about its operation and the prevailing thinking within the body. Some of the things revealed behind closed doors were quite amusing. For example, there was the revelation by a specially appointed commission that a recognised movement for the Liberation of South Africa which had been receiving an annual subsidy of £10,000 was in fact made up of a sixty-year-old man, his two elderly brothers and an uncle on the brink of death. There was also a lot of criticism directed at the extravagant lifestyle of those 'Liberators' who preferred to make a noise from a secure London or Paris base rather than fighting in the bush. And then there were the competing claims of different movements as to who represented who and therefore who should be recognised and subsidised. All told, it was a startling experience to be among all those people – many of whom were far more interested in acquiring power than in the welfare of the people they purported to represent.

I had never seen any country that was being run like Algeria then was. It was under martial law with armed soldiers on motorcycles, scooters, jeeps, tanks – everywhere. No doubt the whole military image conveyed a surface impression of extreme efficiency, particularly for one arriving from a group of carefree islands.

Joubert and I had received a collection of invitations to attend the opening of the summit, a dinner by Diallo Telli, then Secretary-General of the OAU, another one for a reception by H.E. President Boumédienne himself, and one to attend an exhibition in down-town Algiers organised to demonstrate the progress which liberation movements had achieved in several countries still under colonial tutelage. At the Seychelles corner there was a whole collection of blown-up photographs of people who were allegedly demanding independence from Britain. René and his SPUP had employed a clever ploy to deceive first the people of Seychelles and indirectly the OAU and the world. Capitalising on a recent rise in the price of rice, which was imported and distributed by the government, he had organised a procession to protest against it. But when the innocent and illiterate mass had turned up, placards distributed were ten to one about liberation of the islands. Among big bold slogans 'Down with the Union Jack', 'Freedom for our Islands', 'Liberty – Yes, Colonialism – No', 'Down with US Imperialism', were very little ones reading 'Give us cheaper rice'.

Joubert and I were excited about our find. The manoeuvre was a fraud on the OAU and all the way back in our comfortable limousine we discussed and agreed that on our return to the conference hall we would explain the mistake made about our status and all the prevailing circumstances of our case.

Unfortunately as soon as we arrived we realised that we were in serious trouble. Soldiers surrounded our car and we were placed under arrest. A sergeant said that we were to be taken before the Algerian colonel who was in charge of protocol and security.

The man whom we had met on a few occasions before was cool and curt and spoke in excellent French.

'I have received orders that you two must leave Algerian territory immediately.'

'Why?' we asked.

'It has been brought to our attention that you are British stooges, here to spy on our activities.'

'But, sir, we would like an opportunity to state our case ...'

'I am sorry, this matter is not within my discretion. You must leave the village immediately.'

There and then Joubert, who had been making the best of Algerian hospitality, interrupted.

'But, sir, what about our clothes? I have sent all my suits to the cleaners, and it is now nearly midnight.'

'Look,' said the officer. 'Take my advice. The Algerian authorities are grossly embarrassed about your arrival and presence here. We are under great pressure. The sooner you two are out of this country, the better for you and for us.' And then, addressing the sergeant, he commanded, 'Take these two people to their villa to pack their suitcases immediately, and then straight to the airport where they should be put on the first plane out – whatever its destination.'

At three in the morning at Algiers international airport and surrounded by armed soldiers, we learned that there would be no plane out before 9.00 a.m. We were driven a few kilometres away from the airport and locked up in a small room in what appeared to be a rural military outpost. Armed sentries picketed the building. There was only a small single bed in the room and as I lay there with Joubert by my side I prayed to God for morning to come and the earliest possible deportation from Algerian territory.

Without a wash and breakfast, at 9.30 a.m., we found ourselves on a flight of Air Algiers departing for Nice, without any baggage. We did not know where our suitcases were and we did not even care to ask. What we wanted was fresh air and the feeling of freedom. For the first half of the trip we were tense and spoke little. Afterwards we were more relaxed. We knew that if there was any technical problem, we could still head for Nice.

Disembarking at Nice after Algeria – what a contrast! The same sun shines over both countries, and they are separated by only a few hundred miles of sea. Yet what a great difference in the philosophy of life and political system! In Algeria the ladies were veiled and totally inaccessible. In the South of France they were bikini-clad, gay and alive. In Algiers nobody would utter an unpleasant word about Boumédienne and his regime. In Nice the first man we spoke to, the taxidriver, could hardly wait to tell us, 'De Gaulle c'est un salot – la cinquième république c'est pourri.' It did not take me long to realise to which camp I belonged – with or without suitcases.

Some years later I was told that Joubert and I got off cheaply from our Algerian odyssey. It appeared that the radicals on the Liberation Committee wanted the Algerians to arrest and charge us for espionage. Fortunately the Algerians did not wish to get involved in another fracas. They had enough on their hands with the international repercussions that were then resulting from their abduction of Moise Tshombe from his Majorcan hide-out and his subsequent murder on Algerian territory.

On my return I found an invitation from General de Gaulle on my desk to attend an International Assembly of French-speaking Parliamentarians in Paris. Before accepting, I went to see the new Governor, Sir Hugh Norman-Walker, the man who had replaced the Earl of Oxford and Asquith. I anticipated a problem because de Gaulle had recently annoyed the British with his 'Vive le Quebec libre' speech in Canada.

Sir Hugh squinted at the invitation as if it smelled of something nasty. He was a tall man, red in the face, and always wore a monocle. He looked up at me from behind an early morning gin and tonic and shook his head.

'You realise, Jimmy, that the French are breaching protocol again,' he said, flipping the offending invitation back at me. 'This should have been sent through the Foreign Office, not directly to you.'

'I know,' I said, 'but I don't see how this affects my position.'

He shook his head. 'I don't think you should go. Goodness knows what mischief the French are up to.'

I shrugged, picked up the invitation and left. I'd made up my mind; protocol or no protocol, I was not going to miss a meeting with de Gaulle.

On arrival I discovered that the President was underlining the significance of the conference by holding it in Versailles at the Grand Trianon, where he was to be host at an opening *vin d'honneur*. I arrived at the reception to find over a hundred people already waiting in the queue to be presented to the General and Madame de Gaulle, in the presence of the entire French Cabinet. The guests ahead of me were announced, shook hands and passed smoothly into the hall. When my turn came, however, the towering General seized my hand and would not let go. 'How have the British been treating you in Seychelles?' he asked, and proceeded to display a detailed knowledge of Seychelles history and its first habitation by French settlers and their slaves in the eighteenth century. It was five minutes before he released me.

Reporters from the press, TV and radio were there in force and their curiosity was aroused. 'Qui êtes vous, monsieur?' they enquired, and the next day several papers described the special attention I had received and noted that it had been the first direct political contact between France and Seychelles since the territory was ceded to Britain by the Treaty of Paris in 1814.

After the conference I was supposed to return to Seychelles direct from Paris via Nairobi, but I had an idea. Could not the interests of Seychelles be advanced by a little judicious exploitation of Anglo-French relations? I flew to London, taking with me the French newspaper cuttings and a copy of an official booklet, published for the occasion, entitled *The Crossroads of Our Influence* and showing on its cover a map of the Indian Ocean with Seychelles prominent. The following Sunday Colin Legum's column in the *Observer* carried the headline 'De Gaulle has his eyes on Seychelles', which, among other things, made the point that Britain was showing little interest in my integration policy.

News that the airport project was on washed up on our shores a shoal of entrepreneurs and our difficulty was to differentiate between the snapper and the shark. We did not want the fast-buck merchants and we hired Dunn & Bradstreet, the international status investigators, to check every individual and company who arrived with plans and ambitions. The status reports threw up some astonishing backgrounds. Among the 'sharks' were undisclosed bankrupts and a fair selection of wanted criminals ready to take advantage of those whom they thought were still backward islanders. They were soon told to get off the islands but fortunately there were many serious businessmen ready to risk precious capital in the name of free enterprise.

At the time of the announcement there were only 180 hotel beds and these were small cottage hotels. I realised that it would be criminal folly to allow haphazard development and we needed careful planning to provide an essential plan for tourism without spoiling the two basic ingredients of our appeal: the natural beauty of the islands and the natural friendliness of the people.

The London construction company W. & C. French (now French Kier Ltd) was among the first to announce the plans for a major hotel, to be called the Reef, at Anse du Pins. It was to be a luxury hotel with several hundred bedrooms. Then came the Mahé Beach hotel project costing more than £2.5 million pounds. I had several meetings with John Houlder, then managing director of Houlder Brothers, a subsidiary of the shipping company Furness Withy (and now chairman of Houlder Offshore) and convinced him that we represented a good investment area. In return for beach land, which we leased at a nominal rent, Seychelles had secured 15 per cent of the equity in this project.

Suddenly everyone was talking real money, projects with a lot of noughts at the end.

We were all quite aware of the contradiction, that same contradiction I had noticed when I first returned from London; that our isolation had proved our greatest attraction and our greatest drawback. Now it was apparent that the attraction for the new generation of airborne visitors would be that our islands had at the same time everything and nothing; their natural appeal could so easily be scarred by ugly development. The new visitors would need to be housed and entertained, but not in any way that would harm the away-from-it-all appeal. I had seen what tourism had done to other parts of the world and I was anxious to make sure it did not happen to the islands. The new industry could provide a substantial rise in the standard of living but it was something that needed firm control.

We were starting from ground level and could have made mistakes but we were lucky in having the advice of Lars Eric Lindblad, the international expert on travel, a man who had pioneered cruises to the Antarctic and the Galapagos Islands and tours to Tibet. He was quick to see the potential of Seychelles and in the early 1960s had initiated regular cruises on his cruise ship, the *Lindblad Explorer*, from Mombasa to our islands.

He believed that development should not be at the expense of nature, which confirmed my own belief that man can never improve upon natural beauty. Luckily the new Governor, Sir Bruce Greatbatch, shared our feelings and he enlisted the help of Denis Komlosy, an expert from the Ministry of Overseas Development. I was also lucky to have as my secretary Peter Wand-Tetley, a civil servant of high integrity and competence, and total dedication. Together we formulated a comprehensive plan: we stipulated that no hotel would be built higher than the surrounding coconut trees, and the architecture must blend with the natural surroundings; we prohibited the killing or capturing of birds and we made it illegal to catch the green turtles.

This attitude made us many friends, especially in conservation circles.

The SPUP's attitude to the news of the airport was predictably hostile. They knew that it would bring in money and – as they capitalised on dissatisfaction – they had to attack it. René claimed that the airport would have a quasi-military function and that, in any war, Seychelles would be first to be bombed.

And so as the decade came to a close, I continued living a schizophrenic existence, waging a local political battle at home between making trips abroad and consorting with world leaders. I may, on the face of it, have seemed to be a parish-pump politician, but the islands were assuming growing strategic importance, which meant that people in high places wanted to influence me and I, in turn, wanted to make use of their interest to improve the islanders' living conditions.

Chapter Eight

ON THE ECONOMIC horizon there was at last a future, but on the political one still hung a question mark which was getting bigger as Britain debated its policy of withdrawing East of Suez – a withdrawal which would leave the Seychelles as defenceless specks in a huge ocean. Investors were concerned about our future. They wanted security for their investment: something definite.

But things were slow to materialise. Months had passed since the announcement about the airport but there were still no bulldozers. And to complicate matters there was a rumour that the finance for the airport was to come out of the normal aid quota, despite the fact that we had given away three islands.

Once again it was time for me to pack my bags. I cabled London that I was on my way and that I wanted some answers. When I arrived at the Foreign Office it was the same old story. I was greeted by the same old courteous ladies as before who, after a dozen phone calls, finally identified the official who was to meet me. As I waited for him I looked around. The facade of the building was beautiful but the interior conveyed the impression of a shambles. The carpets were ancient, dating from the time when Britain ruled the waves.

'Mr So-and-so will see you now,' said one of the old ladies.

I do not remember the man's name. Every time I went to London there was a new man in charge of the Seychelles portfolio. On one visit I discovered that we came under the Pacific section; on another that we were part of East Africa; now we were attached to Hong Kong. Each time I felt more let down and the institution fell in my estimation by its clear inefficiency and lack of continuity.

Mr So-and-so was another pin-striped anonymity. I had wanted to see someone in government and again I was being palmed off with a civil servant. Again he was polite; again he was noncommittal. I might as well have stayed at home for all the good my visit had done me so far; and so again I thought of the obvious. When the front door is closed, go round to the back. I called a press conference.

It was held at the Reubens Hotel, not far from Whitehall. In front of me sat a group of reporters trying to look interested.

'Gentlemen,' I began. 'Perhaps you have heard about the Seychelles...'

One of the reporters yawned.

'I came over here to clear up a number of points with the British Government but no-one has had the courtesy to see me.'

The reporter stopped yawning and scribbled in his notebook. They began to take an interest.

'It saddens me that our islanders who are in the main patriotic to Britain are considered in Whitehall to be a liability and an embarrassment...'

Now they were interested. I went on to outline the integration question and to tell them that the money for the promised airport was being switched around the books, so that it seemed we had given away our islands for nothing. We wanted to start a tourist industry, so that we would no longer be a drain on the British economy, but we were being held back by the lack of an airport ... I spelled our problems out and they took their notes. The next day we made headlines again.

A few days thereafter there was a debate in the House of Commons in which William Whitlock, Under-Secretary of State for Foreign and Commonwealth Affairs, announced that the airport would cost £5.25 million which was separate and additional to normal aid.

'I want to make it absolutely clear that there is no fraud at all involved in this,' he said. But with respect to the political status of Seychelles he repeated that the wishes of the people would be Britain's main guide. He also announced that Lord Shepherd, Minister of State at the Foreign Office, would shortly visit the islands to discuss matters on the spot.

Thanks to the press conference, the trip had been a great success and now I could go back to the Seychellois and tell them what lay ahead.

Within a few months Lord Shepherd arrived in Seychelles to a tumultuous welcome. Disembarking from the Pan American seaplane, he walked along the pier and through Victoria towards Government House. To his right he saw the SPUP supporters lined up along the road. They were dressed in glittering red and waved their banners at him: 'GIVE US OUR INDEPENDENCE.'

On the other side of the road, the SDP supporters, dressed in blue, waved their banners: 'SHEPHERD, PROTECT THY FLOCK.'

The next day he met representatives of both political parties in separate session before attending a public meeting which had been called to demonstrate their support. The SDP crowd was much larger and more enthusiastic than our opponents and by the time Lord Shepherd left he had no doubt where the heart of the majority lay.

In March 1970 a constitutional conference was held. It was agreed that Seychelles should have a ministerial system of government under which the elected members would be responsible for conducting government affairs in all areas except for defence, law and order and foreign affairs, which were to remain the prerogative of the Governor. But there was still no pronouncement about our future status.

Soon the Legislative Assembly had been declared defunct and the Governor had ordered new elections. We sang our songs and repeated our demand for integration. After months of intensive campaigning, in which we visited most of our islands in search of votes, the result was a majority backing for the SDP which won ten of the fifteen elected seats in the Assembly. On 12 November 1970, in keeping with the spirit of the new constitution, I was asked by the Governor, Sir Bruce Greatbatch, to become the first Chief Minister of the islands.

René's defeat was highly embarrassing for him, particularly because of the high level of financial support he had received from Dar es Salaam. During the election he had been forced to admit to outside support when a consignment of three Land-Rovers and several dozen public address systems had arrived addressed to him, along with a huge cargo of posters, enough to cover an election in New York City. Obviously the benefactor had no real idea how big the Seychelles was! One of the first tasks after the election was to clear the islands' road network and all the shops and buildings of Victoria of these gaudy red posters and put them where they belonged – in the dustbin.

My main problem now was how Seychelles could remain a colony in a world where 'colony' was a dirty word. What I wanted was an arrangement with Britain which would give us a status similar to that of the Channel Islands but we were constantly embarrassed by resolutions passed in the United Nations calling for Britain to grant us independence. The problem was that the Colonialism Committee at the UN – the Committee of 24 – was chaired by the former Tanzanian Foreign Affairs Minister, Salim Salim, who was closely linked with the Liberation Committee of the OAU which were funding René.

Some months before our election I had made a special trip to New York to explain to this committee the circumstances of our case. I remembered at that time a lady delegate representing Sierra Leone telling me that she could not believe we were not viable.

'With all that wine you produce you must be making a bomb,' she said.

I looked puzzled. 'We don't make wine.'

'That's a lie,' she said. 'Follow me.'

I followed her to one of the UN bars and there she ordered a bottle of Chablis. She triumphantly handed it to me and I realised where she had gone wrong.

The label read 'Sechelles' – one of the greatest wine shippers in France.

Such was the calibre of the delegates of this committee that I could not seriously believe that they could take decisions that could fundamentally change different parts of the world. When Britain withdrew from the committee I sent off a congratulatory telegram to the Foreign Office, saying 'This body has been a nuisance for too long'. Unfortunately its nuisance value could not be under-rated especially when its support could bring funds and encouragement to an adverse and vicious political faction.

After his electoral defeat René, having enjoyed the taste of substantive outside aid, was not about to relax. A hundred and one excuses were found to explain his defeat and cables were despatched to the UN and the OAU urging that Seychelles be given its independence. One night in May Radio Seychelles was demolished by a bomb. Again, luckily, no-one was hurt but it was another demonstration of 'positive action', and the latest in a series of invoices to his paymasters overseas. It was another blow to our stability and another question mark in the minds of potential investors.

The SPUP realised that we were capitalising on the coming development. They knew that if tourism was successful then those who were now unemployed and who had followed their bandwagon would end up in our camp, and so they planned other 'positive action'.

One day a group of their supporters was taken by lorry to a deserted beach at Intendance where they were photographed waving placards which read: 'WE DON'T WANT TOURISM' and 'FOREIGNERS ARE EATING ALL OUR FISH'.

The first the Seychelles authorities knew of this was when full-page colour photographs of this fake demonstration were splashed in the German magazine *Stern*. There was an element of farce about the incident but nonetheless the pictures had the effect that René intended, to sow yet another seed of doubt in the minds of investors.

Nothing he could do, however, could stop the airport.

On 2 July 1971 I boarded a British Airways Super VC10 at Heathrow. The passenger list included a director of British Airways and several potential investors. The destination was Seychelles. Throughout the thirteen-hour flight I could not sleep a wink. I thought back to the day six years earlier, 8 January 1965, when I had first proposed a motion that Seychelles should take up the question of an airstrip with the British Government. It had taken years and the loss of three of our islands but finally the runway had been built. For nine months a giant dredger, the *Nassau Bay*, had sucked millions of yards of sand and coral from the sea bed and deposited it off the coast at a spot called Point Larue. Two hundred and fifty acres had been reclaimed. It was a colossal operation and the Seychellois watching it could hardly believe their eyes.

On top of this new land mass a 9,800-foot concrete runway, 150 feet wide, had been laid, a great grey slab jutting into the sea. While such a long runway was essential for jumbo jets, I did not realise at the time the true reason for this extreme example of British generosity. It was another five years before I learned that it was also intended to be used for defence purposes.

For the moment though, on that flight, I knew that the landing of this giant bird on a strip of land which was once ocean would mark the beginning of a new era for our forgotten islands. Yesterday we were a thousand miles and at least three days from anywhere. Tomorrow we could be only hours from Europe, Asia and Australia, suddenly and irrevocably thrust forward into the twentieth century.

Next morning we could see the islands beneath us, strung out in the shimmering ocean, the virgin runway looking like a great white domino stretching into the ocean. As we circled Victoria, it seemed as if the town was empty, the whole population having shifted to the airport to watch us land. Later it was calculated that 10,000 people had turned up, from the town, the plantations, the farms and the outlying islands, each one anxious to be present at the moment when Seychelles entered a new era.

The VC10 made a smooth landing and I was first off. I walked to a dais and made a short speech in which I expressed the hope that the airport would perform the crucial function of raising the people's standard of living and that each visitor would be encouraged to return by the smile of the Seychellois. This hope in the next few years was realised. Before the airport was built less than a thousand people visited Seychelles annually. Five years later there were 75,000 and the airport had become an important civil air crossroads.

However, that very first flight brought a problem. Following me off the aircraft in single file came fifty Italian tourists, each armed with a spear gun. It was obvious that unless immediate steps were taken, all that had been preserved through the centuries could be destroyed overnight. Our government lost no time in setting up a Marine Nature Park Commission and passed legislation to set out areas exclusively reserved for gogglers.

As a keen spear-fishing enthusiast during my younger days I had seen the disappearance over a short period of several species of fish from our coral reefs. In fact, the friendlier the fish, the more vulnerable it was. 'For every person who enjoys killing the fish,' I said, 'there are ten who delight in simply observing them in their natural habitat. Make love to the fish – not war.'

This *avant garde* policy resulted in immediate praise from Hans Hass who, together with Jacques Cousteau, had pioneered spear-fishing. In an article published by the United Nations Centre for Economic and Social Information, he singled out Seychelles as a country on the right track and explained how he, who had fished with a spear twenty years earlier, was now firmly opposed to the sport.

> When I returned to the Great Barrier Reef, Tahiti and Jamaica [he wrote] I was shocked by what I saw. All had changed. The fish were gone. We can of course stick to the view that what matters is our present enjoyment but those who really love

underwater sport feel differently. However beautiful reefs may be, if they are bare of fish they lose their charms.

In no time Seychelles was taking bold initiatives in the various spheres of conservation and planning. So much so that, on a visit to San Francisco, I was described in a newspaper as coming from a country with the toughest planning laws in the world. We were lucky in having had the assistance of Lars Lindblad and we had formed an impressive committee to preserve our natural heritage. The committee included Sir Peter Scott, the naturalist, and Dr Roger Tory Peterson, the world-famous ornithologist. Together they brought us into active association with the World Wildlife Fund and it was not surprising that soon Prince Bernhard of the Netherlands, the President of the Fund, was on his way to visit us.

As would befit his position as consort to Her Majesty the Queen of the Netherlands, Bernhard arrived by a special plane of the Royal Dutch Airforce, guest of the Governor Sir Bruce Greatbatch at Government House.

The Prince had valuable advice with respect to our conservation policy. Beside the millions of terns which nest each year on our coral islands, the Prince was also able to spot some of the rarest birds in the world on the granite islands. On a drive around Mahé, we were able to see a rare Blue Fruit Pigeon which, because of its unusual red, white and blue plumage, is locally named 'Pigeon Hollandaise' after the Dutch flag.

Not only were there spear fishermen and princes flying in, our airport now made it possible for all manner of celebrities to come and sample our delights. Among the first arrivals were David Hemmings who, to my surprise, arrived with his Dutch secretary Cassen Broot, rather than his wife Gayle Hunnicutt.

Hemmings, luckily for him, was not recognised. Cinema was still in its infancy on the islands but with his bald head there was no way of missing Yul Brynner as he relaxed on the beach of Beauvallon with his attractive French wife.

Visits by the great names of show business can be very helpful to a small country trying to get itself on to the tourism map, but they can also backfire. In the early 1960s Noël Coward spent a miserable ten days mostly in bed in the Hotel des Seychelles at Beauvallon, smitten by amoebic dysentery which he had picked up elsewhere but for which Seychelles took the blame. Moreover, an unusually long spell of tropical rain obscured the normally pleasant view from his chalet window. When someone incautiously reminded him that the islands had once been described as 'a string of pearls in a sea of blue velvet', he snapped back that they looked to him more like 'a set of false teeth in a bowl of green pea soup'.

So I was a bit worried, while awaiting the arrival of Peter Sellers, to hear that he had had to be given oxygen during the long flight from London to Seychelles. I remembered the severe heart attack which he had suffered in 1964, soon after marrying the luscious Britt Ekland.

However, he turned up safely with his glorious companion Titi Wachtmeister, a Swedish model whose father was the Swedish ambassador in Washington DC. Sellers was frustrated by a heavy cold, but his spirits revived when he saw the superb view from the mountainside villa where they were to stay, then sank again during the night when the croaking of the frogs prevented his getting to sleep. However, Peter was not to be defeated. Producing his tape-recorder, he captured the sound and played it back to them at full volume, inducing such a frenzy of croaking that the distraught frogs lapsed into silence and he and Titi were soon asleep. I learned later that Peter had a mania for tape-recording and had even recorded every moment, to the last sigh, of his registry office marriage to Britt Ekland. He did not tell me what effect playing it back had on them.

Peter Sellers' immediate motive for coming to Seychelles was neither aesthetic nor amatory, but financial. He had previously invested in some 140 acres of land and believed that the time had come to cash in by promoting its development as a site for a hotel and some expensive villas, making use of his own name and that of his business partner George Harrison, the ex-Beatle, and also of the persuasive skill of his clever New York lawyer, Dennis O'Brien. Our planners were not enthusiastic, since the site was zoned for agriculture, and for the rest of his visit Peter went around muttering angrily through his stuffed-up nose about the evils of bureaucracy. But that did not affect our friendship, which developed over dinners whenever our paths crossed in London or elsewhere. We even spent two days with him on the set in Cyprus, where Heather and I had been staying as the guests of Archbishop Makarios and Sellers was making a film about pirates.

The man who has been called the greatest comic talent since

Chaplin was not an easy person to get along with. His temperament was mercurial to the point of instability. Once, when he was due to dine with me in Seychelles, I asked him to come along first for a drink on board a visiting Royal Navy frigate. The captain and officers were delighted and, after a little wardroom hospitality, he was persuaded to do some of his Goon Show acts, which were a roaring success. Sellers purred. Then we moved on to the petty officers' mess, where the process was repeated to similar acclaim. Finally we arrived on the lower deck, where Peter introduced himself and was welcomed politely. But this time his confident performance landed with a dull thud in front of an audience of a different generation, who looked at Sellers as if his wits had deserted him and sat on their hands. The great clown behaved as if someone had slapped his face. He walked off the ship like an insulted duchess and sulked all through dinner.

The important women in Peter's life have included Britt Ekland, Mia Farrow, Miranda Quarry, Liza Minnelli and of course Titi Wachtmeister. One evening, when we were celebrating the success of one of his Pink Panther films at Annabel's with a little caviar and Dom Perignon, he mused on the subject. 'Jimmy,' he pondered, 'I have known some of the world's most beautiful women, and married three of them. Do you know who has been the most important woman in my life? Well, it is Sophia Loren – the best, the most beautiful and the most exciting. I fell in love with her while we were filming *The Millionairess*.'

A few months later Sellers was married again, this time to Lynne Frederick. He brought his fourth bride to Seychelles on their honeymoon and again we dined together. In contrast to Titi, who had seemed cool and aloof towards him, Lynne treated her complex husband with almost motherly tenderness.

In December 1971 Seychelles got its best ever publicity when the photographer Norman Parkinson arrived with the stunning Dutch model Plonja Van Ravenstein. The result was a thirty-page spread of pictures splashed in *Vogue* magazine. Parkinson's visit coincided with a carnival we had organised and Plonja and I became very close. I remember leading the carnival procession with her, walking arm in arm. What a contrast to Albert René who now has to travel those same streets in a bullet-proof car, arm in arm with armed security men!

This carnival was a dress rehearsal for the festival that was to mark the two-hundredth anniversary of the first landing of settlers in Seychelles and at the same time to express the spirit of friendship and *joie de vivre* which were the essence of our island life. I had spoken to Sellers about the prospect of his friends, Princess Margaret and Lord Snowdon, coming for the occasion and so I was not surprised when, after putting out feelers to Buckingham Palace, Governor Greatbatch confirmed that they would be happy to come.

I looked forward to their arrival with a certain amount of trepidation. Sellers had told me that Margaret could be difficult and that she and Tony were not the best of friends. I was not therefore surprised when the Palace sent an advance notice that the royal couple were to have separate beds and separate bedrooms if possible – although I naturally felt sad thinking that the Princess was not planning to enjoy her stay in the Islands of Love.

However, to my relief, she arrived looking relaxed and radiant and charmed everybody with her lovely sense of humour. She can be very funny, and when she is in one of those joking moods you can immediately tell by the easing of tension in the air around her. After a couple of days I felt that my preconceived idea of Her Royal Highness had been quite wrong. I got along very well with her and thought that she was fantastic company.

One evening during a dinner party which Governor Greatbatch was hosting, the Princess's lady-in-waiting quietly asked whether I could organise a small dancing party 'somewhere on an out-of-the-way beach' to crown the evening.

I was delighted at the request and immediately got on the telephone to make arrangements for a band I knew with a fine repertoire of romantic songs that would set the mood right for a late-night beach party. I thought that Greatbatch would be pleased that things were going so well, particularly with the Princess giving signs that she really wanted to have a good time. So you can imagine my surprise when the Governor's ADC told me that Greatbatch was waiting outside to see me – and far from being elated, he was in an obvious state of agitation. He came rushing into the office red-faced, redder than ever before.

'Look, Jimmy – this is not on!'

'Why?' I enquired.

'I'll tell you later, but please remember I am responsible for the security of these people.'

It was only after the Princess had left the islands that I found out why Greatbatch had vetoed the party. It appears that a man who was besotted with Princess Margaret had followed her all the way from London with the hope of finding some time to be with Her Royal Highness. In fact Princess Margaret, soon after her arrival, had let it be known that this man, 'a close friend of the Queen', was on the islands and should be invited to some of the social functions. But no sooner was this done than Lord Snowdon had his own information to convey: this man was a pain in the neck who was aggressively interfering with his domestic life. Putting two and two together, it was decided to keep the Princess's friend at bay – friend or no friend of Her Majesty. I am afraid I have promised not to reveal the name of that disappointed Romeo – but he was certainly not Mr Roddy Llewellyn.

A prince, a princess, film stars and tourists, entrepreneurs and investors: the queue for airline tickets to Seychelles seemed endless. No longer could any pin-striped ignoramus ask, 'Is it one of ours?' But still there was mischief afoot. At the OAU summit in Rabat, the SPUP had been recognised as a Liberation Movement. It had therefore become necessary to tell friends in Africa – particularly our friendly neighbours – about the political game that was being played on our islands. So I was glad when I received an invitation to visit Kenya.

In Nairobi I was met by Dr Mungai, the Minister for Foreign Affairs, and escorted to the city centre in full VIP style with sirens screaming and motorists of all races driving off at tangents into the bush at our approach. The Kenyan motorist needed no second bidding to get out of our way, having become accustomed to the rather heavy-handed methods of the presidential bodyguard. (A trifle reluctantly I decided that this practice would not work in Seychelles where the terrain was mountainous and the outcome would usually have been fatal.)

I lost no time in addressing a press conference and making my point. I accused the Liberation Committee of wasting precious resources by financing political opportunists. My point was a simple one: don't interfere in internal problems. In Seychelles, the colonial power is ready and willing to leave, so from whom are we being liberated?

Next day at a lunch given in my honour at the Nairobi Hilton, Dr Mungai said in a speech that all countries, large or small, should be able to decide their own destiny without interference and that it was in Kenya's interest, as well as all neighbouring countries, to see that there was peace and stability in the Indian

Ocean.

As I applauded his speech I realised that the main objective of my mission was accomplished. I had gained the support of a powerful neighbour on the African continent whose voice in some way counteracted the squealing complaints of the bankrupt communist regimes which dominated the OAU.

Over the next few days I talked to a number of Kenyan ministers, establishing trade relations and agreeing to collaborate as much as possible towards a tourist scheme which would benefit both countries. Finally I flew to Mombasa to meet the President, Jomo Kenyatta. I presented him with a picture made up of Seychelles sea shells and I remember being impressed with him. His mental powers were certainly failing but his strength of will and his powerful personality were still obvious, even during a simple exchange of courtesies.

The visit was a great success and laid the foundations of what was to become a very friendly relationship, both officially and personally. By East African standards, Kenya was a wealthy nation with a foreign policy that was basically pragmatic rather than ideological.

Its neighbour, Tanzania, was by contrast moving towards Marxism, and Nyerere was becoming increasingly jealous of Kenya's economic success – so much so that later he closed the border, ostensibly to stop Tanzanian produce being shipped across to get a better price in Kenya, but in reality to stop Tanzanians crossing over and discovering a better life under the free enterprise system.

And so, both Joubert and I were in a triumphant – a party – mood when we boarded the flight from Embakassi. As we strapped ourselves into our seats in the first-class compartment we saw two ladies in front of us. They had obviously seen our arrival on the tarmac in the VIP limousine and the line-up of Kenyan officials wishing us farewell. They smiled at us, two slim, very attractive women casually and expensively dressed in shirts and jeans, and sipping champagne. As soon as the seatbelt sign went off I went over to them. Did they mind if we joined them? By all means. One got up and sat beside David while I moved in beside the other. For two and a half hours we enjoyed a gentle flirtation. She told me that her name was Lee. She was American and taking a vacation, and was booked into the Fisherman's Cove Hotel for a week. We drank champagne and swapped stories.

By the time the plane had begun its descent towards Mahé she had agreed to let me show her a Seychelles sunset. I knew exactly where we would watch that sunset. A friend had a small house which was empty at the time – and Jean my chauffeur had put some champagne on ice. As I walked into the hotel that same evening I was no longer Chief Minister Mancham on some official visit. I was just another young man about to go on a date with a beautiful stranger.

At the desk I met the hotel manager. He was English, an old friend. He asked me what had brought me to his hotel.

'Her name is Lee,' I said happily.

'Oh, you mean Mrs Radziwill. Jackie Kennedy's sister.'

I froze. My grin turned into a grimace. When I met her this time I had become formal and polite. Yes, she said, her name was Radziwill, wife of Prince Stanislaw. Her friend was the latest in a series of wives of Alan Jay Lerner, the famous composer.

They had played along superbly with my innocent approach, and we all laughed at my obvious discomfiture.

Chapter Nine

MEANWHILE THE PEACE of our islands was coming under further attacks. An editorial in the *People* suggested that tourists and investors should get off the islands.

'The war is on,' said the writer melodramatically. 'Everyone is beginning to realise that Seychelles are now going through a stage of political turmoil and no stranger wants to be around when this happens.'

I did not take much notice of this nonsense. I knew that the opposition would need to make some noise to counteract the coverage that the Kenyan visit had been given in the international press. A few days later I listened from the sidelines as René addressed an SPUP rally in Gordon Square.

'Too many things are happening in this country,' he said. 'Even God has stated that if an eye causes thou evil, have it removed.'

What on earth was he talking about?

He was about to pass the mike to one of his colleagues when he held up his hand and shouted, as if as an afterthought, 'Soon you will hear, as it was written in the *People*, "The war is on."'

Melodrama, I thought, as I made my way home. But that night, in the early hours, two bombs exploded within minutes of each other, the first in the business premises of an SDP supporter, the second in the Reef Hotel where two bedrooms were destroyed. Luckily the guests were in the bar and no-one was hurt.

It was the most serious bombing incident so far and the Governor brought in Scotland Yard to help. A few weeks later, one of the security guards at the hotel, a man named Guy Pool, was arrested and charged with the Reef explosion.

René recruited a Kenyan lawyer to defend Pool but after an eight-week trial, the longest in Seychelles history, Chief Justice Sir Georges Souvaye found Pool guilty and sentenced him to 12 years' imprisonment. Pool originally made a confession to the police alleging that René had master-minded the explosion. Later he retracted the confession and the Attorney-General never pressed the matter, the Governor having advised him not to make a 'political martyr' of René.

Later, at the time of our independence, I granted Pool a free pardon as a gesture of goodwill towards the spirit of coalition. But the leopard had not changed his spots and he was actively involved in the coup. René made him a captain in the army, 'in recognition of his past services to the state'. Fate, however, has its own way of dealing with people like Guy Pool. A few months after rising from the ranks, this rather dim man was driving a tractor when the brakes failed and the machine plunged into a ravine. He was given a hero's funeral although many believed that the accident was the result of a feud within the army, carried out by those who were incensed by the bomber's sudden and unjustified promotion.

Meanwhile the flow of visitors continued. BOAC announced a new air route linking Europe, Africa and the Far East, and said they were studying the possibility of further flights through Seychelles. The Corporation's chairman, Keith Granville, stated, 'Seychelles is not only our newest and most exciting holiday spot but will also become the air crossroads of the Indian Ocean.'

Almost simultaneously, Buckingham Palace announced that the Queen had accepted our invitation to visit the islands.

On the eve of her arrival in March another bomb went off. It was not very powerful but it was enough to make international headlines. In this way the SPUP had expressed its attitude to the visit. Nonetheless as she drove through the island with the Duke of Edinburgh by her side the crowds stood in silent awe, gazing at her.

The older generation of women were especially gratified. These mothers and housekeepers were the backbone of the islands' society, having learned to be self-reliant because they often lacked regular support from their improvident men. Fervently religious, these women revered the Queen only slightly less than they feared God and to see her in the flesh was the most unforgettable moment of their lives.

For me the occasion was equally awesome. As a youth freshly off the boat in London in my funny suit I had gone to the cinema and saluted the Queen at the end, standing to attention and singing the National Anthem, while all around me people were scuttling out fast. Now I was in the position of being invited to dine on the royal yacht, *Britannia*. I still have the menu: *Consommé Henry IV, Filet de Turbot Florentine, Dinde Poelée Palais, Mousse au Chocolat, Biscuits*.

Despite the formality of the occasion it was amazing how, after a few drinks, the atmosphere became very relaxed and strangers began to talk as if they were lifetime chums. One particular lady-in-waiting kept telling me spicy jokes which encouraged me to tell a few of my own, including one about the Duke of Edinburgh which made her squeal with laughter, especially as we were sitting only a few feet from him.

At the dinner I also had a long chat with Patrick Lichfield. I had seen him during the visit hanging around taking pictures, although at the time I did not realise that he was the Queen's cousin. We discovered that we had friends in common in London. He too was quite a man with the ladies!

Next day the Queen officially opened our airport. Seychelles was firmly fixed on the map ...

When I became Chief Minister, David Joubert, who had been active in the trades union organisation, was appointed Minister of Labour and Social Services. This enabled the SPUP to fill the vacuum, especially as the government was one of the largest employers of labour. From the beginning the SPUP made use of strikes as a political weapon. The first was organised at the tracking station.

The wages of the Seychellois working at the station were among the best on the island, but of course they did not compare with the salaries of the Americans who were mostly experts in electronics. René fed their greed and demanded a 40 per cent increase. Again it was a seductive case, especially put to those who had no conception of what electronics was. If the Americans could earn astronomical sums, why not 40 per cent more for the workers?

And then, to make the strike more general, the government workers were incited to ask for an exorbitant increase.

René addressed them in Gordon Square. For some reason he began by quoting Winston Churchill's 'fight them on the beaches' speech, then he turned his attention to me.

'If you want to see the Chief Minister,' he said, 'you know the way to his office. We are not telling you to go but no-one can stop you if you do.'

They took the hint, two hundred of them. They marched on

my office, throwing stones and overturning park benches. They smashed the windscreen of my car and I was forced to lock the door and keep my fingers crossed. It was my first sight of the mindless power of the mob and I was terrified. René sent them after my blood, fully knowing I was powerless to grant their demands. Seychelles was grant-aided and we had not balanced our budget for years. I could not offer any increase without the prior approval of the British Government which finally had to foot the bill.

Eventually the mob was dispersed by riot police. The Governor condemned the disturbance and that night I went on the air at Radio Seychelles and managed to end the strike by promising that the case would be referred to an arbitration court. I realised it had become urgent to discuss the aid quota with London.

So in August that year I left Seychelles once again for London, this time to try to boost the aid quota. As always I tried to kill as many birds as I could with one stone and had a number of meetings with directors of Hambros, the merchant bankers, to work out some long-term financing for the islands. I spoke at a one-day seminar on Seychelles at the Dorchester Hotel, then went to Brighton as the guest of the mayor to attend a festival and get some ideas for our own forthcoming festival, which was to celebrate the two-hundredth anniversary of the islands' first settlement.

From England I flew to Turin to make final plans for a hotel management course, which the International Labour Organisation had agreed to sponsor for a group of Seychellois, then to Hamburg for talks with Joachim Haase, an astute international businessman of great vision, whose company was financing the building of a brewery in Seychelles. After that came Oslo, discussing with the government and shipbuilders the prospect of a boat to be used for voyages between the islands; then home.

On these trips I felt like a fisherman who had to go out and catch sufficient fish to meet the demands of his growing family. 'Jimmy's gone fishing again,' one of my supporters would say. 'And every time he goes, he comes back with a good catch,' another would echo.

This time I had returned with a good catch. Within a few weeks an economic aid survey was commissioned, a comprehensive development plan drawn up and a team of experienced administrators recruited. Sluggish officials were swiftly jolted out of their lethargy or sent scampering to other pastures, while consultants and contractors were made to understand that there would be no easy pickings.

Seychelles was lucky at that time in having Sir Bruce Greatbatch as Governor. A hard-working, ruthless administrator, he had had a brilliant career in Nigeria and Nairobi, and together we worked on a formula which would make the best use of economic aid, to attract capital without spoiling the natural beauty of the islands.

Seychelles was on the move towards what we hoped would be a better, if more demanding, life and I felt proud to have been chosen as the country's leader at such an important point in its development.

Meanwhile an ATV crew, directed by David Rea, had spent weeks on the island filming a special documentary which was shown at peak time in Britain and later all over the world. When he left Seychelles in July 1972 Rea said that he had thoroughly enjoyed working on the islands. 'We are leaving with not only happy memories but also with affection and respect for Mr Mancham who has been great to work with.'

In October 1972 it was announced that Britain had decided to become part of the European Economic Community. This meant that our cousins in the French Indian Ocean island of Réunion a few hundred miles from us could now enter Britain as and when they chose while we, who were colonial subjects, needed entry permits. It was an ironical example of the topsy-turvy way the world was run that we, who had been taken over by British force, were being deprived of the right to enter the motherland, whereas our relatives, who had remained French, found the door wide open for them. To me and my supporters the question of acquiring integration status now became even more urgent. Coincidentally, at that time the French sent a representative on an official visit, the first such visit since 1794. While he was on the island a French fleet arrived in Mahé followed by a French television crew, causing an irate Englishman to observe, 'Judging by the size of the French element, one might think that they are planning a takeover.'

The representative, Raphael Touze, addressed us at a *vin d'honneur*. Recalling the first French settlers who had arrived in 1770, he said, 'They can be compared to people going to the moon. They left everything including family and land and loved ones to develop their country and promote the glory of France. And France now has no right to forget about her children overseas. I am here to see what France has to offer Seychelles to build a new and noble nation.'

Against the background of Britain's entry into the Common Market, I saw the rebirth of a French-Seychelles relationship not only as a long-standing desire to renew historical and cultural ties, but also as a move towards achieving the same position as Réunion with the EEC. An example of the importance of EEC association could be seen in the price being paid for sugar in three nearby islands. Réunion was selling all its sugar at the top EEC-subsidised price. Mauritius was getting the commonwealth tariff, which was substantially less than the EEC was paying, while poor Madagascar could not sell half its stock at rock-bottom world prices.

Not long after the French visit, Britain sent Geoffrey Rippon, the minister who had negotiated Britain's entry into the EEC, on a tour of commonwealth countries to explain the effects of entry. I found him a jovial, warm-hearted *bon vivant* and with his love of good food and wine I realised why he had done so well in Brussels. However, there was nothing he could tell me about integration, no promises, no encouragement, and so once again a trip to London became necessary.

The chance came when I was invited to a World Travel Congress in Los Angeles. I decided to stop off in Paris and London on the way. In Paris I lunched with Prime Minister Pierre Messmer who agreed to send a mission to investigate areas where French aid could complement British aid. At that time our government had declared a policy of balanced bilingualism and France agreed to provide scholarships in various aspects of technical training. Before leaving, I said, 'Seychelles, backed by Britain and France, cannot afford to fail.'

In London I met Anthony Kershaw, Minister of State at the Foreign Office, who was very forthcoming about aid. The British were going to pump cash into social development schemes, housing, electricity and water. With tourism having taken off so well, both the Seychelles and British Governments wanted to ensure that its benefits be spread as widely as possible among the people. But yet again, on the subject of integration, there was nothing but silence. While Britain had declared a commitment to giving effect to the wishes of the people, our desire for integration still seemed a long way off. I began to worry about what I was going to say on my return, thinking of the crowd who had paraded at the airport when I left with their pro-integration placards, and I continued to wonder what game Britain was playing.

A few days later the Fourth Committee of the United Nations voted in favour of a resolution tabled by Tanzania urging Britain to grant us our independence. Surprisingly Britain did not oppose the resolution, although her representative, Captain Elliott, MP, spoke against it. Going over the recent history, he pointed out that the SDP had gained an absolute majority of votes cast in the recent election on an anti-independence platform.

'Let me reiterate,' he said 'that a system of representative government in Seychelles is designed to make it possible freely to consult the wishes of the Seychelles people. In such a system the victory of the SDP ... is self-evident proof that the electorate of Seychelles was not in favour of independence at that time. This does not necessarily mean, of course, that the electorate will maintain this position indefinitely.'

Although he also criticised Tanzania for conducting a personal vendetta against me, there was one clear point that emerged. Captain Elliott's argument throughout was negative. The fact that the SDP was against independence was made clear but there was no mention of our positive platform for integration.

The message was beginning to filter through. Britain was giving us aid in order that our society would appear reasonably stable on the day that she would ditch us. It was a pay-off. But for how long could this prosperity continue? I recalled the words of the Governor when the tracking station was coming and later when our three islands were taken away – that if we were seeking a privilege we must be prepared to shoulder our burden. Now it seemed that we were about to be left only with the burden.

We had a US tracking station whose purpose no Seychellois understood, and next door in Diego Garcia there was being built a vast naval base. Both were magnets attracting the Russians and drawing them into the arena. Yet Britain was simply waiting for someone to ask for independence, then she would happily get rid of us.

However, I was not about to give up. The UN vote on the Tanzanian resolution convinced me that it was futile to address that body. It was obvious that the vote of a representative was decided back in his capital city and, however convincing an argument was presented in New York, his mind could not be changed. It was also obvious that any resolution adopted by the communist-dominated Liberation Committee based in Dar es Salaam would usually be accepted by the OAU because member states had no notion of the other side of the story. A resolution supported by the OAU was in turn adopted by the non-aligned movement and would then pass the UN because the non-aligned countries were in a majority.

I therefore wanted to make the OAU see me and my Party in proper focus. With the SPUP recognised as the liberation movement, the SDP was taboo. As far as the Secretary-General and his officials in the headquarters at Addis were concerned, we were on a par with the governments of Ian Smith and the Republic of South Africa, simply because of our integration policy. I came to the conclusion that it was necessary to put our case to Africa. I approached Kenya, Zaire, Cameroon, Nigeria, Ivory Coast and Ghana and they all agreed to receive me. Only Tanzania did not respond. They did not even reply to my letter.

Everywhere we went we were received with kindness and courtesy and made official guests of the various governments. We found general sympathy for our policy and realised that in most cases the countries we were visiting had voted in favour of the Rabat resolution (recognising the SPUP as a *de facto* liberation movement and thence providing political and moral support) in ignorance of the situation in Seychelles. Some of the people we met were completely surprised to learn that René was a white man and that his deputy, Karl St Ange, had sent his children to school in South Africa.

Our trip made news throughout the African continent and our message – that the OAU should stop interfering in the internal affairs of Seychelles – came through loud and clear. So much so that when we finally got to Addis we were invited to meet the OAU's political bureau that same evening in Africa House.

Again, as on my visit to Kenya, I put the simple argument. Liberation is meaningful when a minority is suppressing a majority but how could the SPUP – a minority party which existed freely with all legal privileges in a society where the administration had already declared itself ready to grant independence – be called a liberation movement?

The resolution had put into conflict two important principles: the OAU's commitment to the total liberation of Africa – which included the offshore islands – conflicted with the UN principle of self-determination.

It was true that Ian Smith had declared his country independent but this could not be recognised because it was not supported by a majority. At the time the whole clamour over the African continent was for majority rule in such places as South Africa, Rhodesia and the Portuguese territories. How on earth could the OAU associate itself with a minority party? I said that the OAU may wish to see Seychelles independent, that the OAU could advise Seychelles to achieve independence, but where free elections existed, the OAU should fully accept the matter as one to be decided solely by the people of Seychelles.

The officials received my remarks cordially and I knew that my point was beginning to sink in. I was told that the matter would be studied further and that I might be invited to address the next general meeting of the organisation. The officials stressed that they could not overrule a head of state's decision.

A few weeks later, back in Seychelles, at a meeting of the legislative assembly, René asked me to give an impression of the countries I had visited. I told him that they had varying economic, political and social problems but there was one thing they all had in common. They attached prime importance to law and order and dealt very efficiently with trouble-makers. Indeed, I said seriously, in most of these countries, the honourable leader of the opposition would have disappeared from the scene long ago.

After Africa I continued to spread the Seychelles message. When the Mauritian Ambassador to the United Nations suggested during the debate on the Tanzanian resolution that we were being used as a base for the subversion of African countries, I flew to Port Louis to put our case. At a black-tie dinner given in my honour at Government House I addressed two hundred guests and told them in no uncertain terms that Seychelles wanted to be master of its own destiny.

'No two countries are similar,' I said. 'No two countries have been subjected to the same experience and sets of circumstances. There can therefore be no formula applicable to all countries except the broad formula which says, "progress yes, tyranny no".' The point was made and from then on Seychelles had no further problem with her sister island.

Following that visit, I invited Falilou Kane, Secretary General of OCAM, the Organisation Commune Africaine et Mauritian, to visit Seychelles. OCAM represented fourteen francophone countries with a total population of 50,000,000 and if Kane could be influenced, we would have gone a long way towards getting our views across. We wined and dined Kane and showed him round Mahé. He was impressed. He told us that before he came, he thought that Seychelles was like Rhodesia and South Africa but what he found was a country that offered an important lesson for mankind with its happy prevailing state of multi-racialism. He promised that on his return he would tell the facts about our islands.

It was clear now that Africa was starting to understand why Seychelles was against independence.

Soon after Kane's visit, it was announced that Governor Greatbatch was to leave us, to be replaced by Colin Allan, a New Zealander.

I met him in London and frankly was disappointed with the choice. I have no grumbles about him personally. Colin Allan is a kind and intelligent man but his experience at that time was limited to the Pacific Island territories and he had few contacts in the British higher diplomatic circles. Indeed, when I met him, he did not know his way around London and once had difficulty finding the Foreign Office. I thought back to previous Governors. The Earl of Oxford and Asquith was the grandson of a former Prime Minister. He had been replaced by Sir Hugh Norman-Walker, a man of the calibre to become Deputy Governor of Hong Kong after he left Seychelles. Then had come Sir Bruce Greatbatch who went on to be responsible for British aid to Latin America and the Caribbean. Now we were to get this pleasant but unknown New Zealander to guide our destiny.

At a time when so much aid was being poured into the islands, the message from Her Majesty's Government seemed clear. 'Old chap,' I could imagine the Foreign Office mandarins saying to me. 'Isn't it about time for you to take over?'

There and then I made up my mind that I had to find out once and for all what was in the minds of the British.

I thought that an appropriate time would be the swearing-in ceremony of the new Governor. One day in December I stood alongside him in Gordon Square facing a crowd of thousands. He was dressed in the official uniform of tropical white suit and plumed hat.

I welcomed him to the islands and he nodded in acknowledgement. Then I began in earnest. I had decided not to beat about the bush. I said that Britain had a moral and legal duty to us since she had taken us over by conquest. I mentioned the anomaly of Réunion and said that, in seeking European identification, we were not saying that the Seychellois were Europeans. We were simply aiming for a better standard of living.

What we wanted was the right to work in the Common Market countries but this did not mean that suddenly Europe would be swamped with Seychellois. 'If there is a choice,' I said, 'between being a poor independent islander or someone like our cousins from Réunion with their links with France, I would prefer the latter.'

'Of course,' I continued, 'you can make the romantic statement, "better poor but dignified". But I'm afraid I have never seen any dignity in poverty, or begging, or malnutrition or illiteracy or in a future of overall insecurity . . .

'The question today is how long are we to live with clouds of uncertainty hanging over our future? Britain's actual policy as declared in the United Nations, to the effect that she stands ready and willing to grant Seychelles independence whenever a majority would vote for it, presents a situation which can only be to the advantage of the opportunists. The perpetuation of this situation means carrying on living in an atmosphere of uncertainty and fear, of threats and confusion, if not of bomb explosions. We must put our house in order. We must have a clear view ahead. Above all we must forever ensure that the opportunists are never given the opportunity of dominating the wish of the majority. The sooner Britain tells us squarely what she has in mind for us, the better. We want closer ties. Will she give this to us and if so, when?'

The Governor, who had listened without expression, made no reply in his return address on the important issues raised. But a few weeks later he said that I should go to London. My speech had been communicated to Her Majesty's Government and they had made arrangements for two people to meet me there. The Governor thought that these meetings could be most crucial.

Yet again I packed my bags and set off on the 10,000-mile journey that I knew so well.

Chapter Ten

I HAD HARDLY unpacked my bags when the first of the two contacts knocked on my door in the Churchill Hotel and introduced himself as Dennis Greenam. He was a man of medium height. He had a slight limp and a pleasant smile, by no means the stuffy Colonial Office type.

I gave him a drink and waited curiously to hear what he had to say. After explaining who he was – an adviser on decolonisation to Her Majesty's Government, he had been closely involved in the development towards independence of Kenya, Zambia and Mauritius – he wasted no time in coming to the point.

'I've been following the situation in Seychelles,' he said. 'I must tell you that in the light of your speech when you welcomed the Governor...'

I looked hard at him. Were we to get our answer at last?

'All these years you have been speaking about integration. I must make it clear that this is a proposition the British Government is unwilling to consider.'

Briefly I closed my eyes. So, after all these years, I had finally got an answer. And it was the wrong one. There was no doubt in my mind that Greenam was indeed speaking on behalf of the British Government and I listened in silence as he continued. First of all, he tried to soften the blow.

Her Majesty's Government profoundly admired my pro-British stance and felt that, as a gesture of courtesy, I should be quietly informed of its decision. If the policy had been announced publicly, it would embarrass me and allow my opponents to make political capital. An official announcement would appear to be a rebuff.

Then he outlined what he saw as the political realities. Tapping out the points on his fingers he spelled them out.

'Look, Mr Mancham, you have a majority on the islands at the moment but your opponents are receiving massive financial aid from outside, and one day they may well be voted into office, and since integration is not on I suggest you go for a policy of independence as early as possible.'

For a few moments I could say nothing; then I tried another tack. What about associated statehood, I asked. I knew that arrangements had been made with certain Caribbean islands which had become self-governing while Britain had retained sovereignty and the responsibility for foreign affairs, law and order and defence.

Greenam slowly shook his head. 'Not after Anguilla,' he said.

I remembered the story. Britain had granted self-government to the Caribbean islands of St Kitts-Nevis and Anguilla in 1967. In June that year Anguilla unilaterally declared its independence. There was trouble on the island and the British were forced to send a warship.

He shook my hand and left me feeling saddened. I had known deep down for some time that integration was unlikely but had thought that the UK, with all her vast diplomatic experience, would have worked out some formula which would keep us closely linked to her. After all, France had declared Réunion to be one of its *départements* and far out in the Pacific Hawaii had become a state of the USA. It was only a question of will. But no. There was no choice left for poor Seychelles. Independence was inevitable and we would just have to face it with calmness and dignity.

A few minutes after Greenam had left, the phone rang.

'Mr Mancham? Fox Tolbert here.' The accent was clipped, a military voice.

'Who?'

'I think you are expecting me, sir.'

I couldn't place the name. 'What did you say your name was?'

'Fox Tolbert, sir. In the lobby. I'd like to come up and have a word with you. Between ourselves. May I come up?'

I agreed. A few moments later, he walked in, looking for all the world like something out of a James Bond film. He was tall and well-built, smartly dressed and wearing a club tie, very much an ex-service officer.

'May I have a look round first?' he asked as we shook hands.

'Carry on,' I said.

He looked under the table and chairs, checked the television, then disappeared into the bathroom. He returned satisfied.

'In this electronic age,' he said by way of explanation, 'you never know what might be around.' When he was settled, he began to explain. 'I belong to a group of prominent businessmen who are strongly opposed to the spread of communism.'

I looked at him, thinking maybe I was in the middle of a bad movie.

'We have been studying developments in Seychelles,' he continued, 'and we are fully satisfied that Albert René is in the pay of the communists. In view of this, my committee has decided to provide your party with a monthly allowance. Can't say how much this will be yet but if you can give me your London bank account number, I'll see that the money is promptly and regularly deposited.'

'These businessmen of yours,' I said. 'Do I know any of them personally?'

He shook his head. 'Sir, I'm sorry to say that my committee must remain totally unknown. Indeed, if you were to take any initiative to find out who we are, then that would be the end of our association. Nor must you tell any of your supporters about this meeting.'

With that, he wrote down an address and box number in Oxford and left. I sat down and tried to work it all out. I remembered a few weeks earlier meeting a man called Major Geoffrey Dawson. He had been introduced to me by Dougy Mott, our security adviser, who was an Englishman. Later on Mott had whispered to me that Dawson was from MI6 and was known within the organisation as the Galloping Ghost.

Could there be a connection between Mott, Dawson and Fox Tolbert? Could this strange man who had just left be from MI6? It had obviously been a bad news–good news scenario. First Greenam had supplied the shock, then Fox Tolbert had provided the first-aid cream. You have no choice but to go for independence, they were saying, but don't worry, you are not alone; their plan had worked. Before they arrived I was still hopeful about integration but now, only an hour later, I was resigned to independence and relieved that some people were taking an interest in us. Then and there I decided to do as Fox Tolbert said; I never did try to find out who the businessmen were and soon the first anonymous contribution turned up in my account.

Now there was no need to stay longer in London. I cut my visit short, caught the next flight back home and called a meeting of the Party's national executive to tell them Greenam's message.

They were united in thinking that, if Britain was determined to lead us into independence, then we must try to form the first independent government, despite all those years of fighting against it. We had no choice and there was no point beating our heads against a brick wall.

That night I went on Radio Seychelles to explain the situation to the people. I was tempted to talk about Britain's hypocrisy but I said nothing. Fox Tolbert's visit had convinced me that Britain wanted us to win any forthcoming election and I decided that this was not the time to attack her.

The population took the news quietly. Our supporters were naturally profoundly disappointed. Overnight their dream of remaining secure under the British umbrella was shattered and a question mark about our security had appeared on the horizon. It was this question mark which also explained the calm reaction of the SPUP supporters. Although their leaders and a few activists set off fireworks, the majority were subdued. Now that they were about to get what they had been clamouring for, there was a worrying doubt in their minds about what was to happen next.

Events now moved quickly. The Governor announced that an election would be held in April 1974 and the campaign began immediately. It was obvious from the start that the SPUP had massive finance behind it, and that Fox Tolbert's contributions, which were to total approximately £12,000, were a small fraction of what was required to keep up with the pace the SPUP had set. We had no choice but to knock at the door of vested interests who, in the main, were our natural allies. One of our Ministers, Chamery Chetty, a competent man in financial matters, was delegated to collect funds to meet the costs of the campaign. Fun fairs were organised all over the islands and thousands of rupees raised, but the money was quickly swallowed up. It seemed that every night either the SDP or the SPUP was hosting a party somewhere on the islands from the day the election was announced until the day it was held.

We made various approaches to the Americans but, apart from individual contributions quietly made from personnel at the tracking station, no cash was officially forthcoming, despite the fact that there was big-power interest in the result.

During the campaign Chetty and I were called in to Barclay's Bank. The SDP account was deeply in the red and the manager would increase the overdraft only if Chetty and I jointly signed a security for it. It was an expensive election with trips to all the far-away islands to canvass votes, even to the tiniest atoll where there might be only half a dozen people. In my view, the amount spent by both parties *per capita* merits a place in *The Guinness Book of Records*.

Now that the question of independence was no longer an issue, the main argument centred on which party was the more honest, more capable and more fit to govern, which meant that the campaign was a jamboree of character assassination; our support, as always, came from the better-educated part of the community and the women, while the SPUP was strongest among the poorer section where René's seductive rich-versus-poor approach had maximum impact.

If you have not been in politics, it is difficult to explain the psychology of a campaign. There is some kind of irrational energy, some natural amphetamine rush to finish. There is often a passion about running for office, a focus as narrow and intense as ambition, a desire as great as a love affair. Such exciting opportunities naturally disappear from the moment democracy is killed and the one-party-state dictatorship takes over.

On election day, 24 April, there was an air of strange calm, in contrast to the turbulent days of campaigning. Democracy was at work. It was as if a crucial trial had taken place and the nation was awaiting the verdict of the jury. When the results were announced the SDP had won thirteen of the fifteen seats but when translated into popular votes, we had won by only 53 per cent to 47. It was that close. But by all democratic precedents, it was still a clear majority.

That night, hell broke loose. The SPUP had geared themselves for celebration but were also prepared for defeat. More positive action took place. Paid agents started fires, threw stones and damaged buildings in order once again to make headlines in the international press. Excuses had to be found for the defeat. (The occasion was in marked contrast to the election that René organised after the coup which saw him elected by 98 per cent – only the Emperor Bokassa had received a better result before.)

A few weeks later at the first public meeting of the new assembly, I proposed a motion calling on Her Majesty's Government to convene a constitutional conference in order to produce a programme leading to independence. It was unanimously accepted, but those were the days of crisis in Britain. In February 1974, following the turmoil of the three-day week, the Conservative Party had been voted out of office. Harold Wilson had become Prime Minister for a third time but with a tiny, unworkable majority. After making some political capital he announced that a new election was to be held in October, which meant – as far as we were concerned – that our motion had to wait for a more stable climate.

By this time my political commitments were putting a strain on my marriage. There was a never-ending array of social evenings. Weekends were increasingly occupied with work and travel to the other islands. At first Heather came with me on these trips but, reasonably enough, she became unwilling to face the hours of pitching and rolling, breathing diesel fumes in close confinement with seasick passengers.

Then there were the overseas trips. Sometimes she came with me but more often than not I would go alone as they were mostly political trips sometimes lasting only a few days. As an outlet for her energies, and using her experience as a consultant with Cyclax Cosmetics in London, she had opened a cosmetics business in Victoria called Tanny's, which was my pet name for her. Soon she had become the sole agent for Dior, Rochas, Chanel, Rubenstein and Arden – and with the building of the airport her hobby became a full-time and lucrative occupation.

But our lives were drifting apart. Sometimes I met women on my trips and they would come to see me in Seychelles, invited or not. Mahé was too small to play cat and mouse. I was having an affair or two and I knew that sooner or later I would be found out. None of my supporters or any of the local people were bothered by my extra-marital activities. On the Islands of Love such things were taken for granted; it was a way of life.

One morning, whilst Heather was on holiday, I drove to Seychelles airport with pleasurable anticipation to meet Davina Phillips, successful model, actress and businesswoman, who had cabled me that she was coming with her two daughters for 'a complete break with the London scene'. We had met in London when her marriage to property developer Leonard Phillips was on the rocks, and the least I could do was to ensure personally that Seychelles lived up to its 'away from it all' reputation.

Or so I thought, for when the aircraft's door opened the first person to appear was Leonard. A few minutes later I learned that he had telephoned Davina to wish her *bon voyage*, heard that the children's nanny had failed to turn up, been invited to come along instead and had accepted with a view to reconsolidating their marriage. There was nothing for it but to resign myself philosophically to the role of Cupid and conduct the second honeymooners to the Reef Hotel, wish them a happy holiday and step into the hotel restaurant for a solitary breakfast.

A few minutes later, as I sat there reflecting on the curious working of Providence, a cool voice at my side said, 'What a beautiful shirt you are wearing!' I looked up to behold a tall, blonde, classically beautiful woman, her hand outstretched to touch the colourful garment which I had selected to match my earlier mood. I responded suitably and she sat down at my table.

Thus I met Olga Bisera, who had arrived the day before to star in the Italian film *Amoro Libero* which was to be made in Seychelles. She was Yugoslavian, born in the small Moslem town of Mostar, but details such as nationality were of less importance to her than her career as an actress, which had started with her running away from home to attend the Belgrade Academy of Dramatic Art and continued through Hollywood to Rome, which was bidding to become the film capital of Europe if not the world.

With Heather away visiting her family in London there was no barrier to our romance, which blossomed with tropical exuberance. The evenings normally ended at the Reef Hotel where the security guards, delighted that their 'Chief' (as I was often called throughout the islands) should be taking his ease with such a glamorous companion, made it their business to see that we were not disturbed.

Although the people of Seychelles are traditionally tolerant in sexual matters – their colonial masters took a long time to catch up with them – there is virtually no human activity which cannot be used or misused for purposes of political propaganda. And I heard that the SPUP was planning to make capital from the publicity over my affair with Bisera.

I called a mass meeting of the SDP in the main square of Victoria. Thousands turned up, dressed in their brightest clothes, to hear what I had to say. After the usual political harangue which the crowd expected and listened to respectfully but without excitement, having heard it all before, I appealed to them as fellow Seychellois, my brothers and sisters.

'Is it not true,' I asked, 'that our forefathers made it our tradition to be honest and candid in our personal lives, and that we are proud of this tradition?'

'It is true,' they shouted, 'it is true.'

'And did not our forefathers teach us to love beautiful things,' I asked, 'the men to love the beautiful ladies and the ladies the beautiful men?'

'Yes, yes,' roared the crowd, 'it is so.'

'And you have heard,' I went on, 'that I fell in love with a beautiful girl, who was married and now my wife is angry.'

There was silence while the crowd digested this confession. Then an old lady standing near the platform gave the lead.

'Poor Chief Minister,' she said with feeling, 'poor Chief Minister.'

The late Philip Mondon, a close friend and political colleague, was always quick to seize such opportunities.

'Long live our Chief Minister,' he bellowed.

'Long live our Chief Minister,' they echoed.

'And three cheers for his honesty,' added Philip getting into his stride.

The crowd responded heartily. Politically the subject of my affair with Olga Bisera was dead.

After the coup, Bisera was one of the first people to telephone me and commiserate. 'The Leo in you will survive, Jimmy,' she said, 'in or outside Seychelles. Let me know when you are free to go to some more far-away places.' So two months later we went on a fourteen-day Caribbean cruise in a Norwegian ship. 'Cheerio Leo,' said this vivid, unpredictable, moody, passionate Gemini, as she left me at Miami to make her next film, in Nairobi.

Today Olga Bisera has become a top-grade journalist. She may not as yet possess the fame of Oriana Fallaci, but her impressive catalogue of interviews includes President Pertini of Italy, the late President Tito, the late President Sadat, King Hussein and, last but not least, the controversial Colonel Gaddafi.

There was, however, one casualty of my Bisera involvement. I lost Heather. While on holiday at her mother's home, she woke up one morning to find a big picture of me and Bisera in the William Hickey page of the *Daily Express*. She promptly returned to the islands to file for divorce.

At first she was bitter but she soon got over it and moved from

England to Florida; and so, from being a bad husband, I became a good friend and we have remained on excellent terms ever since. I shall always be grateful to her for the happy times we had and, above all, for our children, Caroline and Richard.

Chapter Eleven

WITH OUR CONSTITUTIONAL development in the news and the jet set having discovered us, Seychelles was becoming increasingly well known and consequently the media was taking more and more interest in its Chief Minister.

That summer a BBC crew came to film me for their series 'Lifestyle' – a one-hour documentary featuring the lives of unusual personalities. I was to be the first of the series which included Mary Quant, Freddie Laker, Paul Raymond and others.

My next overseas commitment was to be a guest speaker at a conference of the American Society of Travel Agents in Montreal. I went via New York where I was interviewed by *Newsweek* magazine.

'You have been portrayed as a ladies' man,' asked the interviewer, 'and have been candid about your recent divorce and your active social life. Isn't this politically dangerous?'

This seemed to be a constant source of curiosity.

'Not at all,' I answered. 'For one thing, the Seychelles are so small that everybody knows everybody else's story. So there is no point in Jim Mancham trying to pretend that he is someone he is not. Elsewhere, a man is likely to have two identities – his own self and a public image. In the Seychelles we prefer to state what we are candidly: that we are trying to do good, that we work hard – but that we remain "sons of men on the road of life". We in the islands don't think there are many saints in the world, or at least we don't know where to find them. And as for my divorce, in New York I noticed that everyone is getting one. I think that shows that the world should make a new assessment of the institution of marriage. The contract is all right, but once the spirit of marriage is gone, then there should be open valves to make it easy for people to breathe fresh air.'

After the ASTA conference I decided to go to Ottawa to

discuss with government officials the prospect of Seychelles benefiting from a new aid policy, under which the Canadian Government would subsidise development projects on the understanding that the subsidised country would import Canadian goods and materials.

During these discussions I received an unexpected invitation to have lunch with Prime Minister Pierre Trudeau. It was a British newspaper which had first referred to me as 'Trudeau of the East'. Since then the cliché had been adopted by several papers and magazines, particularly in Third World countries. I was naturally flattered to be compared with the charismatic Canadian leader who had always stood high in my estimation as a respected world statesman. And so I was delighted with the invitation which was awaiting me at the Château Laurier Hotel.

'It is a long time since I've wanted to meet you,' Trudeau said, as he welcomed me to his official home, explaining that since the British press had started calling me 'Trudeau of the East' his High Commissioner in London had kept sending to his office a constant supply of cuttings about me. 'You see, I know quite a lot about you and I have particularly enjoyed some of the lines you have written,' he said, pointing to a copy of my book *Reflections and Echoes from Seychelles* which lay on a side table among far more serious works.

Reflections and Echoes from Seychelles. I remember it well, that little book I had written mostly in the early hours of the morning at the time when my marriage was collapsing. The book represented some moods I had lived through – some moments of happiness and of disillusionment, of comfort and confusion, of deep thoughts and honest questioning. Suddenly it occurred to me that some of the feelings I had known, some of the sentiments I had expressed, could somehow be shared by my Canadian host, for after all didn't we both belong to the same wonderful, confused, glorified and suffering humanity?

As Mr Trudeau led me to a sofa, a little boy ran towards him, screaming, 'Papa, Papa, Papa.' He must have been about five years old. 'Mr Mancham, let me introduce you to my son, Justin,' the Canadian leader said, as he lovingly fondled his eldest child.

Mrs Margaret Trudeau, twenty-nine years her husband's junior, was at that time away in Japan on what the press had described as a 'photo-journalistic engagement'. Only a few months before there had been stories about her suffering a nervous breakdown.

The way Trudeau spoke to me, by his looks and the tone of his voice, it was immediately obvious that here was a man questioning life at the top, particularly with his wife far away and the handsome little Justin bidding for warmth and affection.

Lunch comprised vichyssoise, poached Nova Scotia salmon and wild berries, all served with a well-chilled Chablis. Pierre Trudeau and I had really hit it off. We were speaking about politics, double standards and prevailing hypocrisy.

'In our democratic society the man who has charisma, who is flamboyant and popular with ladies, gets elected to public office, but then the people who elected him expect him suddenly to behave like a priest ...' I was saying, when interrupted by the arrival of the butler.

'Sir, Mr Mancham's car has arrived.'

'Tell him to go back to the hotel. I will drop Mr Mancham off later on my way to the office,' Trudeau said.

Thus, in this very informal way, I spent another hour discussing life and the burden of political leadership with the Canadian Prime Minister.

I discovered that although some had painted him as a cool intellectual, deep inside he shared with me, and indeed with other men, the urge for loving arms, the warmth, the reassurance and the relief from tension which results from a satisfying encounter with the right lady. Whichever way one may view his politics, Trudeau remains fundamentally an individual with a great Canadian soul.

A few days later I found myself in London where Paul Watson, the BBC producer, wanted to put the final touches to the 'Lifestyle' programme. It was Friday night and a pleasant weekend was in prospect. I was relaxing in my hotel looking forward to seeing Ursula Roistsch – a beautiful German blonde whom I had met in Montreal. She was due in London the next day. I had arranged a dinner party for her and Paul Watson, together with my old friends George Rassool and Edi Camille.

Then the phone rang. It was Geneva.

'Chief Minister, my name is Gerard Boissier and I am the Geneva representative of the Triad Corporation. Our chairman would like to invite you to Cannes for the weekend.'

'And who is your chairman?' I asked.

'He is Mr Adnan Khashoggi.'

I called to mind what I had read about this fabulous character in press articles which had called him 'the Supersalesman', 'the Arab Rockefeller', 'the Top Wheeler-Dealer', and focussed on his enormous wealth and lavish lifestyle.

'But today is Friday. How does Mr Khashoggi expect me to get to Cannes?'

'Sir, our chairman will send his plane for you.'

This became interesting. No-one had ever sent a plane for me before.

'I'm sorry,' I said. 'I'm entertaining some friends tomorrow night.'

'Sir,' said Monsieur Boissier without a moment's pause, 'your friends will be the welcome guests of Mr Khashoggi.'

Clearly this was an invitation which could not be refused.

Next morning three Rolls-Royce limousines – AMK1, AMK2 and AMK3 – pulled up outside the Churchill Hotel and in walked Gerard Boissier and two Triad executives, who had flown from Geneva to escort us. At Heathrow we collected Ursula on her arrival from Paris and a few minutes later we were airborne in Omaria 3, a DC9 equipped with every modern aid and comfort and manned by two pilots who had previously flown President Johnson in Air Force One. As we drank Dom Perignon and ate Beluga caviar, a steward slipped a video cassette into a TV set and we watched a documentary film, which had first appeared in New York a few days before, about the impact the new Arabs were making on the western world.

'We Americans,' the producer was saying, 'have been brought up to think of Arabs as people who live in the desert, eat dried milk and onions and travel on camels' backs. But during the past few years, since the oil phenomenon, a new kind of Arab has been descending on our shores.

'These Arabs are now busy. They are busy buying our cattle ranches, they are busy buying our hotel chains, they are even buying our banks. And the most flamboyant of them all is a 42-year-old Saudi Arabian, Adnan Khashoggi ...'

Our reception at Nice airport was no less impressive than our departure from England. Bob Shaheen, AK's trusted adviser and personal assistant, immaculately dressed, was there to meet us with another contingent of Triad executives and more champagne. Instead of Rolls-Royces there was a line of gleaming Cadillacs. We drove to the sumptuous Carlton Hotel, overlooking La Croisette, where an entire flower-filled floor had been reserved for us.

'Royalty could not have been better treated,' remarked Paul Watson.

'Royalty could not have treated us better,' I replied.

The scene had already been set. I could not wait to meet the great man himself.

At twelve thirty our host walked into my suite. Casually dressed in black shirt and trousers, he wore round his neck a gold zodiac sign of Leo, the unconquerable. He was somewhat stout, with a round cheerful face.

'Mr Mancham,' he said, holding out his hand. 'Welcome to Cannes.' The voice was deep and resonant with vitality. He wasted no time in explaining why he had invited me.

'I have heard a lot lately about the Seychelles and I think you are doing a good job.'

I thanked him. Already the man's personality was captivating me. His eyes missed nothing. His smile was warm and friendly.

'From what I understand Seychelles is one of the most beautiful spots on earth,' he said.

So that was it, I thought. Here was a man who was reputed to fly 60,000 miles a month in his private Boeing. Obviously he was thinking about an out-of-the-way place where he could relax and recharge his batteries.

'I would like to contribute something to your islands,' he continued.

I was delighted but, as always, just a little wary. Many people had wanted to exploit Seychelles and not always with the best motives.

'I'm flattered by your interest,' I said. 'But I must point out that we have a very strict development code. Nothing can be done which would scar the beauty of the islands.'

His smile widened. 'I cannot agree more. I have seen places massacred by uncontrolled development. The natural beauty and way of life must be the overriding consideration and in the end your people must preserve their smiles. Indeed, if you wish, I could easily find the expertise to help you achieve this. I leave you to think it over.'

Before leaving he gave me a silver coin, depicting on one side Medina, where he was born, and on the other Mecca, the holy city of Islam, and said that he would send a car to take me to his Cannes home.

I was making tracks for the bedroom when the telephone rang. 'Mr Mancham,' a voice said. 'I am Mr Khashoggi's personal masseur. After every trip Mr Khashoggi enjoys a massage. I would like to offer my services.'

'Thank you,' I replied, looking at Ursula through the open door, 'but could you please make it six o'clock?'

Escorted by AK and his lovely and graceful companion, Countess Lamia Biancolini, now his wife, we arrived at a restaurant which displayed a notice: 'The management regrets to inform its faithful clients that the restaurant is closed tonight because of a wedding party.' The forty or so guests included Harold Robbins. It was an evening of gaiety and laughter, and I recited a hymn which in a moment of exhilaration I had written in praise of Liberty. It was not good verse but it came from the heart and gave pleasure to my host, who clearly shared my love of that condition.

So began a relationship which was not only of great value to me personally but also highly beneficial to my country. After visiting it, AK soon came to adopt it as a retreat from his business cares and a target for his benevolence. When we became independent, still without adequate means of transport and communication between the islands, AK sent his yacht *Khalidia* to Port Victoria and allowed it to be used for official purposes. He paid $80,000 to French *Vogue* to include special coverage of the independence celebrations and hired an American TV crew to record the occasion on film. Sometimes he sent the government one of his aircraft, the Boeing 727 AK3 or the DC9 Omaria 3, and twice they came to my rescue when I had been left stranded by a national airline. Once we loaded AK3 with fruit and vegetables from the islands and sent it with three of our ministers. Like the three wise men from the Bible, they descended on Riyadh, with my message of goodwill to His Majesty King Khalid, who received them courteously and accepted my invitation to visit Seychelles later in the year.

Khashoggi's adoption of Seychelles, and Triad's plan to construct an extensive hotel and recreational complex at Beauvallon, sent a current of interest through the international investment community which would certainly have sparked off some excellent development if the *coup d'état* had not put an end to such prospects. With AK's support I was planning to make use of our first independence anniversary celebrations to attract some of the biggest names of the industrial world. What little

1. Called to the Bar, Middle Temple, 1961

2. With my wife, Heather Evans, on our wedding day

3. With my arms raised, leading a demonstration against independence

4. Discussing the Indian Ocean's strategic importance with Senator Tower, chairman of the Senate Armed Services Committee, in 1966

5. Responding to the crowd's acclaim as Sir Bruce Greatbatch (*left*) and I escort the Queen and Prince Philip

6. On the beach at Beauvallon, Mahé, with Olga Bisera

7. At State House, Mombasa, meeting Mzee Jomo Kenyatta, with David Joubert (*right*) and Peter Wand-Tetley (behind Kenyatta)

8. Sir Seewoosagur Ramgoolam, Prime Minister of Mauritius, provides a head of state's welcome for me

9. Escorted by Sir Colin Allan, then Governor, I become the Seychelles' first Prime Minister

10. Minister for External Affairs Chevan greeting me on arrival in India with Seychelles Minister G. D'Offay and Helga Wagner

11. Meeting Indira Gandhi

12. With Adnan Khashoggi and his brother Essam in my office

13. Attending the Non-aligned Conference, Sri Lanka, in 1976

14. Joachim Hasse (*left*) introduces his Seychelles Brew to the Duchess of Gloucester, Minister André Uzice (*right*) and his wife (*second left*).

15. Independence: Albert René swears allegiance to the constitution

16. Dancing with the Duchess of Gloucester at the Independence Ball

17. At the Franco-African summit in 1977, listening to the chairman President Leopold Sedar Senghor of Senegal. Beside him is Valéry Giscard d'Estaing

18. President of the Malagasy Republic, Didier Ratsiraka, and I discuss regional issues

19. Meeting President Marcos of the Philippines

20. Addressing a press conference in London the day after the coup

21. René (at the back) poses with his guerrillas

22. No rejoicing in Victoria on the first day of René's rule

23. My children, Richard and Caroline

24. With Catherine Olsen

Seychelles needed, I thought, was sponsors of that calibre, men who, like Adnan Khashoggi, might see themselves not only as investors of money but also as guardians of the country's natural heritage and of the welfare of her people. And, if any of them should decide to build a nest in Seychelles, he would not wish to see it fouled ...

I have tried to write down what I feel about the man; it came out in a kind of verse:

> History will one day see him as he is –
> Tireless Ambassador of his great native land.
> A force to be reckoned with on whichever side he may be
> A man who has made a 'village' of this world
> But adamantly refuses to make his world a village –
> An individual who cannot stop moving –
> Because his soul cannot stop seeking.
> Every day he works as if he is going to live for ever
> And plays as if he is going to die tomorrow.
> Epitome of Kipling's prince among princes
> And common man among common men.
> He is a boss whose entourage with affection style 'Our beloved Chief'
> A son, a father, a brother with equal grace
> And to me – a loyal and respected friend.

(On 1 June 1982 AK invited me to the ground-breaking ceremonies for the Triad Centre in Salt Lake City, Utah, which one of his companies is financing. Five years before, his father, the late Dr Mohamed M. Khashoggi, had offered dedicatory prayers at the beginning of the Salt Lake International Centre which he dedicated as a symbol to the brotherhood of man. I could not go to that ceremony but today the obvious success of this enterprise stands to be admired. Over sixty major national and international companies have already built their headquarters or important branches there and the overall development concept falls within a planning framework which pays highest respect to the environment. This is indeed proof, if proof is at all needed, of the Khashoggis' commitment to 'excellence'. With such an achievement behind Triad Utah Corporation (which is ably presided over by AK's younger brother, Essam) it is no wonder that all influential groups in the state of Utah, from the mighty Mormon Church to the state Governor and other elected representatives, gave prompt enthusiastic support to the company's plan for the rebirth of what was once 'the gathering place' of their capital city.

The Triad Centre, to be built at a cost of over $450 million, will cover an area of 26 acres, providing 4,500,000 square feet of office, residential, retail, hotel, historic, entertainment and recreational space. The centre will have an international bazaar with food, goods and entertainment from many lands to emphasise the concept and spirit of man's brotherhood. It will stand as a monument to free enterprise and international commerce – typifying for Utah a bright future rising from its proud past. This is the sort of 'dream and vision' AK and I had talked about and contemplated for Seychelles on the many occasions when we drifted on his yacht *Khalidia* over the calm turquoise sea around Mahé.)

Chapter Twelve

BY NOW THE airport staff reacted automatically when I turned up; they snapped the LHR tags onto my bags and nodded towards the London flight. As our constitution came under review in Whitehall, I was like a commuter on the Brighton-Waterloo run.

In October 1974 Labour had been returned with a workable majority and the question of our constitution could now be considered. I arranged early meetings with Joan Lestor, Under-Secretary of State for Foreign Affairs, and a date in March was fixed for the constitutional conference.

One thing, however, was bothering me. Independence was inevitable but we had to have a treaty of defence with Britain. With the growing interest being taken in the Indian Ocean I assumed that Britain would go for the idea enthusiastically but, to my surprise, there was no immediate positive reaction from Joan Lestor. I was so worried that I raised the matter with Dennis Greenam. He was no help. I met him regularly during this period, either in London or Seychelles, and whenever the subject was brought up, he looked uncomfortable. These non-committal replies once again seemed like echoes of the past, but the press got wind of it and made the points in several articles.

However, I was quite confident when I travelled with members of my party and René and his supporters to the constitutional conference, to be held in Marlborough House between 14 and 27 March and chaired by Joan Lestor. After her speech of welcome it was time to make my address. I spoke about the circumstances which had led to the conference and proposed that the constitution should guarantee fundamental human rights and uphold the law under an independent judiciary, finishing with a request that a date for independence should be fixed that very day.

I sat down and the chairwoman stood up. 'The time has come,' she said, and we waited for her to give us a date, 'when everyone can enjoy a cup of tea.'

I laughed aloud. These British, I thought. For years they have been trying to get rid of us and now that we are here, everything stops for tea.

The meeting adjourned but I had hardly had time to look for a cup when Dennis Greenam appeared at my side, asking for a private word. I took him into a room which was reserved for the leader of the delegation.

'Jim,' he said, shutting the door. 'What do you think about a national government of both parties?'

I shrugged. 'There are a number of advantages but what about René?'

'If you don't take him in,' Greenam said quietly, 'he could really turn out to be a pain in the arse with all those hooligans on his side. There could be a lot of problems, and more bombs.'

'Can I think about it?' I asked. 'At any rate, I'll have to discuss it with my colleagues.'

'Fine,' he said.

We left the room and I went to the tea room to arrange a meeting with my friends. As I tried again for the cup of tea that the chairwoman had suggested we enjoy, I looked back and saw Greenam slip stealthily into Joan Lestor's room. A few minutes later a conference official told me that she wanted to see me. Off I went again.

'Mr Mancham,' she said, as I walked in, 'we are of the opinion that Mr René and yourself should work together in a coalition government.'

By now I had had a chance to think it over. 'A good coalition can't come from outside pressure,' I said. 'You pushed us to go for independence. We fought an election on that platform and won an absolute majority. Now instead of agreeing on a date, to which we are entitled, you are telling us other stories.'

'This is true,' she said sweetly, 'but you only had 53 per cent of the vote.'

'And you, in the previous election, had only two seats of a majority,' I said. 'What's the difference?'

She refused to acknowledge the point.

'I suggest that you think about it,' she said, 'but we don't feel we could give a date until the matter is settled.'

I left the room boiling with rage. Duplicitous bastards, I

thought. I grabbed hold of each of my colleagues and took them to my room. The sooner this matter was thrashed out, the better.

I knew that there had been private meetings between members of the two parties on this subject and I was just about to break the news to them when the conference official I had met earlier came in, this time with a letter. It was from René:

Dear Jim,

In the past few months you and individual members of your Party have discussed with me and individual members of my Party the possibility of a national government in the interest of Seychelles as a whole.

The National Executive Committee of my Party now feels that the time has come for both Parties to meet as Parties. As we are all in London we feel that this provides an ideal opportunity for such a meeting in the course of which both Parties will have an opportunity to air their views and attempt to find a solution to the critical situation in our country.

A very early reply will be appreciated.

I read the letter and told them what Greenam and Joan Lestor had said. The reaction was mixed. Some were enthusiastic, others downright hostile.

Robert Frichot, an articulate lawyer and ardent supporter, spoke up. 'This could be the best thing that could happen. There has been enough turmoil. René sharing power could be far less vicious than René in opposition.' He had a point but David Joubert reacted angrily. He got to his feet and thumped the table.

'René is a snake in the grass,' he shouted. 'The British are playing with our future. If we go to bed with a snake, we will wake up one day with our balls bitten off.'

Listening to the arguments, I could see both points of view. Perhaps, I thought, by showing magnanimity, we could achieve a situation of national reconciliation, which could be the best thing for our islands.

The party struggle had seen leadership qualities and national interest sacrificed for petty partisan consideration with the result that the people were greatly confused and sadly divided. However, I could not work out which argument appealed to the majority and so I called for a vote, saying that I would accept a majority decision. A big majority voted for coalition and I returned to Joan Lestor with the news. It was the biggest political blunder that the SDP, under pressure from the British, had ever committed, and events were to prove how right Joubert had been.

If I thought that by agreeing to a coalition we would get our date for independence, then I was wrong. If it is naivety to expect people to act honourably, then I was naive.

The outcome of the conference was a constitution that would see Seychelles become internally self-governing. I was to become Prime Minister but the date for independence had to wait for a second conference sometime in the next year.

In agreeing that I became Prime Minister, René asked to be made Minister of Lands and Works. With law and order and foreign affairs still the responsibility of the Governor, this ministry held by far the most important portfolio. René had control over all aspects of development. Any foreigner wishing to buy land needed René's permission; any developer wishing to build a hotel needed René's okay.

On 1 October 1975 I was sworn in as Prime Minister. Watched by a crowd of 6,000 in the new stadium, I made my speech of acceptance. Explaining why the two parties had gone into coalition, I said, 'How can we build a nation if part of it tears down what the other part is trying to construct? How should we find time and energy to tackle the problems which human existence imposes if our efforts are expended in difficulties that we ourselves have created?'

Pointing to recent history, and Angola in particular, I said that cruel dramas beset a country which finds itself on the road to freedom and divided into hostile factions. Looking at René, who was sitting beside me, I realised that trust had to be a two-way channel and I wondered what was crossing his mind.

'I would like to assure everyone,' I continued, 'of my personal conviction that a country can only be as happy as the individuals who inhabit it. Far too many countries have gone in pursuit of technological advance and so-called progress at the expense of the vital soul. We must avoid this mistake.'

Looking straight at René, I continued. 'A tranquil mind and quiet conscience are assets of no mean value. Whilst the heritage of the past is the seed that brings the harvest of the future, let us face our deficiencies and acknowledge them and not let them master us.' The crowd clapped. René smiled.

Messages of goodwill poured in from all over the world and all manner of governments and that night, after all those years of turmoil, the supporters of both parties joined together in festivity. For the first time the blues and the reds were as one and few could have believed that behind René's smile lurked a deep sense of hostility. As if to reassure me and the doubting Thomases in the SDP that things had been patched up, he gave a big party in his luxury villa, built on top of the highest mountain in Mahé. As the wine and the conversation flowed, everyone forgot that René had acquired a priceless estate in this area of national parkland under questionable circumstances when he was chairman of a government committee.

At the time I was only too glad that things were working out. I realised that the period of self-government was something like an arranged marriage, a trial marriage, and for those nine months it was a honeymoon period. René was as good as gold. He co-operated politically and was socially amicable. If my acceptance speech had been the equivalent of a wedding speech, if I was playing the part of reluctant bride, then René was certainly proving to be the perfect husband. Little did I know that, all this time, he had rape on his mind.

During this period Dennis Greenam kept in constant touch. We met regularly, either in Seychelles or in London.

There were several matters I had to clear up with him. What organisations were we to belong to? How would a tiny country set up diplomatic representation world-wide? What position would René occupy in an independent government?

At that time it had become obvious that the power retained by the Queen on her independent dominions had become largely illusory. Only a few months before the then Governor-General of Australia, Sir John Kerr, had dismissed Gough Whitlam's Government before the Queen or her closest advisers knew about it. I knew too, through a common friend, that René wanted a republican status. He realised that I wanted to keep responsibility for foreign affairs and had said that he would be satisfied as Prime Minister, if this would include the development portfolio.

I asked Greenam about the possibility of republican status and to my surprise he was most enthusiastic, saying that it would not diminish the links of understanding between Britain and ourselves.

Fine, I thought, that will keep René happy, and I then turned to the most important question, that of defence. Granting republic status could be a cosmetic, painless act, but defence was a question of commitment and responsibility.

He shrugged his shoulders.

'Her Majesty's Government won't agree to enter any such treaty,' he said. 'Britain doesn't want to be sending warships all over the world. Look at Anguilla. We had to send a ship there. No. The government is dead against any such commitment.'

Again I was horrified. There it was again, on the line. We were being pushed into independence with no back-up if there was trouble.

'This is totally immoral,' I told him. 'You have burdened us with an American tracking station and you have allowed the Americans to build a base next door. You know very well what this means. We are now in the middle of a strategic area with the Russians keeping a close watch on us. It is so unfair to leave us in the wilderness.'

We really had a battle of words. Again he shrugged, dismissing my fears as paranoia. 'This is what our withdrawal policy East of Suez is all about,' he said. 'We simply don't have the will nor the ability to patrol this part of the world. Anyway I don't think there's any question of you being invaded. Your problems are internal. So we shall arrange for the government to provide sufficient aid so that you can modernise your police force, build up a para-military unit and an intelligence section, all to be ready before independence.'

I thought about it. I had no choice but to agree again. Beggars cannot be choosers.

'If this is the situation, then we have no option but to go for a policy of non-alignment.'

Greenam smiled. He knew that this was the very thing that René had been suggesting. 'Her Majesty's Government will fully support and understand such an argument,' he said happily.

And so in January 1976 we found ourselves once again in London for the second Seychelles constitutional conference, this time under the chairmanship of Ted Rowlands, the Welsh MP who had replaced Joan Lestor. Studying the conference papers, I noticed that the question of internal security was not on the agenda. Immediately I phoned Greenam, who came over to my hotel. I pointed out the omission and said that I would raise it at the conference.

He shook his head. 'Better not,' he said. 'I think Ted Rowlands wants to talk to you about it.'

Sure enough, on the morning before the conference began, Greenam told me to meet Rowlands in his office at Marlborough House. He was most friendly.

'Do you mind if I call you Jim?'

'Of course not.'

'I'm Ted.'

We shook hands.

'Look,' he said. 'I've discussed the question of help for your internal security. We are of the opinion that since as President you will yourself be in charge of law and order, we will leave this outside the orbit of the conference. We want it to go smoothly and without fuss.'

In other words he did not want René to oppose it on the grounds that the money should be spent on social needs.

'I undertake,' continued Ted, 'to see that necessary funds are provided and we will start working on this soon after the conference and everything should be ready before independence.'

I agreed. What he said made sense.

Appropriately he opened the conference by referring to the statesmanship of the coalition government in working so well together. 'Had there not been such a partnership, the conference could not have taken place,' he stated.

Everything went as planned without fuss. On 2 January Ted Rowlands MP, Under-Secretary of State for Foreign and Commonwealth Affairs, on behalf of Her Majesty's Government, I, as representative of the Democratic Party, and René, representing the SPUP, solemnly – in front of press, cameras and television – signed the agreement which, after passing Parliament and obtaining the Queen's assent, would make Seychelles independent no later than 30 June.

The constitution made provision governing 'citizens', 'the Cabinet', 'Parliament', 'judicature', 'public service', 'finance and pensions', but above all dealt with fundamental human rights – to life, personal liberty and the protection of law, freedom of conscience, expression and assembly of association and of movement; protection for the privacy of a person's home; protection of deprivation of property without compensation.

As first President, full executive power was to be vested in me. I was to be responsible for foreign affairs, defence and national security. Provision was made for my removal by the National Assembly for violation of the constitution or gross misconduct, a procedure requiring progressively greater majorities in each of three stages. The Cabinet was also empowered to remove me on the grounds of mental or physical incapacity. Under my direction, the Prime Minister became the principal minister and leader of government business.

On our return to Seychelles, our officials promptly started work on the requirements for internal security, within the framework of the Foreign Office's undertaking. When this was submitted, we were amazed to learn that the Treasury would not make specific appropriation to the Foreign Office for that purpose. According to the British Treasury this was a matter for the Ministry of Overseas Development. But the Labour Government had split up the two ministries and had given the latter autonomy.

And the minister, Dame Judith Hart, had her own philosophy of the distribution of aid. Time and again she made it clear that she was concerned only with giving funds on social and humanitarian grounds and would not pay for guns or policemen.

Some British officials argued on our behalf that social development could not take place unless it was against a background of stability. They even quoted Churchill, 'If you want peace, you must be prepared for war'. But the Dame would not be moved. There was certainly a stench of hypocrisy in the air. (Later the same lady had no hesitation in keeping British aid pouring in to Tanzania although that country had seen fit and proper to send a large military contingent into our islands.)

The whole thing smelled. The tug-of-war between Seychelles and the Foreign Office on one end of the rope, and the Ministry of Overseas Development on the other, went on right up to the coup but the promised help never arrived. Perhaps if it had, things might have been different.

The question of the return of the three islands was brought up at this last conference but it took a three-party meeting – bringing in the Americans – to work out an agreement. With the construction of Diego Garcia in progress, the British persuaded the Americans, who had finally financed the BIOT deal, that the islands should be returned in order to keep us happy. However, there was a condition attached, that the islands were not to be given away to other powers.

In addition we were to receive an annual rent averaging $1 million spread over ten years for the tracking station, so long as we respected the original commitment.

'What commitment?' we asked.

That in time of war, we respect Britain's agreement with America to allow American aircraft to use the airport.

Ah! Now we understood. This was the reason why the runway was so long; but it was the first we had heard of such a commitment.

Again, what could we do but go along with it? We signed. As always I looked on the bright side. Now we had our date for independence when Seychelles would become a republic. We also secured British aid of £10 million for the next two years with a further £1.7 million budget support over the following four years.

René and I agreed to maintain a coalition government until 1979. Seychelles was about to go it alone.

Chapter Thirteen

IT HAD BEEN a long, hard political struggle and I needed a break. With René on his best behaviour, it was safe enough to leave the islands for a while and make new contacts. So far most of my diplomatic efforts had been made in Africa. Now there was a need to meet friends on the other side of the Indian Ocean. An itinerary was worked out which would take me to Mauritius, Delhi, Bangkok, Kuala Lumpur and Penang, Singapore, Hong Kong, Seoul, Tokyo and Manila.

The question of a travelling companion was no question at all. It had to be Helga. We had met a few months earlier in New York. A friend, Nancy Cath, the wife of a Dutch banker, had written to me saying that the next time I was in New York I had to meet this incredible woman called Helga von Mayerhoff Wagner. She was Austrian and divorced from an American shipping magnate. She had her own business, designing jewellery, and was stunningly beautiful. She had also, apparently, read my *Newsweek* interview and agreed with everything I had said.

I took up Nancy's invitation and one night in El Morocco, the nightclub on Manhattan's First Avenue, she introduced me to Helga. I was entranced by her. She was petite, blonde and well-endowed.

It was an instant mutual attraction. We danced cheek-to-cheek by candlelight and reached a decision that needed no words of confirmation. There was no time to waste. A few days later we spent an idyllic weekend in Bermuda together. She fascinated me. I discovered that she spoke several European languages fluently and that she held a helicopter pilot's licence. I had met a number of dumb blondes in night clubs but she was not one of them.

I called her and told her about the grand trip to the Orient and within a few days she joined me in Seychelles.

The first stop was Mauritius where we stayed at the official residence of Governor Osman as his guests while Sir Seewoosagur Ramgoolam gave us the red carpet treatment. From there we went to India and spent two weeks travelling around the sub-continent, discovering its ancient past, its varied culture, its vastness, its achievements and contradictions. It was a journey of discovery, worthy of a book in itself, and the highlight was a meeting with Prime Minister Indira Gandhi.

I had followed her career closely since my student days when I had twice attended talks by her father Jawaharlal Nehru. We had been introduced at Zanzibar's independence celebrations but this was the first time I had the chance to talk to her. Before seeing the Prime Minister, I met a number of her ministers and I was not all that impressed with them. Most had been elected on local rather than national issues and seemed to be narrow-minded and parochial. Mrs Gandhi by contrast was hugely knowledgeable of world politics.

We met in her office in Delhi. As I shook hands and smiled into the well-known face, with its imperial nose and brooding eyes, my first impression was of a small, nervous woman, too frail, it seemed, to be the leader of the largest 'democracy' in the world.

We spoke mostly in English, occasionally lapsing into French which she also spoke well. We discussed Seychelles–Indian relations in general and the Indian Ocean in particular. She was highly critical of the American build-up in Diego Garcia and I discovered that her idea of a zone of peace was an ocean under the dominant influence of the Indian Navy. And with the Pakistan war only just over, I wondered how 'peaceful' belligerent India might turn out to be.

The meeting lasted forty-five minutes and when I left her office I was joined by the naval officer who had been assigned to escort us around. I was intrigued by Mrs Gandhi and I idly asked him who was closest to her.

'She is close to everyone and she is close to no-one,' he said curtly; an enigmatic answer about an enigmatic woman, a frail creature of amazing stamina. Was she the reincarnated Hindu divinity, as one artist had portrayed her, or a notorious fascist, as her enemies claimed, or the saviour acclaimed by her adoring millions? I had no answer.

Outside a lone press man was waiting for me.

'What do you think about the state of emergency?' he asked, his pen poised over his notebook.

I had been prepared for the question. The state of emergency had been declared only a few weeks earlier and was the centre of controversy. I had thought hard about it and I could not see how this huge country, with its vast social and economic problems, could make much progress under a liberal, democratic system which, in the case of India, at times gave regional consideration more importance than the national interest.

'In my view,' I told the reporter, choosing my words, 'under certain circumstances, such a thing could be justified.'

He nodded, asked a few more questions, thanked me and scurried away. An hour later, and at regular intervals throughout the day, All-India Radio flashed the message, 'Mr James R. Mancham, visiting Prime Minister of Seychelles, a British Commonwealth country, said in Delhi today that the declaration of emergency was totally justified.'

What the newsreader failed to point out was that I was the representative of less than 75,000 people and that Mrs Gandhi's emergency was affecting the lives of some 600 million.

There was to be no meeting with officials during our stay in Bangkok but Joachim Haase, who runs a medley of breweries world-wide and had built the brewery in Seychelles, had excellent connections with brewers in Thailand who lost no time in extending bountiful hospitality. This included a visit to a massage parlour. Both Helga and I thought that after all this flying we could do with some relaxation. When we arrived, I was escorted by a young lady to a private room.

'Sir,' she said very politely, 'I want you to know that everything is available here for your pleasure.'

'What do you mean?'

'If you want a girl you've got to tell me what you like best and I'll find one for you. We also have a selection of boys. It's up to you.'

I thought this special attention was only going to be made to me and was anxious to tell Helga but a similar offer had been made to her which included – if she had wanted – a special massage from the matron who ran the parlour and who had been particularly impressed by Helga's fine figure.

Leaving Bangkok, we headed east and eventually landed in Singapore. While friends took Helga to tea at Raffles Hotel, I met Prime Minister Lee Kuan Yew, a man for whom I have immense respect. His common-sense approach has made a success of the little island where its 2.2 million people had the highest *per capita* income in the East.

Our meeting lasted an hour and he told me about his political confrontations with the communists over the years.

'Today,' he said, 'they are having a harder time convincing people that history is on their side. It would be criminal folly to allow them to get into a position where they can psychologically dominate men's minds and where they can intimidate men into believing the myth of rewritten history with different sets of heroes and villains.'

After discussing the political problems of Seychelles, this political philosopher turned practical ruler continued. 'The communists would exploit contradictions within societies but the West seems unable or unwilling to exploit the communist contradictions with the same emphasis. Unless the West takes a more sensible approach, more countries in the Third World will fall to the communists by default.' How true!

In Hong Kong Helga and I looked up some friends who made our visit unforgettable. There was a sixty-plate dinner which made a lasting impression, but whenever I hear the words Hong Kong, I think of the frightening experience of being piloted by Helga in a helicopter which buzzed like a demented hornet among the skyscrapers. I was terrified and Helga was exhilarated.

Day to day living in Hong Kong with its teeming millions has always seemed like a miracle to me. Nothing could be a better testimony to their industriousness than the fact that no work permit was needed. In Hong Kong the philosophy was if you can survive in Hong Kong, then you are good enough for Hong Kong.

In Seoul the Koreans provided the sort of welcome typical of a divided country where two factions are bidding for international friendship. The controversial issue of reunification was due on the UN agenda and the South Koreans wanted all the friendly votes they could get. After a fact-finding tour of the demilitarised zone, I met President Park Chung Hee, while Helga went off to the National Museum. Such security reminded me of my visit to Algeria.

The President's predecessor, Syngman Rhee, had been deposed in 1960 and deported to Hawaii following a violent uprising of students. President Park had not forgotten this and consequently he kept a tight rein on the opposition, to the extent of adding a novel innovation to authoritarian rule. He presented South Korea with a new constitution, then imposed draconian emergency regulations, one of which prohibited people from discussing the constitution.

There was evidence everywhere that he trusted hardly anyone but in the end, all this paranoia became self-fulfilling. He was deposed and assassinated by the very people he had hired to protect him.

From Seoul we flew to Tokyo, where I met representatives of Japan's leading tuna fishing company to discuss a joint Seychelles–Japanese fishing venture, then to Manila. For the first time on the trip Helga accompanied me to see a head of state. She and President Ferdinand Marcos shared a passion for water-skiing and had common friends in America. With the President's wife abroad on a mission on his behalf, the meeting was the most informal of the trip.

When we arrived at his office we found twenty-five people lined up in the corridor under military guard. They were dissidents from the island of Mindanao and Marcos was about to grant them amnesty. They were Moslems and the President's clemency was a gesture pointed at the growing influence of the oil-rich Arab nations.

Our final stop was the island of Cebu, a colourful island with a reputation for spectacular sea shells. As I lay on the beach watching Helga select shells from the reef, I reflected on the lessons learnt from the trip and I also thought about Helga and myself.

She was a truly remarkable woman. In the past few weeks she had been almost constantly full of energy, almost always smiling. The only time she had been low was after visiting a soothsayer in Delhi. She had gone to him when I was meeting Mrs Gandhi and whatever he had told her had shocked her. She did not tell me what it was and I did not intrude on her privacy by asking, but it had taken her several days to get over the visit.

She was the sort of woman any man might fall in love with, a little strange, like many of the most fascinating people. She once woke in the middle of the night saying that she was the reincarnation of Nefertiti – and she was not someone a man could easily forget. She ran over to me with the shells and began to enthuse about them. She said she would take them home and make jewellery out of them, and she did. Her designs were taken up by Saks Fifth Avenue, Harold Grant of Palm Beach and the Lyford Cay Club in the Bahamas. Soon they had become a talking point among the cosmopolitan ladies of Manhattan and a slogan was born, 'Diamonds on Monday, gold on Tuesday and shells by Helga on Wednesday'.

Helga, in fact, had everything, but the only problem as far as I was concerned was a man called Ted Kennedy. The first time I realised that she was involved with him was when I woke up in her Manhattan apartment with Helga asleep by my side and her little poodle, Putsi, leaping around the bed. The dog jumped off the bed and knocked a photograph frame off the bedside table. When I bent to pick it up, I saw myself staring into the smiling face of the famous Senator from Massachusetts.

I did not ask Helga about him at the time. We were getting along fine and there was no need to delve into such a delicate subject. Then, during the trip, I noticed that at each airport Helga would rush to the news-stand and hunt out copies of *Time* and *Newsweek*, then carefully read through the section on US affairs. If there was any mention of Ted Kennedy she would read the article two or three times.

I felt very close to her and shared her enthusiasm for the good life but, despite wonderful moments, I came to the conclusion that deep inside she had one burning desire – to be in Kennedy's arms again.

That day, on the beach at Cebu, she told me about him. At that time she had been seeing him for ten years. They had met briefly in 1962 but had not got to know each other for another four years. She was then married to Robert Wagner, the Texan shipping magnate, and one day the phone rang in their Miami apartment. It was a friend asking if they could entertain the young Senator and his wife. Shortly afterwards, in great secrecy, they arranged to meet in London. It was the beginning of a relationship that for a long time was known only to Kennedy's closest friends. Neither Robert Wagner nor Joan Kennedy knew of their surreptitious meetings in Palm Beach, New York and Miami.

The romance blossomed during Bobby Kennedy's presidential campaign in 1968. According to Helga, the best campaign organiser was a girl called Mary Jo Kopechne. A few months later Mary Jo was drowned at Chappaquiddick in Ted's car and the controversy has haunted the man ever since.

Since that night Helga has consistently been asked the same

question: why did Kennedy telephone her immediately after the accident, before he notified the police? She told me that she sticks by her answer, that he called to get the number of his brother-in-law, Stephen Smith, who was vacationing in Europe. Soon after his call, Nancy Cath came on the line, almost hysterical. She had heard the news and assumed that the drowned girl was Helga.

To this day, perhaps not surprisingly, Helga says she is certain that there was nothing going on between Kennedy and Mary Jo.

I spent many more wonderful times with Helga after the Orient trip. She taught me to ski in her native Innsbruck during the Winter Olympics and we met again in the Bahamas. For a time she tried to interest me in one of her other passions, the cult of Scientology. She enrolled me at the Scientology New York headquarters in Celebrity Centre and I went through the first stages of what they call the process. However, I was soon disenchanted. The organisation was keen to accumulate data on the past lives of its followers and seemed able to exert a strong and continued influence over them. I met people on drugs and others with deep emotional wounds, and I was concerned about their fanatical devotion to their leader, Ron Hubbard, a man whose whereabouts were never disclosed. Finally, when a controversy arose and the State Department began investigating the cult about some missing papers, I decided it was not for me.

Helga was philosophical about my decision to quit and we remained the best of friends. She introduced me to Jack Needham, the American oil tycoon whom she later married. It did not last. Fiercely independent, Helga could not adjust to the domesticated life of a housewife. Then later her name was linked with that of Prince Charles, and the gossip columnists had a wonderful time tracking them down in Gstaad and Palm Beach. 'She is,' wrote one, 'quite a lass.'

'Charles seemed particularly smitten by her. He chatted with Helga in confidential whispers, bopped and laughed with her on the dance floor, and rubbed knees and shoulders with her on the polo ground the following day,' wrote William Hickey of the *Daily Express*.

Last summer we lunched together at Mr Chow's in Knightsbridge. Helga was as radiant as ever, a walking advertisement for good living, but when I asked her about Ted Kennedy, her smile faded. She was worried about him, she said. Ted is a natural charmer, a master campaigner and a shrewd and skilful politician, but she did not like his policies on welfare and was even less impressed with the crowd of leftists which surrounded him.

'And what about the rumours of marriage?' I asked.

She was silent for a moment. 'Ted is the greatest love of my life,' she said quietly. 'He remains very close and dear to me. He is a great man with tremendous qualities and I believe the US does need him, but I don't think we will ever be married.'

Chapter Fourteen

AS WE MOVED towards independence the British Government was anxious to see us establish friendly relations with the Iranians, who were being encouraged to fill part of the gap created by the British decision to pull out East of Suez. This idea was fully in accordance with the ambitious plans of His Imperial Majesty the Shah to transform Iran into a powerful modern state and to make it a dominant influence in Middle East politics. We soon began receiving regular visits from units of the Imperial Iranian Navy. While their officers entertained us with caviar and champagne, the ratings spent Iran's oil dollars freely on expensive presents for their wives and girl-friends. It was all designed to impress our people with Iran's wealth and power and it did just that.

There was, however, one Iranian visitor who was not seeking to attract attention. He was the Shah's nephew, His Highness Prince Sharam Pahlavi Ria, son of the Shah's twin sister Princess Ashraf, and his mission was to buy an island where the Shah and Empress Farah could enjoy undisturbed peace when in need of rest and meditation.

He found it in D'Arros, a group of three extremely beautiful coral islands encircling a large lagoon in which a flotilla of seaplanes could land safely. It was also rich in bird and marine life, and our official planners were aghast at the prospect of its being sold to a monarch over whose use of it there could be no effective control. Nevertheless the sale went through for $1 million and approval was given for the islands' development as a 'private holiday resort' including an airstrip. The Seychelles Minister of Works and Land Development, who was responsible for dealing with the matter, was none other than Albert René, the declared socialist, who assured the public that the project had been approved because it 'will provide employment for many people' and that the change of ownership 'does not mean that D'Arros no longer belongs to Seychelles'.

In the following months I entertained Prince Sharam regularly during his frequent visits to Seychelles and came to look on him as a personal friend. On short business visits he would be accompanied by his German financial adviser, Baron von Behren, but when he came for rest and recreation he would bring his wife, Princess Minoufe, and their American friend, Carlos Veranjo. The three were such close companions that the Seychellois labourers working on D'Arros referred to them as 'the inseparable trio'.

In due course I received an official invitation to visit Iran as the guest of the Prime Minister, Amir Abbas Hoveyda, who had been the Shah's right-hand man for thirteen years. He was articulate in several languages and seemed very much in charge of day-to-day affairs as, during our discussion of Iran's future role in the Indian Ocean, he was constantly interrupted by demands for this or that decision. At lunch with some of his ministers it became clear that Prince Sharam's purchase of D'Arros was regarded as a private matter, not to be discussed openly in Tehran, but on the subject of future relations with Seychelles Hoveyda was eloquent. He offered to send an economic mission within three months, to investigate the possibility of Iranian investment in fishing and other industries, and at the end of the meal he dictated an agreement to that effect which both of us signed. I left Tehran much impressed by this demonstration of Iranian efficiency, and richer by two kilos of beluga caviar and signed photographs of Hoveyda and of the Shah and his consort in imperial splendour.

Back in Seychelles, I gave orders for preparations to be made for the mission and left the civil service in no doubt of the importance which I attached to it. Everyone worked hard and all was in readiness when, two days before the mission was due, a message was received from Tehran regretting that it would be delayed for six weeks. Five weeks later we got a similar message, this time promising that the mission would arrive before the end of the year. And so it went on, up to independence and a year afterwards, by which time I had acquired a better understanding of Iranian efficiency.

Another country with which I wanted to develop closest possible ties was, of course, Australia, which is home to an estimated

10,000 Seychellois who had immigrated there in search of a better future – mostly before our airport was opened.

After the Second World War, Australia saw a rapid decline in British influence as she turned politically more and more towards the USA and economically more and more towards Japan and south-east Asia. These developments gave the impression that Australia considered herself a Pacific Ocean nation. I was therefore eager to remind Australian leaders that the waves of the Indian Ocean wash the coast of its great western state – an area which is sparsely populated but rich in minerals. Moreover, Seychelles could offer Qantas an ideal stopover point on a Perth–London flight should demand for such a route ever arise.

I had visited Australia several years before when I had gone to Sydney to receive a tourism trophy at the American Society of Travel Agents Convention. At that time I had befriended Stephanie Meurer, a former Miss Australia who had made me discover Sydney oysters, Morton Bay bugs, Great Western champagne and other Australian delights.

This time the visit was to be much more formal. I was, after all, arriving as the Prime Minister of a country on the road to independence. An official reception greeted my arrival at Perth airport, an airplane of the Royal Australian Air Force was to take me across the huge island-continent, there were to be official discussions in Canberra and a special dinner hosted by Governor-General Kerr. It was at this dinner that Kerr asked what prompted the Seychelles to seek a republican status on independence.

'You, sir,' I had answered.

Kerr did not take the point. 'I was asking why the Seychelles wants to become a republic,' he asked again.

'Yes, sir. I understood your question; the answer is you, sir.'

Finally Kerr got the point. Only a few months before, contrary to established practice and convention, my host had dismissed from office the Prime Minister who had appointed him – and when the matter had gone to court, the judiciary had ruled that he had acted within his legal powers.

The dismissed Prime Minister Gough Whitlam called on me during my stay in Sydney at Kirribilli House (the Australian Prime Minister's official residence in Sydney). Very understandably, there was only one thing Whitlam wanted to speak about – Kerr's outrageous breach of convention. Whitlam was, of course, a controversial Prime Minister. Not only did he order Australians out of Vietnam and wanted to replace 'God Save the Queen' as the country's national anthem, but he also went out of his way to criticise South Africa's apartheid despite Australia's own problems with the aborigines and its much criticised 'White Australia' immigration policy. However, one could not help appreciating the down-to-earth friendliness of this very tall individual.

It was in Sydney too that I met the man who had replaced Mr Whitlam – Australia's present-day Prime Minister, Malcolm Fraser. Mr Fraser took due note of the growing strategic importance of the Indian Ocean and responded positively to my request for some aid by agreeing to the Federal Government subsidising the Australian Rice Growers' Association so that Seychelles could import its annual rice requirements at a price it could afford.

The closer we came to independence, the more aware we became of the vital strategic importance of our islands. This was clearly demonstrated by the sudden interest of the super powers. Besides Britain and France, representatives from China, India, the USSR and the USA now began to arrive at Mahé airport. They were high-level diplomats, all wanting the same thing – to set up embassies; all this on these tiny coconut islands with a population of less than 75,000!

One morning in my office I found myself facing a middle-aged American who had arrived. To my secretary he was the First Secretary at the US Embassy in Nairobi, but he lost no time in telling me who he really was – an employee of the CIA. Somehow that organisation had got wind of the tug-of-war between the Foreign Office and Judith Hart and it knew that independence would make my government vulnerable.

'In the long term,' said the American, who shall be known as Mr X, 'we have our own plans for the Indian Ocean. Iran will be used to fill the gap caused by British withdrawal. In the short term we want to secure your independence.'

I listened fascinated as he continued. The hour was grave, he said, and his point was clear.

'You have the tracking station on Mahé. We are busy building our base on Diego Garcia next door. We want to keep it this way. But the Russians and their proxies will plot for your overthrow.'

Proxy, I thought; a good word. I had never thought of René as a proxy.

'Mr Mancham,' he continued. 'We want to secure your position.'

He wanted me to sign a document authorising the CIA to organise our intelligence system, which would allow them to keep an eye on local groups which, in his opinion, were out to make trouble for us, the region and therefore the USA. In addition he wanted to support a para-military unit.

'The sums involved,' he added, 'for such an operation would have to come from Washington, but within the Nairobi budget I can arrange to train a small nucleus of bodyguards for you and subsidise the *Seychelles Weekly* by a few hundred dollars a month.'

I signed the document. Judging from past experience, I could not have much faith in the British ever keeping their promise about our internal security and, even if they did, it would do no harm to have additional American backing. The bodyguards, I thought, were hardly necessary but I agreed. What could I lose?

As for the *Seychelles Weekly*, the CIA was concerned that René and his party, although apparently collaborating totally with us, were still publishing anti-American articles in the *People*. Since it was not possible for the coalition paper, the *Nation*, to refute these articles, Mr X thought that we could use the columns of the *Weekly* to do so.

With my signature on his document, the 'First Secretary' left my office. A few weeks later three men arrived and began to train ten members of our intelligence force, as well as my chauffeur and the man who was to become my ADC, in protection measures and the use of small arms.

Although the people of the islands did not realise it, they were living in an Eden which was rapidly tasting of the Tree of Political Knowledge and would soon learn the ways of a not very honest world.

For the moment, though, the air was crackling with excitement as plans were made for our independence celebrations. A British Army officer, Colonel E. A. Hefford, a man who had helped several countries with their celebrations, was recruited. A flag had to be designed and an anthem composed. Festivities had to be organised, not only on the main island but also on the smaller islands. Then there was the question of the invitation list.

This was a very delicate matter best illustrated by the China situation. Throughout my early days in politics I had managed to foster close links with the government of Nationalist China and had become friendly with Mr H. K. Yang, a man who had earned himself the name of 'Mr Africa' because of the huge efforts he had once made to keep Taiwan in the United Nations. However, when Richard Nixon made his overtures to communist China, poor Seychelles was left with an embarrassing friendship. We may have been heading towards independence but we were still under pressure from Britain.

The Governor, when we were discussing the invitation list, made it quite clear that Her Majesty's Government would have no enthusiasm to be present if Taiwan was invited. I recognised the realities. Seychelles should not haphazardly incur the wrath of such a mighty nation as Red China but, on the other hand, was not Taiwan a model of efficiency and economic success? In addition, Mr Yang had promised that, if we wished, Taiwan would provide us with special training in security. Was not, I wondered, a little bird in the hand worth a big bird in the bush?

I tried to think of a way out but I realised that I could not win, and so for the first time I saw myself, too, sacrificing principle on the altar of political expediency. My friend Mr Yang never received his invitation.

The apparent success of the coalition had fostered an image of a stable paradise and our airport became busier and busier. Every month as we moved towards the big day in June, our hotel beds were at a premium.

A fantastic investment climate prevailed; there was no unemployment; the standard of living shot up; new houses sprouted out of the ground like spring flowers; more cars appeared on the roads and traffic was a new problem. And, most of all, the Seychellois were becoming proud. The happiness of the people was a prime objective of our policy. Many islanders, after a history of slavery and years of neglect, had been left with feelings of inferiority. It was important to promote that certain smile which said, 'We really now feel free.'

One of the most enlightened measures our government took was aimed at encouraging social contact between visitors and locals. I had seen places where the tourists were kept apart in their air-conditioned corrals, seeing only servants, while the locals watched from outside, with increasing envy and bitterness. And so we issued strict instructions to all the hotels to grant easy access to all Seychellois to their facilities. There was, for example, to be no entrance fee for hotel dancing. Any Seychellois could enter providing he or she was dressed decently, behaved properly and could pay the bill. In that way our pleasure-minded people were made to see tourism for what it should be – an industry which could bring untold fun and happiness not only to the affluent visitors from overseas but to the locals. In this way many a friendship developed between the visitors and the people.

Seychelles was getting top marks in the glossy brochures of European travel agents. Typical of hundreds of letters was one I received from David Kevan, planning and marketing manager of the travel company Rankin Kuhn: 'Your islands have been for us the success story of 1976, both in terms of the number of clients we have sent and the highly complimentary comments we have received.'

There was no reason, if things carried on like this, why Seychelles could not be a true success story.

PART II

Chapter Fifteen

IT WAS MONDAY 28 June and midnight was almost upon us. The royal party had long since taken their seats in the new stadium. There had been stirring performances from the Royal Marines Band and the band of the Indian Navy. Local children had given a display of club twirling. Police dogs had gone through their paces. The Roman Catholic and Anglican bishops had each offered a short prayer. René and I had made our speeches. And now, at precisely thirty seconds to midnight, in total darkness, the flag party, made up of members of the Seychelles police, made its way to the centre of the stadium.

The place was packed but there was not a whisper. Precisely on time at one minute to midnight a spotlight was snapped on, illuminating the flagpole in a single beam, picking up the Union Jack. Simultaneously the Marines Band started up with 'God Save the Queen'.

I stood beneath the pole, next to Governor Allan, with René on his left, watching as the Union Jack was slowly hauled down. Beyond I could see the harbour glittering with floodlit warships from five countries, the USA, France, Iran, India and Australia; yet there was not one vessel from the nation that had once ruled the waves of the Indian Ocean. Not a single name from that never-ending list which constituted the Falkland Islands' armada. The Royal Navy had been invited but had not been able to send a single ship. I was sad. As a boy I remembered the harbour regularly visited by British ships; but not today, even though the ocean was now of far greater strategic importance.

As the Union Jack disappeared out of the spotlight, the new Seychelles flag appeared in its place, red and blue with a white diagonal cross, and our new crest – a giant tortoise and a coconut palm in the centre, rising slowly up the pole. Once it was secured, the band struck up our new anthem.

It was zero hour. Our little group of islands had been born a nation. My feelings were mixed. In that half second, I had left behind the role of Prime Minister in a colony and become President of an independent republic. Suddenly Seychelles was alone in a world of conflict and pressure.

It was a well known fact, though, that my newly-declared stand of 'friend to all and enemy to none' was more the result of pressure and circumstances. Although I was officially non-aligned, deep down I remained very much pro-West.

The next day my presidential flag was raised over what was until then Government House and which now became State House, and Governor Allen became my guest until he left the country some days later. That afternoon we assembled once more in the stadium for the independence ceremony. I arrived in a Seychelles-blue convertible Rolls-Royce Corniche which had been gifted to the government, for the use of the President, by an English entrepreneur. My mother was by my side, thus ending press speculation about which lady would have the honour. The *Daily Express* had favoured Olga, with Helga a possibility and Fiona Richmond an outsider. But I had played safe; there were many women around but since my divorce I had had one commitment – to my country.

As President I had been made a Knight of the British Empire. Seychelles having become a republic, the knighthood was an honorary one. Thus I joined Alistair Cooke, Douglas Fairbanks Jnr and a select group of other foreign citizens who, though knighted, are not expected to use the prefix 'Sir'. I saw in the knighthood the seal of friendship with the British people despite the couldn't-care-less attitude of the Foreign Office.

The Duke of Gloucester handed me the document which made our independence and new constitution official and two judges arrived, perspiring under their long spaniel-like wigs and robes, to legalise the transfer of power.

Welcoming the Duke and Duchess, as the Queen's representatives, and Lord Shepherd as representative of the British Government, I said that our march to freedom had not been simple. The debates had been hot and sometimes bitter, but, repeating what both I and René had said the previous night, this was now a matter of history.

'The difficulties and misunderstandings of the past are behind us,' I said into the microphone, my voice echoing in the hills. 'Today we start on the great adventure of building the

Seychellois nation.'

I looked at René as I continued. 'Our destiny is henceforward in our own hands. I call on every Seychellois to join me today in this great adventure of nation building. In the spirit of 'En Avant' [the title of our anthem] let us all work together in order to mould our country so that it will set an example to the world in progress, toleration and high endeavour.'

As the crowd applauded, I held out my hand to René ... and the bastard shook it.

The islands erupted in festivity. There were carnival parades with each community putting on a show. A Chinese dragon was followed into the square by a motorised giant tortoise. Pretty girls were pulled in rickshaws. There was a float decorated by members of the Baha'i faith and another with the strange message 'Local herbs good medicine'.

To most Seychellois, it seemed that we did not have a care in the world.

With the festivities came telegrams of congratulations from capitals all over the world. Ironically, one of the first was from Julius Nyerere.

A few days after independence I was on my way to Mauritius to attend the summit conference of the OAU, this time not as a party leader but as a head of state. Immediately I noticed a subtle difference in my reception, something to which I was to become accustomed during the next twelve months. From then on, it was a case of ADC, motorcade and national anthem.

The conference was being presided over by none other than Field Marshal Idi Amin who had assumed the chair during the previous conference in Kampala. I had first met him at Mogadishu in an OAU meeting. By then he had already acquired a certain notoriety, not least for addressing to his fellow politicians in other parts of the world uncomfortable telegrams like the one to President Nixon which read, 'I am sorry what they are doing to you. These people will cause you to commit suicide.'

For the opening session I was seated in the gallery for distinguished visitors with a clear view of the rulers of Africa who had gathered for the occasion. There was even the ageing Emperor Haile Selassie, who had arrived unexpectedly on hostile territory to state his country's case in the dispute with Somalia. There, too, was General Gowan from Nigeria, unaware that the next OAU summit would see him toppled from power. All were assembled when, ten minutes late, Idi Amin strode into the hall, wearing field marshal's uniform, followed by numerous acolytes and raising first his right hand, then his left, in the manner of a bishop blessing his flock. The sour expressions on the faces of his contemporaries, notably that of Nyerere in his dowdy Mao-style uniform, left no doubt of their feelings at being upstaged by this giant of a man, who clearly regarded himself as the superior of everyone present.

On this Mauritius trip I was not particularly anxious to meet him because I had not responded positively to his desire to attend our celebration. He had bombarded me with a series of messages suggesting that he came along with a troop of African dancers, but both the British and I thought that our independence was a purely Seychelles show. We could not allow an unpredictable Amin to arrive and spoil it. In the end I had sent him a cable:

> Your Excellency, my Government and I have been extremely touched by the personal interest your Excellency has taken and is taking with respect to our coming independence. It would have been our dear wish to specially invite Your Excellency but considering Your Excellency's international prestige and in the light of prevailing local circumstances our Government feels it will not be able on this occasion to provide Your Excellency with the undivided attention which Your Excellency rightly deserves. In the circumstances we are of the opinion that it would be more opportune for us to arrange for an appropriate visit at a mutually convenient date in the not-too-distant future. May I avail myself of this opportunity to convey to Your Excellency my highest consideration.

He did not acknowledge this message but on Independence Day sent me a telegram of congratulation for having finally got rid of the yoke of colonialism, Zionism, fascism and neo-colonialism.

Fortunately we were spared the embarrassment of a confrontation. By the time I had reached Mauritius, Amin was on his way back to Uganda to deal with the problem caused by the sudden arrival in Entebbe of an Air France aircraft hijacked by Palestinians, the first act of that extraordinary adventure which led to the successful raid on Entebbe airport by Israeli commandos.

As I was being driven to the conference in Port Louis, I

remembered the last time I had stopped off at Entebbe on an Air France flight, only a few days after Amin had overthrown Milton Obote while Obote was attending the Commonwealth Prime Ministers Conference in Singapore. I was tired that day and had no intention of leaving my comfortable seat during the short stop at Entebbe, but as soon as we landed three army officers boarded the aircraft and loudly demanded to know which of the passengers was the Prime Minister of Sicily. The hostess pointed at me and the senior officer drew himself up, saluted and said, in the manner of the commander of a guard of honour, 'Sir, on behalf of His Excellency President Idi Amin Dada we welcome you to Uganda. Please, sir, to follow us to the VIP lounge where champagne is awaiting you.'

The lounge was tastefully decorated but the air-conditioner was not working and it was infernally hot and sticky. On the table stood a magnum of Moet & Chandon and four glasses advertising Tusker Beer. There was no sign of any ice. I thought sadly of the glass of well-chilled champagne I had consumed before we landed.

The senior officer took a long and suspicious look at the cork in its wire cage. At length he seized the bottle, put the cork in his mouth and twisted left, right and left again. A cascade of warm champagne descended on the room, some of it landing in the Tusker Beer glasses. 'To your great country, sir,' said the officer triumphantly. 'And to yours,' I replied politely. Another officer sought to open the conversation. 'Is it true,' he enquired, 'that by this time of year the snow on your mountains has started to melt?' In this one's mind I seemed to have been identified as the President of Switzerland.

I reflected that Uganda was reputed to have the best university and the most able local civil servants in eastern Africa, and that these officers had perhaps been promoted rather rapidly from the ranks in step with their leader.

As it transpired, our last encounter took place later that year at the Afro-Arab summit conference, shortly after Amin had again made the headlines by murdering the Anglican archbishop. It was noticeable that, contrary to usual practice, the story of this atrocity was on open display even in our hotel bookshop, and that the other heads of state did their best to avoid personal contact with the President of Uganda.

At President Sadat's dinner on the opening night of the conference, I found to my amusement that I had been seated between

Idi Amin and President Numeiry of the Sudan. I tried to make light of it.

'Your Excellency,' I said to Amin, 'how is it that you manage to keep fit under so much pressure?'

'My brother,' came the answer, 'in my country I have many swimming pools and I also control all the lakes.'

'And the crocodiles,' I said, 'I suppose that in Uganda even they must respect the President?'

Numeiry was trying hard to stifle his amusement as Amin replied, 'You have a point, my friend, you have a point.'

Idi Amin was not the only notorious leader I met during my crusade in Africa, beating the SDP's integration drum. An even stranger personality – if that were possible – was Jean-Bedel Bokassa, President of the Central African Republic, a man who took the wind out of the sails of his fellow despots by proclaiming himself Emperor instead of merely arranging to be returned to power every five years or so with more than 90 per cent of the votes, as is current practice. The target of much severe criticism from the West, not least for his reintroduction of outdated punishments such as cutting off an ear for a second offence of larceny, he himself remained unmoved by it. 'Imagine,' he said, 'the plight of a poor farmer who, after months of hard labour, wakes up in the morning to find that thieves have reaped his harvest.' A cruel tyrant he may have been, but perhaps he understood his people.

His charm when in a good mood was matched by his fury when crossed. He once ordered forty Mercedes cars to be delivered by air from West Germany. The agreement specified that twenty should be paid for in advance and twenty on arrival but before delivery. When the second batch arrived, the local manager of Air Afrique declined to release them without payment. The luckless man quickly found himself in one of Bokassa's very unpleasant prisons. A few days later he was whisked out of jail and into the presidential palace for lunch, which was covered live by Bangui TV. After lunch, Bokassa kicked him in the face before he was taken to the airport and deported to France.

Bangui is, I think, the only capital in the world where television was used as a normal means of communication between the President and his ministers and senior officials, who alone could afford to own a set. 'You, Minister of Transport,' Bokassa may announce on the screen, 'I have a bone to pick with you. I want you in my office first thing tomorrow, and you had better make sure that you have all the information I need.'

To offset his small stature and impress his loyal subjects, Bokassa wore resplendent uniforms adorned with medals acquired from antique shops all over Europe. When I come to think of it, westerners are not being quite fair to scorn a poor African for employing his own version of a technique which European states, and particularly Britain, have been using successfully for centuries.

Bokassa's *folie de grandeur*, combined with his extravagance, was a heavy burden on his poor, landlocked country's exchequer. When attending an OCAM conference in a village which he had had built especially for the occasion, I found in my room tulips from Amsterdam, Chivas Regal whisky and two dozen bottles of claret labelled *Cuvee speciale de la cave Jean-Bedel Bokassa*. Once he presented me with an affectionately inscribed photograph measuring six feet by five, which proved an embarrassment because I could find nowhere to put it without giving the impression that Bokassa was my hero. As I looked at it, I wondered what his lifestyle would have become if oil had been discovered in his country.

As well as the gigantic portrait, he gave me a book which outlined his political philosophy. It was called *The Myth and Reality of Operation Bokassa; Volume One*. In bold capitals the book asked the question, 'Who is Jean-Bedel Bokassa?' before supplying the answer:

> A very simple man of noble bearing. The national and international press have made him so popular that there is no need for us to describe him in detail. Whether Bokassa wears a soft felt hat with a grey lounge suit or a general's five-starred cap with his khaki or dark blue uniform, the man remains astonishingly unpretentious. He is frank and easy to approach, though, at times, impulsive and familiar. His eyes sometimes wide open, sometimes half-shut, shine suddenly with unexpected brilliance and you discover the strong will of a man trained in the hard school of statesmanship at the head of a nation.

I shall never forget the parade which Bokassa had ordered to celebrate National Day, the anniversary of his republic's foundation. Every inhabitant of Bangui was present, if they knew what was good for them. I had been placed near the President's seat on the dais, from which a red carpet had been laid for at least a hundred yards right up to the Avenue Jean-Bedel Bokassa, along which stood L'Université Jean-Bedel Bokassa which was itself not far from L'Hôpital Jean-Bedel Bokassa. Five minutes before the President was due to arrive the heavens opened and down came torrential rain. Thunder and lightning greeted the glistening Mercedes as it drew up alongside the red carpet, which the deluge had turned into what looked like a river of fresh blood. But, like a true soldier, Field Marshal Bokassa waded straight through it, heedless of the damage to his splendid uniform.

His method of averting a possible coup when travelling abroad was simple. He made sure that all the potential instigators were on the aircraft with him.

However, one day after rejecting his Christian names – he converted himself overnight to a Moslem before flying to Tripoli to meet Gaddafi to discuss the Chad problems – the French, who had been the power behind his throne, decided they had had enough of his blackmailing attitude. A military coup was promptly engineered and the Emperor finally found himself homeless.

Africa is a continent where it is almost suicidal for any up-and-coming politician to outshine the President-for-life. The story of Karl i Bond, Minister of External Affairs in Zaire, is a case in point.

On arrival in Kinshasa I was met by Karl i Bond, who escorted me to the OAU village where I was to stay during my visit to Zaire. The government had prepared an elaborate programme which brought home to me the great size of the country and its vast agricultural and mineral resources.

Everywhere I went groups of women and children chanted songs which welcomed me to Zaire and at the same time praised God for having given Zaire a leader such as President Mobutu Sésé Séko. Television programmes were punctuated every fifteen minutes by representations of the President appearing like a messiah among the heavenly clouds to the accompaniment of hymns extolling his virtues and qualities. This kind of promotion became more understandable when one remembered Zaire's conglomeration of hostile tribes and troubled colonial history.

Mobutu received me in his luxurious palace overlooking the Zaire River, which separates Zaire from the People's Republic of the Congo. With him was his Minister of External Affairs, Karl i Bond. Mobutu, good-looking and dynamic, was charming and witty. Karl i Bond was impressively articulate and courteous. It was difficult to judge who was the more intelligent, but in later years I met Karl i Bond at several international gatherings and formed a very high opinion of his ability. In his interventions at these conferences he displayed wisdom, realism and maturity, and at the Franco-African Summit in Dakar in 1977, following the first invasion of Shaba province by rebels from Angola, he made a brilliant address to justify French intervention on behalf of his government. It seemed to me that he invariably defended the actions of his President vigorously and with transparent loyalty, and I was shocked to read a few months later that he had been arrested, convicted of treason and sentenced to death.

Later, following appeals from the Pope and different heads of state, the death sentence was commuted to life imprisonment. After a few months, Bond was pardoned by his President and reinstated as Prime Minister. A few months after that he went to Brussels on an official visit and remained there as a political refugee.

However, there are also several outstanding leaders in Africa whom I profoundly admire; statesman-like Félix Houphouët-Boigny of the Ivory Coast is one. A man of strong principles, he has always held firmly to his convictions regardless of the changing winds of opinion among his counterparts in other countries. When most African countries decided, at the time of the oil embargo, to break their links with Israel, Houphouët-Boigny declined to follow suit. Similarly, when the majority of OAU members recognised Peking, Houphouët-Boigny remained loyal to the Republic of China and President Chiang Kai-shek. His moral courage has been further demonstrated by his granting asylum to leaders who had been overthrown in neighbouring countries – besides Bokassa, a former President of Togo, a former President of Upper Volta and General Ojukwu were allowed to start new lives in Abidjan following their loss of power or defeat – and by his public advocacy of dialogue with racist South Africa as the best means to combat apartheid. A master of diplomacy, he sympathised with me in my problems with the OAU and afforded me every facility when I arrived in Abidjan to present my case to members of his government.

One day I asked him what he regarded as his most useful asset as President and he answered without hesitation that it was his ability to see himself first as a farmer. In fact he has always maintained a farm in his home village and spent as much time as possible on it. This example has helped to encourage agricultural growth, which is largely responsible for the Ivory Coast's development from a poor country to a relatively stable and prosperous African state.

Then there is Leopold Sedar Senghor, former President of the Republic of Senegal, who is undoubtedly Africa's most intellectual leader. A man of charm and wit, and a renowned scholar and poet, he seemed more suited to an academic life in France than to the leadership of an African nation. Indeed, he gave an impression of remoteness from the people around him and his famous philosophical treatise, *Negritude*, is more an intellectual concept than an essay in practical politics. The palace where he and his elegant French wife had their official residence, and where we lunched and dined during the Franco-African summit conference in early 1977, reflected more the culture of Versailles than Dakar. This was not surprising as the palace had been the residence of the French Governor-General before Senegal achieved independence in 1960.

Senghor left a singular mark on the history of Africa. In 1981 he voluntarily retired to make way for Abdou Diouf who had been his able Prime Minister for several years. It was an exemplary and, indeed a unique, transfer of power in the Dark Continent.

(Just after Diouf took over, neighbouring Gambia was threatened by a René-type coup while President Sir Dauda Jawara was playing golf in Britain. Diouf did not hesitate in sending troops to restore constitutional legality and I was so impressed that I promptly wrote to him, telling him how much I admired this demonstration of solidarity. Diouf replied, 'The understanding and moral support you have provided towards our action in Gambia proves, if proof was needed, your continual commitment to our common struggle to build a strong and respected Africa.')

Even within the OAU secretariat, which had once been so hostile, I discovered that there were men of logic and principle, who were not only able to see that there were two sides to every argument, but who had the courage to put career and personal safety at risk for their principles.

I had met such a man at the OAU summit in Mogadishu when I had been invited to put the SDP's case. The Tanzanians were insisting that I speak only to the Liberation Committee and not to the Plenary Session of the Heads of State, arguing that the question was to do with liberation. Naturally the moderates within the organisation realised that, with the Liberation Committee as it was constituted, this would be the end of the matter and there would be no redress of our grievances.

An OAU official approached me in an empty corridor. He had a plan and he spoke in a whisper.

'Let's not make any fuss about the matter at this stage. I will make sure tomorrow that the public address system in the Liberation Committee room is broken. Since the Seychelles question is on the agenda and since the heads of state are under pressure to return home, the secretariat is bound to suggest that you be allowed to address them directly.'

'Yes, but who will do it?' I asked.

'Sir,' he said, 'it will have to be me. This organisation is riddled with communists. Naturally I expect you to keep this between ourselves. But I want to assure you that a lot of us are on your side.'

The plan worked. My arguments were the same as those I had previously made over Africa and as we had now moved to an independence platform the OAU decided that we too should be recognised as a liberation movement. Such was the crazy logic which sometimes prevailed in the OAU!

Africa is truly a schizophrenic continent and if the Amins and Bokassas are the Mr Hydes, then men like Senghor, Diouf and Boigny are the Doctor Jekylls. Julius Nyerere, however, is both.

After the SDP had been recognised as a liberation movement, I visited Dar es Salaam with a group of colleagues to meet some officials of the Co-ordinating Committee for the Liberation of Africa. The capital during colonial days was clean and full of life but since Nyerere's imposition of his African socialist philosophy, 'Ujama', it had become shabby and dead. The contrast was so obvious that it was understandable why Nyerere had closed the border with Kenya. There is not much in the shops and there were few good restaurants left. The day after our arrival, my friends and I decided to have a curry lunch at an Indian restaurant. It was five minutes to three. The Indian who opened the door looked at his watch.

'You've arrived just in time,' he said. 'We stop taking orders at three.' As he turned the sign to 'closed' I asked him why they were so strict with their time-keeping.

He shrugged. 'Since Ujama it's hard to get staff to work extra hours.'

We sat down and ordered our lunch, relaxing over good Indian food. Half an hour later there was a bang on the door. Then three more bangs. The Indian opened it and looked into the faces of six Africans all dressed identically in Mao-style uniforms.

'A table for six,' said the first African in an arrogant tone.

The Indian apologised and repeated what he had told us; they stopped taking orders at three.

'You imperialist Indian bastard,' shouted the smallest of the group.

'You capitalist exploiter,' yelled another.

'You white suckers,' roared a third.

As they stood at the door shouting insults, a photographer appeared and began swooping around, recording the scene. Next morning the country's only newspaper, a government-controlled rag, carried the pictures under a headline: 'Indian Restaurant Close By Government Orders.' The story said that the owners were being deported for racial discrimination.

We had witnessed a minor but squalid piece of Nyerere's positive action.

A few weeks later the restaurant opened again and one of my colleagues who had been at the lunch returned. An African in a Mao suit was running the show. A huge photograph of Nyerere dominated the place. The menu was the same but the chicken curry, according to my friend, tasted like a Mexican pea soup. Nyerere's socialism had worked wonders...

Julius Nyerere – 'Mwalimu' to his sycophants – has ruled Tanganyika, later Tanzania, for more than twenty years but the much-vaunted popularity he is said to enjoy simply does not exist in his own country. Despite the speeches he has delivered in international forums and the books he has written, he remains a ruler who plays to the international political gallery. He gets upset by unfavourable articles in *The Times* or *Guardian* but the sufferings of thousands behind bars in Tanzania does not touch a single chord in his Christian soul. The Tanzanians regard his speeches and writings as a load of rubbish. To them they mean nothing for they have never done anything to stop the economic chaos into which his leadership has so energetically and systematically plunged the country.

Oscar Kambona, who was his Minister of Foreign Affairs when Tanganyika became independent and who now lives in forced exile in London, told me, 'This paragon of virtue has done more harm to the people of Tanzania in twenty years than all the colonial years put together, both German and British.'

During my visit to Tanzania, his preventive detention act (which René has copied and introduced) was in full swing. It was a licence for secret police brutality and indefinite detention in solitary confinement. There were thousands of political prisoners lingering in jail without trial. The country was being ruled by terror. Idi Amin may have stolen the limelight but Nyerere is doing as badly in the darkness.

Nyerere's Tanzania sadly characterises conditions in several other unfortunate African countries. They are all overtly committed to the struggle for majority rule in South Africa but I believe, as I said in Dar es Salaam, 'In Sharpeville the bullets which killed black schoolchildren were fired by white police, but in Dar es Salaam and elsewhere in free Africa, it is black police and soldiers who fire on black citizens. The bullets are just as lethal irrespective of the colour of the fingers which pull the triggers. If it is a shame for a people to be ruled by another people, as President Nyerere rightly asserts, then it is a greater shame for them to be oppressed, humiliated and denied their dignity as human beings by their own kith and kin.'

Chapter Sixteen

IF THERE IS one thing in which all members of the Organisation of African Unity find unity it is most definitely apartheid.

I was at the Intercontinental Hotel in Paris, some time in 1975, being interviewed by *To the Point International*, a Brussels-based weekly magazine, which gave a lot of space to African affairs. The interviewer was particularly interested to know what our policy would be towards South Africa when we became independent.

I enlightened him. 'No, we shall not sever our trade links with South Africa. If we do so, we would be acting against our own vital interest, as a small state faced with economic problems, especially inflation, which have been imposed upon us from outside and over which we have no power or control. South Africa produces a steady stream of tourists during the European summer which enables us to operate our hotels throughout the year. South Africa also supplies consumer goods at a price which keep inflation down. We cannot afford to forgo these benefits.'

'What about apartheid?' the interviewer enquired.

I was only a child when I first heard about the word apartheid. At that time South Africans used to arrive for holiday by slow boats. My impression of them was of a cocky, loud-mouthed and, on the whole, arrogant lot. One day I was having lunch with my father at the Hotel des Seychelles when I saw written on the menu in bold letters, 'This hotel is under European Management'. Upon enquiring why this inscription was necessary, my father proceeded to explain about South Africa and apartheid. 'I do not know whether it was General Smuts or Daniel Malan who started it, but it was certainly the worst thing that they ever invented for their country.'

He then told me the story of a visit to Bombay and the restaurant which carried a notice: 'South Africans and dogs not allowed'. 'Obviously,' he explained, 'the reaction of someone who had suffered under the system.'

'But the majority of the world population is not white. Why should they want to offend all these people?' I asked.

'Obviously they are interested in staying at the top, but by aggressively promoting the doctrine of white supremacy they now have the whole world on their back. Take New Zealand where there are Maoris who are good rugby players. The New Zealand Government's policy is to promote multiracialism. But suddenly New Zealand is to play a rugby match against South Africa, and there crops up the big question of what to do with the Maoris ...'

Belonging in what was more or less a happy multiracial community I was, to say the least, deeply hurt and horrified by what I had heard about the system.

Several years after that unforgettable discussion with my father, I had returned home from my studies when, one evening, father turned up, pleading with me to accompany him and two of my younger brothers on a visit to South Africa. 'The system is changing fast,' he said. 'The Japanese are now classified as honorary whites and there is an unquestionable presumption that all Chinese are Japanese.'

I would have loved to go and see things for myself, but I was too busy. A few weeks later, with my brothers Micky and Frank, he left for Durban. After two months they returned with a glowing picture of what they considered one of the most beautiful countries in the world. They had been well received. The Africans were well-off although they had heard about some small-scale riots in some suburbs.

Some time later I was visiting the USA and arrived in Dallas, Texas, where I was to meet a friend in a downtown hotel. I caught a taxi driven by a black man.

'How is life in Texas?' I asked him, as we drove towards the city centre.

By his accent I could make out that he was neither American nor Caribbean. 'Where are you from?' I asked.

'Nigeria,' he curtly replied.

As the car sped along this highway of white opulence and wealth, I wondered why this son of Africa would have chosen to come to Texas, the heart of southern racialism, of all the states in the USA.

'My friend,' he answered, 'do not speak to me of racialism. I am from Biafra and what I suffered for that, in my own country, was worse than anything I ever encountered. Here nobody bothers me. I came here to study economics, I ended up with a degree from the University of Texas, together with one wife, two children, a house, two cats and a taxi driver's licence. Now my wife is damn lazy and wants more and more money. Also once in a while some police officers would give me a hard time. But otherwise I am at peace with the world here in Texas.'

'But what about your degree in economics?' I enquired.

'Well, here in Texas it doesn't take me very far. I am hoping one of these days to be employed by one of those big oil conglomerates. Nigeria is an oil country, but also tough and rough for the average American visitor. I could make a perfect travel representative for them.'

A man with hindsight and vision, of realism and balanced judgement, I said to myself.

That night in my hotel, I had thought a lot about the problems of southern Africa. The South African tourists who had visited us since the opening of the airport were not the same as those who arrived by slow boats fifteen years before. These people were now on the defensive. The past arrogance had vanished. They were conscious that they were living in a world that was hostile to them because of apartheid, and on many occasions I had personally witnessed them going out of their way to make friends with our local people just to show that the presumption that they are all racist was not true. In my own social encounters with South Africans I found most of them down-to-earth and friendly. None, of course, was friendlier than Vera Johns whom I met one evening at the Mahé Beach Hotel and, after a dance, learnt that she was Miss South Africa on the way to London to attend the Miss World contest. (Vera had something extra special about her ... and luckily when she got to London she was disqualified from participating because of her Rhodesian background. Luckily, because I was a judge at the Miss World contest and could have easily been accused of favouritism!) In fact most of the visitors in conversation would give the impression that they supported the opposition party. Obviously this was not the case. One could see that these people were caught up in a great dilemma.

The problem of southern Africa undoubtedly poses the greatest threat to peace on the African continent and, if it is not solved, can escalate into a war far more vicious than that of the Israeli–Arab conflict, with many countries becoming involved. The point is that there are two sides to the story. This must be recognised. In my own experience with the OAU, and particularly with the Liberation Committee, I can see signs of a terrible and dangerous confrontation ahead. South Africa has tremendous technical knowhow and an economic basis which could help bring better living standards to many other parts of Africa, where today millions are living below subsistence level.

Apartheid, I explained to the interviewer, is based on the assumption that people of different races cannot live and develop harmoniously together. Seychelles, however, provides living proof that they can do that. I see no reason, therefore, why the South Africans cannot come and see for themselves how wrong their doctrine is.

The interviewer put down his microphone, switched off the tape-recorder and asked, 'Would you be willing to meet the South African Minister for Information?'

When I nodded assent, he continued.

'As it happens, Dr Connie Mulder is two floors above you. I interviewed him before coming here and he said he would like to meet you. Shall I find out if he can come now?'

And so ten minutes later I was shaking hands with Dr Mulder and his chief executive Dr Eschel Rhoodie, who were to become the two leading figures in the famous Muldergate scandal. Mulder was plain, portly and blunt; Rhoodie, good-looking, athletic and eloquent, but there was no doubt who was the boss.

'Mr Mancham,' Dr Mulder began, in his thick Afrikaans accent, 'as you know, our Prime Minister has over the past few months taken certain initiatives in an attempt to promote a better relationship with our black African neighbours. We believe the essence of international understanding is communication and we were therefore happy when Ivory Coast advocated dialogue with us.'

I interrupted him, stating, 'In my own view dialogue is essential to resolve the problem,' adding that there could be no winner in a confrontation.

'Because of apartheid everyone is at our throats,' Mulder said, adding, 'our blacks are the most advanced in all Africa.'

I replied, 'This may be so but I can never condone apartheid because it hits at a man's dignity. My own idea is that South Africa should drop apartheid fast and then apply for membership of the OAU, since OAU's policy is non-interference in internal affairs. The system you devise to stay in power, provided it is not another form of apartheid, will be a matter for you and you alone.'

Mulder interrupted, 'I see what you mean. The world is really not fair to us. Black African governments are allowed to rule their countries without interference. Some of these leaders oppress and butcher their subjects without an African voice being raised in protest. Yet we want to have good relationships with black Africa, especially with our neighbours.'

Dr Mulder then spoke about Mauritius, stating that the UN representative of Mauritius was spending his time abusing South Africa, although the South Africans were always the first on the scene whenever a cyclone hit the island.

I told him that he could count on me to support a policy of dialogue aimed at doing away with apartheid and bringing an entente with black Africa.

Dr Mulder stood up, put his right hand in his trouser pocket and pulled out a Krugerrand. 'This is gold, Mr Mancham, gold! Please accept this as a memento of our meeting and a reminder of South Africa's principal export.'

Resisting an impulse to hand it back, I accepted this rather tactless gesture in the interests of diplomacy.

Some months later, on a visit to Seychelles, Dr Rhoodie came to see me. He was concerned about the campaign of vilification against South Africa which was being conducted by the *People*, organ of René's party. 'Look, Mr Mancham,' he said, 'my department is in a position to provide some help if any means could be found to counteract the situation.'

I answered that in principle I would not suppress publication in the *Seychelles Weekly*, which I own and control, of any criticism of apartheid, nor indeed would I endeavour to publish any editorial that tended to justify or condone it. However, I agreed, there were also several blatant violations of human rights in other countries in Africa which could be better exposed in order to put South Africa's situation in a more balanced perspective. On the question of help, I told him what had then become public knowledge, that the government of Tanzania had over the years not only provided a press to the SPUP, but also generous financial support. I mentioned that the last election had left the SDP with an overdraft of nearly 200,000 rupees and asked whether he could make a contribution to the Party's funds and help me acquire a new printing machine for the *Weekly*. Dr Rhoodie said that he thought he could help in both areas. But, he added, these are extremely sensitive matters and consequently must be left strictly between the two of us.

Eventually Dr Rhoodie contributed around 12,000 Rand to help us settle the election overdraft. Subsequently, too, I received printing machines worth several thousand pounds which had been consigned to me from Holland. One morning, two or three months after independence, Margaret René, my private secretary, told me that Dr Rhoodie was calling from Pretoria. He said that a South African newspaper had published an article saying that Guy Sinon, one of our ministers, had said in Dar es Salaam that we were about to cancel South Africa's air traffic rights, in deference to an OAU resolution calling for an economic boycott of South Africa, and that Dr Mulder wanted him to fly to Seychelles to discuss this and other matters with me.

Despite his party's strong link with Tanzania, René, who was then Prime Minister, had come out as a firm supporter of our policy on South Africa, which briefly said: No to apartheid, Yes to tourism and commercial contact.

I therefore told Rhoodie that it would be a good thing for him to come so that we could discuss the whole matter with René, but I added that he should arrange to come discreetly, as if coming on holiday with his family.

'With our new membership of the OAU I don't think it would be wise for me to extend to you an official invitation,' I explained.

On the morning of Rhoodie's arrival, I telephoned René and told him of the South African concern about their traffic rights and of Rhoodie's arrival to discuss the matter with us.

'It is this baboon Guy Sinon who doesn't understand the doctrine of ministerial responsibility. He is always making statements on subjects outside his portfolio,' said René.

Sinon, a hugely built black Seychellois, was the Secretary-General of SPUP and Minister of Education in the coalition government.

René accepted the invitation to meet Rhoodie at dinner.

The gathering consisted of René, his wife Geva, Dr and Mrs Rhoodie, Rhoodie's deputy, Les de Villiers, and his wife, and a South African couple who were in his party. After dinner, Rhoodie, de Villiers, René and I went to another room and I assured the South Africans that it was not our intention to withdraw their traffic rights nor to sever our commercial and tourism links with them.

Rhoodie looked pleased and said that he wanted to raise two rather delicate matters. First, he wondered whether there was any possibility of getting Seychelles passports for a few South Africans to enable them to travel to African countries which were at present barred to them. Secondly, he had been asked by a fertiliser tycoon, Mr Louis Luyt, who wanted to promote his business in black Africa, if it would be possible to register an aeroplane in Seychelles.

The passport request I turned down flat. As it happened, two Hong Kong Chinese had approached us a few days before with a scheme whereby some 200 of their wealthy compatriots, nervous about Chinese designs on the colony, should each deposit £25,000 interest free in a Seychelles Development Bank, thus securing it £5,000,000 overnight, in return for Seychelles passports.

I had to tell them we were not in the passport business since our constitution clearly laid down who was entitled to Seychelles nationality, and this I explained to Dr Rhoodie. On the question of aircraft registration, neither René nor I had the position at our fingertips, but we agreed to look at it. Not very much else was said that night. We joined the rest of the guests until we said goodbye.

A few months after the coup which deposed me I received a telephone call from South Africa. It was from Kitt Katzin, deputy editor of the Johannesburg *Sunday Express*. He said he had discovered that Dr Rhoodie came to Seychelles on a private plane when he had got his department to purchase commercial tickets for himself and the family. 'Did he visit you when you were President? Was he on holiday or on official government business?'

'As far as I am concerned he came on official government business.'

'Do you remember what was discussed?'

'There was the question of South African Airways landing rights and some other matters.'

'Can you tell me about the other matters?'

'No, I do not think that I can reveal to the press the nature and details of confidential discussions.'

'OK, Mr Mancham, that will do for today. I will call back another time. Thank you.'

That was investigative journalism at work. Apparently, a week before, Katzin had cornered Rhoodie who said that his visit to Seychelles was a holiday. Katzin was to make bold headlines: 'RHOODIE IS LYING – MANCHAM SAID HE CAME ON OFFICIAL GOVERNMENT BUSINESS'. Poor Rhoodie, there was no way he could win on this issue. A week later he contradicted himself, stating that he had come on 'a delicate and secret mission', which formed the basis for another *Express* article, this time under the headline 'WHY THE CONTRADICTIONS? THE SECRETARY QUALIFIES FOR A NAME CHANGE FROM DR RHOODIE TO DR RIDDLE'.

Whilst the question of whether Rhoodie came to Seychelles on holiday or on business was the straw which broke the camel's back, it was a small matter when it became known that a mysterious company called Thor Communications was a front for the propaganda activities of the South African Government's Department of Information. Later the South African Parliament got a shock when Prime Minister Vorster admitted that he was personally responsible for the secret funds used by the Department. Then there was the allegation that huge sums had been spent in the United States to improve the country's image. And when investigative journalism gathers momentum, as in Watergate, it does not stop at one issue. Suddenly Rhoodie had to admit what a hostile world already knew, that South Africa had for years undertaken sensitive and highly secretive counter propaganda operations abroad, and that these activities were paid for from a secret fund. 'I was authorised by the Government that counter action was to be taken as if we were in a state of war, and that no rules or regulations would apply,' Rhoodie said.

I could not help feeling some sympathy for Rhoodie when he added, 'South Africa's enemies must be laughing their heads off at the way the Auditor-General and sections of the press have destroyed an apparatus which, unknown to the public, had in secret achieved incredible success.'

Chapter Seventeen

AT THE TIME of our independence, Monsieur Jean de Lipkowski, leader of the French delegation, brought me a personal invitation from President Giscard d'Estaing to attend the 14 July celebrations as his special guest and then fly to Nice for a naval display. I was particularly flattered by this singular manifestation of friendship, especially as the human adventure of Seychelles had begun with the arrival of French settlers, the influence of which was still very much alive in the islands.

Everything went according to plan. We signed an agreement for future bilateral co-operation, under which the French were to send an aid mission to help diversify our agriculture and develop our fishing potential. We were also presented with a number of cars for our VIP pool and arranged for a group of Seychellois teachers to come to France so that upon returning they could help put into effect our new policy of 'balanced bilingualism'.

On a PR level I met Yves Rousset-Rouard, head of Trinacra Films, and agreed that he should film *Goodbye Emanuelle*, starring the vivacious Sylvia Kristel, on the islands. I also arranged with Robert Caillé of French *Vogue* that a fashion *rapportage* by Roman Polanski, starring Natasha Kinski, on the theme 'The Pirate', should be produced against the colourful background of our beaches and mountains.

It was a most successful trip which augured well for Franco-Seychelles friendship!

There have been many stories in the international press about Roman Polanski and his affair with Natasha Kinski since the release of the film *Tess*, which Polanski produced, starring Kinski, based on Thomas Hardy's novel *Tess of the D'Urbervilles*, about a very young girl who is sexually violated by an older man. The whole affair started in Seychelles.

When Polanski agreed to produce the 'Pirate' fashion *rapportage* for French *Vogue*, he insisted that he could choose the model. Natasha is the lovely daughter of Polanski's friend, the German actor, Klaus Kinski. When the two, together with the *Vogue* team, got to Seychelles I hosted a welcoming lunch and discovered that the famous producer had a budding interest in the young lady. As a matter of fact, friends with *Vogue* and staff at the hotel told me that, until Natasha started co-operating, Roman was often found to be noisy and quarrelsome. But once his obsession had been satisfied, he earned the respect and affection of all by his sharp intelligence, obvious inspiration and great sense of humour.

In 1978 the part-time liaison became full time when Roman fled to France to escape charges that he had raped a thirteen-year-old Californian girl. In an interview Natasha gave, she said, 'I just hope the worst won't happen to him. He has too much to offer, he teaches you to have courage, to rely on yourself and to take risks. . . .'

That line about 'risks' reminded me of the night of their departure from Seychelles with the *Vogue* team. I was at the airport to see them off when it was announced that the plane was one hour late. It was a wonderful moonlit evening and no one can blame Polanski for leaving the VIP lounge to take a breath of fresh air and a last look at our tropic sky before the trip. But half an hour later I was with the rest of the group when a police inspector called me aside.

'Sir,' he said, 'that short man who was with you. He is a very naughty fellow. I want to charge him with indecent exposure.'

'What do you mean?' I asked.

'Well, he was having it with the young lady not far from the runway,' he said. 'A constable and I saw it all. But this is a small country and it could be most embarrassing. I think we should give him a chance.'

'OK,' I said. 'But I will have a word with him.'

Roman then arrived with a big smile. Natasha too looked happy. But then the *Vogue* photographers wanted some last-minute pictures and soon afterwards the plane arrived. A few weeks later when the *Vogue rapportage* appeared Polanski had devoted one full page to depicting his 'special friends' – and there among the group was a photo he had personally taken of me on the lawn of State House!

*   *   *

On returning from France I heard that a Russian research vessel, *Kallisto*, was about to visit us. The ship belonged to the Academy of Sciences and on board was Dr Valentin Stonik, Director of the Far East Scientific Centre. We were told the ship was exploring the ocean, and the scientists would provide our government with a report of their findings. We had had hardly any visits from the Russians during the colonial days, yet now that we had just become independent they had arrived to take full advantage of our declared policy of 'friend to all and enemy to none'.

We gave them a party and toasted the health of the President of the USSR. Next day the Russians invited us on board. It was a Saturday night and I went with my chauffeur, my security guards and a group of colleagues to the ship which was anchored five miles out by the reef. As soon as we boarded it became obvious that the Russians had taken notice of my reputation as a *bon vivant* who enjoyed the company of women. A group of us were entertained in the close quarters of the director's cabin. There was an impressive gathering of glamorous lady members of the crew. Caviar, crab and champagne were served in prodigious quantities. With two of my ministers and my ADC I had a lavish time, eating and drinking and singing. Yet I could not rid myself of a feeling of unease, despite the champagne. There was a strange atmosphere on board, unlike any other ship I had visited. My hosts were friendly enough, but as we were being escorted to the director's cabin, I noticed that the sailors were either deeply engaged in games of chess or studying. While our hosts made a special effort to be warm in their greeting, there was not one spontaneous smile of welcome from the rest of the crew.

Watching all these chess games and seeing these sailors' noses deep in books, I found myself impressed and frightened at the same time. It was all so different to the Saturday nights when French, American or British ships were in port and when everyone went out on the town and made sure that a good time was had by all. I could not understand why, after months exploring the bottom of the Indian Ocean, these men and women were not permitted to stroll singly or in couples around Mahé. Why did they all have to move around in packs, like a group of tourists off a bus? It was very strange. And it was incomprehensible to the Seychellois that these poor Russians were under orders – on a Saturday night – to be back on board ship before sunset.

On the launch taking us back from the party, my chauffeur asked a question.

'Sir,' he said, 'how did you enjoy the party?'

I told him it was quite good. I told him about the pretty women, champagne, crab and caviar.

For a moment he was silent, staring into the spray, then he looked back at the Russian boat. Eventually he shook his head.

'We got peanuts, sprats and terrible beer,' he said. 'I always thought that under communism, a chauffeur could eat with a President.'

He had learnt, that night, the difference between theory and practice.

My year as President consisted of constant work at home, punctuated by trips abroad. There was no breathing space, and no time off, but it was exhilarating. The work pumped the adrenalin through my veins. It was a most exciting year, with meetings and conferences all over the world.

At the Summit Conference of Non-aligned Countries in Colombo that August the main preoccupation of some eighty heads of state was how to keep their shaky edifices together when internal disagreements were tearing them apart. Moreover it was becoming difficult to ignore the fact that some countries were less non-aligned than others and that others were not non-aligned at all. It seemed that much of Mrs Bandaranaike's hard work to make the conference a success was destined to be wasted.

One such disagreement concerned the Polisario Front. The previous OAU meeting had avoided upsetting its own leaky boat by deferring the matter for investigation and report. The Algerians were displeased at this decision and had sent Foreign Minister Boutlefika to Sri Lanka to lobby for debate. The Moroccans and the Mauritanians were also active, however.

Since I had participated in the OAU decision and sincerely believed that this was an African problem, I had agreed to co-sponsor a Moroccan resolution to that effect, but was soon reminded of the political realities. Scarcely had I signed the Moroccan motion when President Boumédienne of Algeria invited me to meet him for discussion. I had intended to break the ice by referring lightheartedly to my Algerian experience, but he was in no mood for frivolity. 'What is small Seychelles doing meddling in North African politics?' he demanded menacingly.

'Do you realise what supporting the Moroccans could cost you?'

Later the same day I was approached by President Gaddafi of Libya, who wanted me to support his motion condemning French activities in Africa, especially in the Comoro Islands and Réunion. It seemed that he and his aides had failed to notice the rosette of an officer of the Légion d'Honneur, which President Giscard d'Estaing had recently bestowed upon me and which I was wearing in my buttonhole.

That night I pondered deeply on these matters and decided that the following day, and indeed for the rest of the summit meeting, I would serve the interests of my small country better by remaining in the hotel swimming pool than by going to the Bandaranaike Memorial International Conference Hall.

But one event I had no intention of missing. President Tito, co-founder of the Non-aligned Movement, was to give a party. His sumptuous yacht, decorated with coloured lights, contrasted with the drabness of Colombo harbour. Respectful silence greeted the entrance of the great man, eighty-five years of age, beautifully tanned, wearing a white suit with white shoes and a diamond tie pin, his hair thinning but immaculately groomed, and smoking a large Havana cigar, as he moved slowly among his deferential guests. For my part, I ate caviar and drank champagne from crystal glasses, and once again wondered how the principles of socialist equality applied between rich and poor and large and small nations, and what the unemployed of Sri Lanka were expecting from this exalted meeting.

A few weeks later I accepted the invitation of British Airways to fly Concorde to Washington where Seychelles was to be admitted as the 145th member of the United Nations.

I boarded this unique aircraft at Heathrow, marvelling that in only three and a half hours we would have crossed the Atlantic and would be touching down at Dulles International in Washington.

The blonde air hostess brought a tray of goodies, a wonderful glass of champagne and a collection of magazines. I flipped through them and saw three stories that interested me. President Ali Bhutto of Pakistan was having problems, Shirley Bassey was ill and Vivianne Ventura had given an interview about her jetset life. I recalled Bhutto's generosity on the eve of our independence when he sent a ship fully loaded with rice to us – a gift from the people of Pakistan to the people of Seychelles.

It was a gesture which touched me profoundly particularly because Pakistan was a poor country. But then Bhutto was waking up to the fact that Indira Gandhi was sending several warships to our celebrations. Pakistan would certainly not be happy with Seychelles under India's influence.

Bhutto later sent one of his ambassadors to present me with the Quaid-i-Azam gold medal of Pakistan – one of the country's highest awards. Now I read that the poor man was in trouble, threatened not by Mrs Gandhi but by his own people. Reading about Bhutto reminded me of one of my oldest friends, Cappi Badrut. She was American, a former Hollywood actress and estranged wife of Andrea Badrut who owns the Palace Hotel in St Moritz, a place his family has run for generations, not just as a hotel but more like a country club for sophisticates. I met Cappi one night in Regine's in Paris and we ended the evening at my apartment in the Hotel Crillon. Next morning when I woke up, Cappi was gone. I looked round. There was no message. It had been a ships passing in the night affair, I thought. However, an hour later in the bathroom was a message I could not miss, written in lipstick on the mirror: 'Jimmy it was a lovely evening', followed by her phone number and surrounded by kisses.

I had a lovely affair with Cappi and we always met when I was passing through Paris. Often we would go to eat at Maxim's with Dewi Sukarno.

On one occasion Cappi had arranged to visit me in Seychelles and was to send her yacht. However, the vessel never finished the voyage. It ran aground on the reef of Djibouti. She was trying to get it lifted off when René's coup occurred and so she never made it.

At the Palace Hotel, Cappi had met everyone – Charlie Chaplin, Noël Coward, Henry Fonda, Count Theo Rossi, Somerset Maugham and most of the crowned heads of Europe, but her most cherished statesman was no doubt Ali Bhutto, whose charm and personality had left a deep and lasting impression on her. (Cappi loved Bhutto. She was full of tears when he was hanged. Poor Cappi herself passed away recently – another sad victim of cancer.)

The story of Shirley Bassey reminded me of a flight I had taken a few months earlier with her and Soraya, the first wife of Adnan Khashoggi. I had met Soraya at a party in London given by Lloyds Shipping for Adnan and she told me that she was leaving the next day for Seychelles in one of her husband's planes. As I was waiting for the next British Airways flight, which was not due to leave for three days, I asked if I could hitch a lift. Within a few hours we were leaving Heathrow on Omaria 3 with Soraya and Shirley. We flew all night, refuelled in Khartoum and woke to a champagne breakfast. We were all in a party mood. Shirley was singing 'I've got you under my skin' when she was interrupted by the captain telling us to fasten our seat-belts as we were about to land at Mogadishu.

Omaria 3 was a US-registered aircraft, the two pilots were American and the Somalis – at that time under heavy Russian influence – were claiming that we were violating their airspace. Our captain had told them over the radio that we had clearance, but they were adamant that we land. We watched as three Russian MiGs buzzed round us and forced us down. Shirley had stopped singing. The champagne had gone flat and we were all nervous. On landing the aircraft was surrounded by armed soldiers as the captain and his co-pilot were taken for questioning. We sat there sweating for an hour as the tropical sun rose, then the door was pushed open and we stared into the faces of a group of armed soldiers.

The leader stared at us. 'Where is the Prime Minister of Seychelles?' he asked.

I stood up and introduced myself, trying to control my nerves.

He saluted and smiled. 'My apologies, sir, for keeping you here,' he said. 'On behalf of the Somali Government I welcome you to Mogadishu. The Minister of Foreign Affairs is on his way to greet you, and all your friends are invited to join us for lunch.'

We were escorted to the airport lounge where we discovered that the pilot had been asked for a passenger list. When the Air Force realised that I was on board, they were worried that there might be diplomatic repercussions and had phoned Foreign Affairs Minister Arteh, a man who had often been hostile to me at OAU meetings. Now, however, he was about to put himself forward as a candidate for Secretary-General and so he took the opportunity of making up with me.

'Oh, my brother,' he said, as he arrived in his limousine. He shook my hand as if we were long-lost friends and within the hour we were feasting in a corner of the airport on three barbecued goats. Shirley had rediscovered her voice and was singing 'Over the Rainbow'.

Vivianne Ventura was another lady of social graces with whom my name had become linked. We first met at a dinner party she was hosting at an Italian restaurant in London's Bayswater when we danced until the early hours. Next morning the *Daily Express* Hickey's column was already announcing that 'Miss Ventura was so engrossed with the Mancham charms that she left the restaurant forgetting to pay the bill of more than £200 . . .'.

At any rate a few days later I had a *rendezvous* with Vivianne at her apartment in Flood Street. I did not remember the exact number of the place. When I rang the front-door bell of the house in front of which the chauffeur had stopped, the maid who answered politely told me that this was the home of Mrs Margaret Thatcher, then a bright star within the British Conservative Party and now Prime Minister. I soon found out that Vivianne lived only a few doors away.

That evening as we drank white wine and ate tit-bits, Vivianne told me some wonderful stories of her amazing life. There were pictures everywhere of those she particularly remembered – King Hussein of Jordan, the millionaire financier, John Bentley, who was the father of her daughter Sheherazade, and of Anthony Quinn, opposite whom she appeared in the film *A High Wind in Jamaica*.

There is something about air travel which stimulates the imagination and encourages a person to philosophise. Perhaps it is the fact of being sealed in a tiny capsule so far above the world that gives a sense of detachment. Flying at twice the speed of sound and higher than any other commercial aircraft, I began to ponder on the state of the world below.

Funny, I thought; here is my tiny nation about to join the most important international organisation in the world where its vote could neutralise that of the USA, the USSR or China. Already we were being fêted. It was no accident that British Airways were flying us free to the US, and I was reminded of Colonel Gaddafi who had sent a special plane to pick up the Maldivian representative so that the man might vote alongside Libya at the UN on an issue close to the Libyan ruler's heart.

Landing in Washington, I was made even more aware of the new privileges of and pressures on a head of state. Following the assassination of the Kennedy brothers and Martin Luther King, Congress had ruled that any visiting head of state should be afforded full security protection. From the moment we stepped off the plane until we boarded again several days later, we were surrounded by security men. No less than fifteen met us at Dulles. This contingent guarded the VIP lounge during a two-hour meeting I had with State Department officials, then accompanied me to Kennedy Airport, New York, where they were joined by another ten who stayed with me until I checked into the Hilton. During my stay the security was impressive. Two men stayed outside my suite at the hotel. They wanted to know which restaurant I was to go to. When I arrived, a group of them would be eating at the next table. When I brought a girl back from a party, two more accompanied us in the car and rode the elevator with us, leaving us only when we reached the door.

And so, on 21 September, flanked by my guards, I drove a few blocks from the Hilton to the great green domino on First Avenue to represent my country as Seychelles joined the United Nations.

Opening the thirty-first session of the General Assembly, the Luxembourg delegate, Gaston Thorn, spoke lengthily about human rights. Following his speech the assembly paid tribute to the memory of Chairman Mao Tse-tung, who had just died.

Then it was my turn. I congratulated the Sri Lankan Ambassador who had assumed office as President of the thirty-first session. I expressed my sentiments of condolence to the government and people of China at the death of their leader, then went straight into my speech, watched by delegates from all over the world, many of them wearing earphones as my words were translated into dozens of languages.

I once again outlined our policy of friend to all and enemy to none and stated that Seychelles could be a shining example to the world of the ability of different races to work together:

'We do not have to look very far or very closely to see that there are simple and natural laws which work as surely in human affairs as they do in the rest of creation. If you sow a mango seed you get a mango tree. If you sow maize you get maize. No exception to this simple law has ever occurred or ever will. By the same token, if you sow the seed of contention, the seed of violence and hatred, the harvest will be more contention, more violence and more hatred.

'Society can only change by first changing the attitude of people who live in it – among whom, to begin with, I repeat, the attitude of those who have the responsibility to guide and to lead those people. To guide and to lead the people where? Towards progress – which means peace – which is, after all, an essential condition for real, true, lasting progress.'

Looking back, I realise how quickly I had forgotten about René and his bombs, how sometimes the head can get lost in the clouds of righteousness. It was, I think, the speech of an idealist; it was sincere, optimistic, yet ultimately naive.

That night, still buoyant with that optimism, we hosted a party in one of the UN halls. I had invited a gorgeous blonde Texan socialite called Janet. She had spent some time before with me in Seychelles.

After the party we went back to the Hilton chaperoned until we reached my door by security men. Three hours later, naked and fast asleep, we were startled by a bang on the door. My security guards wasted no time bursting in.

'Follow me,' said the biggest. 'Quick.'

If he was in any way fazed by the sight of us, he did not show it. He threw us two towels and rushed us out of the room. There was no time to ask where we were going. The man had the sort of authority that defied any questions. We simply did as we were told. We ran past the elevator to the exit doorway and barefoot, followed our guards down the concrete stairs; down, and down and down – all forty-five floors to the street. The night was hot and humid and the staircase seemed endless. Clutching our Hilton towels round us, Janet and I made rather an incongruous sight as we eventually reached ground level. Only then were we told as we were escorted into the nearby Americana Hotel that Puerto Rican dissidents had exploded bombs in the Hilton after a party given in honour of the Governor of the island. Luckily no-one was hurt and luckily for us, there were no photographers around to record Janet and I hobbling into the Americana wearing our Hilton towels.

Next morning I could hardly move, I was so exhausted. When the security man knocked, I crawled to the door and opened it on my knees.

The man looked down at me and grinned.

'What's wrong?'

I rubbed my calves which had knotted with cramp from running down all those stairs.

'Charlie Horse,' he said in his broad Texan accent. 'That's what you've got. Charlie Horse.'

I had never heard of the term but Charlie Horse kept me hobbling for the next few days.

The story did not get back to the islands but if it had, most Seychellois would have enjoyed the irony. Here was its President accepting membership of the UN and making a speech of idealism in a most dignified setting, yet within a few hours caught in a towel with a blonde on the New York sidewalks. Yet this was nothing compared to the embarrassment of one of my ministers who, only a few weeks later, met a high-class New York hooker in his hotel bar. She smiled at him. He bought her a drink. She slipped something into his drink. He became dizzy. She suggested a massage in his bedroom. An hour later he woke up naked without passport, money or watch. An easy-going, trusting islander with no experience of the devious ways of the world, he had made the classic mistake. We had quickly to get him a new passport and some money so that he could fly home.

After New York I was invited to be guest speaker at the thirtieth anniversary celebrations of UNESCO in Nairobi. Three thousand delegates packed the Uhuru Hall and, as I stood to make my speech, I looked down at all the faces; black, white, brown and yellow, the representatives of almost every nation in the world, and I realised how far Seychelles had come in such a short time. How many of these people, I wondered, would have been able to find our islands on a world atlas ten years earlier?

The same thought occurred to me a few weeks later when I received an invitation to Mexico as the guest of President Miguel Aleman. This man, the first civilian President of his country, was undoubtedly the doyen of international tourism. During his period in office he had supervised the build-up of the industry from some 400,000 visitors a year in the early 1960s to four million by the mid 1970s. It was Aleman who had seen the potential of the fishing village of Acapulco and had turned it into a playground for the jet-set. In his letter of invitation he recalled our first meeting at the World Travel Conference there some years before. Since then he said he had watched our development and now he wanted to present me with a gold medal in recognition of the work I had done to put Seychelles on the international tourist map.

In Acapulco the vivacious Karin Aleman had arranged a lavish reception for me at Villa Alejandra, the Alemans' plush beachside residence. Fifty guests turned up from different parts of the world, including such international jet-setters as Bruno and Kika Paglia, Vicky and Oscar Oberfeld, Baron Enrico di Portenova and his wife, Sandra.

It was an extravagant evening and I made new friends, but the lady who most interested me was an attractive and magnetic

Frenchwoman who was introduced to me as la Comtesse Jacqueline de Rochambeau, who had come to the reception on the arm of an elderly gentleman named Charles Lachman, the founder of the Revlon cosmetics empire.

After the gala dinner, a small group went on to a discotheque. It all proved too much for Mr Lachman. He was soon sound asleep at his table while I was left to dance with the Comtesse. I learnt that she was finalising a divorce from the Count and intended marrying Lachman afterwards. I also knew that we would meet again.

Sure enough, a few weeks later she wrote to me, saying she would like to see me. She had enjoyed my book of poems. What were my travel plans? I checked my diary. In March I was due to go to the Afro-Arab summit in Cairo, and Cairo was only a short hop to Paris.

We met and dined at Maxim's. She told me that her divorce was coming through and asked me to recite some of my poetry. I was a happy man, dining with a beautiful woman in a superb restaurant in the most romantic city in the world, the worries and responsibilities of my work momentarily forgotten. The idyll was interrupted only briefly when a waiter brought me a message. Prince Talal of Saudi Arabia was in Vienna and wanted urgently to see me. I slipped the note into my pocket, putting aside the affairs of state for as long as possible.

Next morning, I was boarding a private plane at Le Bourget sent for me by Prince Talal. As I fastened my seat-belt, I looked again at the note he had sent to Maxim's and wondered why he was taking the trouble to fly me to Austria. I had met the man only once, a few weeks earlier when he had visited Seychelles as the guest of both Adnan Khashoggi and myself. He was interested in buying the Bay of Port Launay where he wanted to build hotels and a marina, to develop the place into a complex which, in his own words, 'would rival Marbella'.

I remembered him as being a quiet man and very shrewd. I learned that he was the brother of King Khalid and the favourite son of Abdul Aziz. He was most definitely a man to be taken seriously.

Soon I found myself at the Imperial Hotel, opposite him dressed in flowing robes. He told me that he had come to Austria for a medical check-up. I nodded and waited for him to come to the point.

'Mr President,' he said, 'I want to thank you for the welcome you gave me in Seychelles. It is a beautiful country and I like your people. As Adnan must have told you, I want to invest a lot of money, but there is a problem ...' He was looking directly at me, watching my reaction.

'Your Prime Minister,' he said. 'I don't trust him.'

'In what way, Your Highness?' I asked. What on earth had René done now, I wondered.

'I remember the dinner you gave for me. You put the Prime Minister's wife by my side. This woman made the point of adapting her voice to the level of the music. When the music was loud she was loud – when it was low she whispered.'

So what? I thought to myself. She was just trying to make herself heard, maybe ...

'I think, President, she did not want you to hear what she was telling me. And then there is your Prime Minister. I did not like the look in his eyes. He never looked at you straight in the face.'

And that was virtually the end of the conversation. We exchanged a few pleasantries and within the hour I was back in his plane heading for Paris again to catch my flight to Seychelles. I thought back to what the Prince had said. On the face of it, there was nothing sinister in his warning; the tone of voice of René's wife, the look in René's eyes. That was it. Yet he had taken the trouble to fly me to Vienna to tell me this. I thought of the instinct of the Bedouins, sharpened by centuries of desert warfare and intrigue; these people lived or died by noticing such things as the expression on a man's face. They had a sixth sense, an invisible antenna which picked up trouble. I knew nothing of such things. I had had too peaceful an island upbringing to understand. All I knew was that this was a warning, the latest in a series. It called, I thought, for a call to my CIA contact.

As soon as I got back, I looked out Mr X's number. In the few months since his promise of help for our internal security I had regularly been in touch, asking him to tell me when something concrete would happen. The first time I called him, he was apologetic.

'Look, Mr Mancham,' he said, 'President Ford has got Senator Church looking into the CIA. We are being torn apart at the moment. With the disgrace of Watergate and the guilt over Vietnam, the country wants to have a go at us.' He became quite poetic as he continued. 'The country is flaying itself with moral whips. It's become fashionable to purge every part of the system.'

'I understand,' I said. 'But where does this leave us?'

'At the moment in limbo,' he said. 'We've been told here in Nairobi to delay submission of the project for three months until things calm down.'

That had been the first phone call. But it was not the last. I had called him again in the autumn. This time the problem was the presidential elections.

'I'm sorry, Mr Mancham, but the climate isn't right. During a presidential election, Washington doesn't give high priority to foreign policy matters.'

Jimmy Carter's victory in November 1976 led to yet another call.

'As you know,' said Mr X, 'during the election campaign, the role of the CIA became a controversial issue. We now have to wait for President-elect Carter to evolve his philosophy towards us.'

I think I swore down the line.

'We guarantee, however, that in two or three months' time, things will start moving.'

Two months later things did start moving but in the wrong direction. In January Carter's nominee for the directorship of the CIA, Theodore Sorensen, asked the President to withdraw his nomination. Sorensen had run into opposition from some Senators who objected to him on the grounds that, as a confidante of the Kennedys, he had taken classified material – when on the White House staff in 1964 – and used it in a book he had written on the Kennedy administration. He was also unfit, in the minds of these Senators, because he was inexperienced in foreign intelligence, he had helped Edward Kennedy explain the Chappaquiddick incident, he had been a conscientious objector to military service, and he had been employed in a law firm representing multinational firms and foreign governments.

And so, with all these problems, Sorensen had to go. I had been invited to Ethiopa by General Taferi Bante, a man I had met and grown friendly with during the Colombo conference. Bante had taken over the country after the overthrow of Haile Selassie in 1974. I knew little of his politics but on a personal level I found him friendly. And so on 3 February I was ready to accept his invitation to see him. I was flying to Rwanda to attend an OCAM summit meeting and had to stop off in Addis Ababa.

As I was driving to the airport, I heard on the BBC World Service that Bante and six of his supporters had been killed in a gun battle that had broken out between different political factions. The victor, said the BBC, was a certain Colonel Mengistu. My immediate reaction had been to give Addis a wide berth but there was no other way to get to Rwanda in time. The airport authorities assured me that Addis airport was still open and so I carried on with my itinerary.

As we came in to land at Addis, I was apprehensive but as I got off the plane I found a guard of honour lined up to greet me. The soldiers were wearing red caps and scarves and I thought: 'Oh God, more leftists.' Maybe they were going to throw me in jail for my friendship with Bante.

Instead a short man, one of those wearing the red cap, saluted me and shook my hand, introducing himself as Haile Mariam Mengistu. Over his shoulder I could see the Seychelles flags fluttering and banners saying 'Long live Seychelles–Ethiopian friendship'.

For a few minutes, before Mengistu left, we made small talk. I made no mention of the coup. Nor did he.

As we waited in the VIP lounge for our connection we were well enough treated. Even in poverty-stricken Ethiopia there was the usual champagne and caviar, but I could not relax. In the wastepaper-basket I had glimpsed two photographs glued side by side – one of Bante and the other of me. I could not get out of Addis fast enough and that experience led to another phone call to Nairobi.

The same question: 'Are we any further forward with our security plans?'

'Haven't you heard?' said Mr X, and now there was a note of exasperation in his voice. 'There's all sorts of problems here. Sorensen's out. We'll just have to wait for a while.'

'Okay,' I said, and hung up.

What next?

A few days later Admiral Stanville Turner, a former classmate of Jimmy Carter, was nominated as CIA director. Surely now, I thought, we could go ahead. I waited. There was no news from Nairobi. Meanwhile something was bothering me on the island.

On 12 February Gilbert Morgan, a young supporter of the SPUP, vanished. He had been drinking in the Reef Hotel when he got a message that someone wanted to see him outside. He left a full glass of whisky, two packets of cigarettes and his matches on the counter and went out. That was the last anyone saw of him. At first there was no concern. Morgan was a good-looking young man and there were a number of yachts in the harbour with women on board and there was no lack of parties.

However, when he did not show up, a security meeting was held. The police went to his room and found a copy of the Seychelles constitution open at the page dealing with the presidential office. A reward for information was offered but nothing turned up. Gilbert Morgan had vanished off the face of the earth. What bothered me was that, although he was a prominent SPUP activist, very little play was given in the *People*. (After the coup there was no mention of this once gallant supporter. No memorial service was held; there was no hero's bugle; no street was named after him as was the case with others.)

I was worried. Morgan was unpredictable, a loud-mouth. Whenever I saw him at the Reef, he made faces at me. The conclusion was inescapable. He knew something that the SPUP was planning and he was silenced before he shot his mouth off.

Again I phoned Nairobi.

'Haven't you heard?' said my contact again. 'The *Washington Post* has come up with all sorts of stories about CIA payments to Hussein, Kenyatta, Chiang Kai-shek, Synghman Rhee, Bhutto and God knows who else. It's all over the front pages. How the hell can you work an intelligence agency when it gets splashed all over the damned papers?'

There was no answer to that. Mr X was angry. It was no time to ask about Seychelles. Again I hung up....

... But now, in April, with Prince Talal's warning in my mind, I decided to have yet another try. I picked up the phone.

'You must have read what Carter's done now,' my man said. 'He's appointed Andrew Young to the UN and he's agreed with Young's statement that Cuban troops have stabilised the situation in Angola. *Stabilised*! Jesus! How dumb can you get?'

I took the hint. Washington was in total confusion. Seychelles therefore was way down the list. God knows when their commitments to us would be fulfilled. We never did get our security system. Perhaps if we had, things might have been different.

Yet, as we approached high summer and the first anniversary of our independence, we could congratulate ourselves on the fact that things were progressing. We had no internal security system to speak of and no defence against the outside world. Our only defence was the smile of our people; but we had made progress. For six months we had worked on a five-year development plan, the details of which I announced over the radio.

We had worked out how to develop fishing. We had an agriculture scheme which included reafforestation and the building up of the coconut plantations. Inter-island communication was to be improved. Land was bought and a plan made so that every family would own its own house; a new hospital was to be built, free health service having been introduced two years earlier; the airport was to be expanded, a sewage system to be installed in Victoria, an electricity network built on Mahé and electricity introduced in two of the outer islands; compulsory primary education was introduced, along with more streaming in the secondary schools; a dam was being built and the roads were to be sealed.

It was hard, exhilarating work and I had organised a strict routine for myself. I was up at dawn, ate a hearty breakfast, then went to my office, which was situated in the same compound as State House. The mornings were taken up with meetings with various ministers and investors. Lunch would be with some local group or with visiting VIPs or ambassadors; a half-hour nap, then back to the office by two-thirty to work for three hours, after which I would pick up Richard from school and we would go to one of the beaches for a half-hour swim; another nap before dinner at State House or at one of the hotels.

Hosting dinner parties could be very tiring but I wanted to do it as often as possible because it was the way Seychelles should be. Invariably at dinner I had a lady as my guest among the groups, but I never heard anyone complain, not even the bishops who were regular visitors. René and his wife Geva were always invited to important functions and they came promptly and formally dressed. Geva seemed to pay particular attention to the way State House was decorated and once took her son Francis to see Richard's room.

At the end of the evening, around eleven thirty, I would insist that the guitarist played the national anthem and everyone would stand and sing. It was essential that I had a full night's sleep. It was a tight, regular schedule and I enjoyed every minute of it.

At least once a week I called a cabinet meeting, the ministers being responsible to the National Assembly. Only when a bill got through the Assembly could it obtain my assent and become law. It was a good system in which the politicians were all held to account. The finances were also strictly controlled, the books being the responsibility of Chamery Chetty, who was accountable to the National Assembly. On top of that the Public Accounts Committee was itself subject to public scrutiny.

During that first year, we had organised ourselves properly. Our house was in order and investors were happy with us. My dream was to turn Seychelles into a small Switzerland, taking advantage of our geographical position and staying out of the tug-of-war of power politics. There was widespread support for this idea and no-one was more enthusiastic than Abbas K. Gokal, chairman of the Gulf group of companies which he ran from his headquarters overlooking Lake Geneva. With estimated assets of $750 million, Gulf was involved in shipping, trading, insurance, banking and travel. It employed more than 4,000 people in forty countries and when the backers of a prestige office and shopping complex in Victoria ran into financial difficulties, Gulf took over.

I was particularly interested in finding jobs for young Seychellois on Gokal's world-wide fleet. When you are born on small islands, there comes a time when you want to opt out for a while in order to see for yourself what the big world outside is all about. Personally I always believed in an outward-looking policy for our young people. Experience had taught me that the great majority of those who sought positions beyond our shores would finally return to the islands, convinced that 'east or west – home is best'. Naturally Abbas was quick to see my point and oblige, and in no time a considerable number of Seychellois had been recruited to work on various vessels flying the Gulf flag.

On 13 May the Citibank of America, the second largest banking group in the world, announced that it was to open up an offshore branch on Mahé. Seychelles was on the brink of becoming a tax haven, with the potential of the Bahamas and the Cayman Islands. With the wealth of the Middle East nearby, with an advantageous time difference from New York, Geneva and Tokyo, and with air links to capitals all over the world, we were in an ideal situation spot to become a financial centre rivalling the others.

There was also considerable interest from German investors led by people like Dr Heinrich Bischoff of Bremen, then head of the flying section of Hapag Lloyd, now owner of a charter airline company, Dr Heintz Koester, managing director of the Zurich Insurance Company, Mr Adi Dharboven, the German coffee king, and Mr Robert Vogel, the famous property developer of Hamburg, to finance additional tourism infrastructure as well as a modern fishing industry.

With the backing of men like Gokal, with Citibank poised to come in, with our development plan ready to be put into operation, with help and encouragement from people like Khashoggi, Seychelles in June 1977 had a very prosperous future ahead. All it needed was an assurance that people would not be frightened off by a return to the old divisive politics. As I was about to go to London I felt that I needed René's assurance, and so I invited him one afternoon to State House.

He had been as good as gold ever since the coalition. Indeed he and his party had hardly criticised a thing. If anything, it was a group of my own supporters who provided the only voice of dissent and criticism.

I put it to him. The next election was due in September 1979. What were his plans? Were we about to go to political war again?

He looked at me as if I were crazy.

'Don't be stupid, Jimmy,' he said. 'How can there be anything else but a coalition? How can we get back to strife?'

It was the answer I wanted to hear.

'Okay,' I said. 'I'll get Bernard Lousteau-Lalanne [the Attorney-General] to look into the matter and report to us after the Commonwealth Conference.'

As I watched him go, I thought that here indeed was a man many had misjudged. He was, after all, the man Bruce McKenzie wanted me to shoot; I must have been mad to listen to the South African, I thought. Everything was going to be all right.

And so, one June evening, I hosted my last dinner party before leaving for the Commonwealth Conference. René and his wife were special guests. It was a pleasant night and we sang together. After the coup, one of the guests, Debby Lousteau-Lalanne, Bernard's English wife, recalled a whispered aside that Dr Ferrari, one of the conspirators, made to René.

'They're singing their last song,' he said.

At the time Debby thought it was some kind of joke.

Next morning René accompanied me to the airport and kissed me on both cheeks.

'*Au revoir*, Jimmy. *Bon voyage.*'

I had no conception that this was the Judas kiss and that last night's dinner had been the Last Supper.

Chapter Eighteen

AFTER THE FIRST shock of René's coup had worn off, I got to work, phoning around the London hotels to tell the others in the delegation what had happened. Before dawn they had turned up in my suite, haggard and uncomprehending.

The first person I wanted to contact was Dennis Greenam. We had lunched together only the day before when he had made certain suggestions about the speech I was to deliver at the conference. All the time I had known him, he had been associated with James Callaghan, first as his adviser on African affairs, when Callaghan was Secretary of State for Foreign Affairs, and now as Prime Minister. I phoned Greenam's flat but there was no answer. I left a message at the Foreign Office but there was no response.

At ten o'clock someone from the Foreign Office turned up. He was tall and handsome and there were tears in his eyes. He looked like a surgeon who had performed an emergency operation and was coming to announce that his patient had not survived. But immediately he could see that I was already aware of the news.

'I am sorry,' he said. 'My instructions are to inform you of the position as reported to us by the High Commission in Mahé.'

I asked him if he had met Greenam. He shook his head.

'Will you please ask him to get in touch with me?'

He nodded, turned and left the room. I watched him go and looked at his little brown Civil Service brief-case with its crest of the British crown, little realising that this was my last official encounter with a representative of Her Majesty's Britannic Government after more than fifteen years of association and avowed friendship.

Meanwhile the telephones in the bedroom and the lounge kept

ringing. Friends all over the world wanted to know what was happening, but from Greenam and the government there was not a breath of life.

Yet time was of the essence. With the international media reporting that hundreds of Tanzanian soldiers were flying to my country, it was obvious that any initiative had to be taken quickly. I rushed to our High Commission in Mill Street to address a press conference. I did not have any time to prepare for it. I knew that the coup must have been planned and executed for geo-political reasons. After all Nyerere was flying his troops in quickly, yet I had had no confrontation with him.

After the press conference I met David Dale, secretary to our Cabinet (now Governor of the British colony of Montserrat in the Caribbean). Luckily he happened to be holidaying in Britain and so at least I had one friendly contact.

I came straight to the point. 'Will the British Government help to bring back constitutional legality?' I asked. 'After all, they were a vital party to our constitutional agreement.'

He shook his head. 'Look, Jimmy, the priority of the government now is with the success of the Jubilee celebrations. Several leaders here are themselves products of *coups d'état*, so I don't expect any initiative from the UK.'

Again I mentioned Greenam. I had to speak to him. Again Dale shrugged and wished me luck.

Back at the Savoy, I phoned and phoned and phoned. Still nothing. When the phone *did* ring, it was Adnan Khashoggi again, asking if the British were helping me.

'So far, nothing,' I said.

'Can I be of help?'

'I don't think so,' I said. 'I'm thinking of going to see Giscard.'

'In that case I will send you a plane ...'

And so a few hours later I was being whisked in a Lear-jet over to Paris. As the aircraft cleared the grey skies of London, I thought about my relations with France and felt a surge of optimism. I had, after all, been the first to re-establish contact with them and I had initiated the policy of bilingualism. Back in my office I had a letter from President Pompidou, framed and prominently displayed.

'Believe me,' he had written, 'my country has not forgotten the people of Seychelles which in the past has been so closely linked to our destiny and who today contribute to the glory of the French language in the Indian Ocean.'

I had been decorated by President Giscard with the ensign of Officier de la Légion d'Honneur, and less than a year ago I had been so well feasted at the Bastille celebrations.

The French, I thought, were bound to help.

What I did not know was that there was an important nucleus within the government which was tainted with duplicity and conspiracy and to whom the terms francophone and francophile were incompatible with anglophone and anglophile. To them, my policy of integration had branded me as too close to the British. To these prejudiced politicians, if you were pro-British, you were anti-French. It was they who had pushed de Gaulle to cry 'Vive Quebec Libre'. To them the policy of bilingualism was not enough. They wanted French to be *the* language. Nor did I realise at the time that they could be stupid enough to believe that the imposition of their language was far more important than the risk of throwing a democratic ally into the Soviet camp.

I had sent a message to the President that I was coming and when I arrived at the George V Hotel, I was told that René Journiac, his adviser on African affairs, would be coming to see me that day. I had met him at the Franco-African summit in Dakar and found him to be warm and friendly, but when he arrived, he seemed nervous.

'A friend in need is a friend indeed,' I said.

He smiled.

'All the pro-West countries admired the bold initiative you took alongside Morocco to help Zaire.'

Again he smiled an acknowledgement.

'You know that the Indian Ocean has always been a crossroads of French influence. You must help my government to get back and restore the country to democracy.'

'Mr President ...'

'Don't call me that,' I said, interrupting him. 'You know I'm no longer President.

'In France you are,' he said. 'Like the USA, France considers that once a President always a President. I will promptly convey your request to President Giscard.'

With that, M. Journiac left. Three days later, France was second only to Idi Amin in backing René's regime stating that she 'recognised the state but not the government', meaning she recognised the country but not those who ruled.

I was sickened by the news and it was not until later that I understood what had happened, that there had been a long thought-out conspiracy.

Soon after our independence, Monsieur Alain Brugère, the French Chargé d'Affaires, was replaced by the Marquis de Choiseul Praslin who, it was said, was related not only to the man who had given his name to our second largest island but also to two French Ministers of Foreign Affairs. I had asked why Brugère had gone so suddenly but I did not receive a convincing reply. Only later did I realise that it was Dr Maxime Ferrari, the most anti-British politician in the Seychelles, who had been responsible for this changeover.

Ferrari, I also discovered, had been adopted by M. Bernard Dorin, Chef du Service de la Francophonie at Quai D'Orsay, as his lieutenant in Seychelles. Dorin was one of the anti-British group in the French government and a man who dreamt of French dominance at all costs. Soon after the coup René sent Ferrari to France to solicit necessary manpower, to replace the British advisers and officials who had been arrested and deported. Hence, while the Tanzanians were in military control, the French were flying in to fill the administrative gap. It was an unholy alliance, to say the least.

Welcoming Ferrari, Dorin, said: 'Thank you dear friend, for chasing out the British and for having returned Seychelles to its family.' Then he kissed him on both cheeks.

Present at this ceremony was Madame May Moine, our Chargé d'Affaires who had elected to remain in office under René. She was stupefied by what she had heard. Recently she told me at her home in Cannes that René and his wife had been received in France a few weeks before the coup when he was supposed to be in Vienna negotiating over aid from OPEC. They were welcomed on arrival by Praslin's wife, then became the guests of Yvette Chassagne, Director of Economic Development at the Ministry of Cooperation, who hosted a lunch for them. The next day they attended a dinner at Maxim's with Dorin and other French officials. Mme Moine noted all this and became so convinced that something sinister was going on that she called at the British Embassy. She met the First Secretary M.D.J. Wright, and informed him about René's activities so that he would, in turn, through the Foreign Office inform me what was going on. Unfortunately, the British Government was so busy with the Jubilee celebrations that the message never got through.

Returning to London after the French visit, I found at the Savoy a long list of messages and cables. One was from Shridath Ramphal, Secretary-General of the Commonwealth Association. He wanted to see me first thing next morning.

He turned up promptly. I had met him a few times and he had attended our independence celebrations. Again I met a slightly nervous man, a man concerned about whether I should turn up at the opening of the Commonwealth Conference. I was due, after all, to make the return address to the Prime Minister's speech of welcome.

'The Queen is head of the Commonwealth,' he said, 'and this is the occasion of her Jubilee. We must avoid any possibility of a walk-out which could cause embarrassment. My suggestion is that you stay away from the opening session. We could then get the Seychelles matter openly debated under the "any other business" item on the agenda.'

I felt instinctively that the British were behind this. Moreover, friends from Mauritius had already told me about an active campaign by the Tanzanians to keep me away. Feeling let down by the silence from Greenam and the British Government, and out of deference to the Queen, I decided to take Ramphal's advice.

Pierre Trudeau, Lee KuanYew, Seewoosagur Ramgoolam and a few others wanted me to turn up as expected, but as far as Britain was concerned, the government was too busy with the success of the Jubilee celebrations. It was another blatant example of principle being sacrificed on the altar of expediency. My friends from the African continent were also dismayed and confused. Brigadier Joe Garba, then Federal Commissioner for External Affairs and head of the Nigerian delegation, later explained his position in a letter.

'My dear Jimmy,' he wrote, 'Roger Felly [the Ghanaian Foreign Minister] and I tried to contact you in London during those dreadful days but we were advised that it would be misinterpreted as interference in the internal affairs of your country, so we stayed away. I hope you did not feel abandoned by your friends.'

(Poor Roger Felly. Little at that time could he have thought that worst things were awaiting him on the political horizon of his beloved Ghana. A few months after the Seychelles coup, Flt Lt Rawlings overthrew the Ghanaian Government and Felly was one of those who was publicly executed by firing squad.)

However, in the list of messages, there was one ray of hope. Baron von Behren, personal assistant to Prince Sharam of Iran, got in touch with the news that the Prince, who was in South America, wanted to see me next week in Paris.

Again I prepared to fly the Channel, this time to the Intercontinental Hotel. Again I felt a ray of optimism. Iran, after all, was being prepared by the West to play a dominant role in the Indian Ocean. She was undoubtedly the best-armed country in the zone, with an important naval capability. In addition she was closely aligned with America and I thought that the CIA might have been behind von Behren's phone call.

However, as I drove to Heathrow, I heard the news on the radio: 'The Shah of Iran has commented on the *coup d'état* in Seychelles. His Imperial Majesty, in a statement to the international press, has said that the change of leadership in Seychelles is of no importance to Iran so long as Iranian national interests are not threatened.'

He was responding to a cable of goodwill sent by René. (Little at that time did His Imperial Majesty realise that later President Carter would be adopting the same attitude towards him as he was showing to me.)

Sharam never turned up for the appointment. Three months later I happened to meet him and realised sadly that he had been a friend of President Mancham but not of Jimmy.

So there I was abandoned by the British, tricked by the French, let down by the Iranians and forgotten by the Americans. In a phrase, the West was letting down a sincere and faithful ally.

Throughout our move towards independence, I had worked hard to promote a UK-Seychelles parliamentary association which would group together members of the British Parliament who had visited the islands and who were otherwise keen in following developments there. One of those MPs was Mr Carol Mather, Conservative MP for Esher, who had visited Mahé just a few weeks before. While the British Government was busy with the Jubilee euphoria, on 11 June Mather made the following points in the letter columns of *The Times*:

> Those who know and love the Seychelles will be deeply saddened by the events of the past few days which culminated in a *coup d'état* and the overthrow of the one-year-old constitution.

The only crime of which the deposed President was guilty in the eyes of the authors of the coup was to be unashamedly pro-British and pro-West. But this was unforgivable and had to be changed even at the point of a gun.

There is no doubt that the coup was inspired from outside by Marxist interest, through the agency of Tanzania, with whom Mr Albert René's party had close contacts. The coup would certainly have had no popular support in Seychelles as Mr J. G. Rassool, High Commissioner in London, makes clear in his recent letter to *The Times*.

There are, of course, strategic implications to these events which would very much please Moscow. The Seychelles group of islands lies adjacent to the West's oil sea route to the Gulf.

But those factors apart, it is above all a sad thing for the Seychellois who were loyal and intensely patriotic towards Britain. The Seychellois accepted independence reluctantly, believing they were freer under British protection than any neighbouring African states, where freedom means dictatorship. How ironic that they should be the ones who now suffer.

Pertinent words indeed, but within the euphoria of the Jubilee celebrations, how many in Britain were there who would bother to follow the points? His realistic appraisal was comforting to me but it was still no substitute for real action that had become necessary.

However, I then received a letter which radically changed my mind. It was from Felix Paul, the Roman Catholic Bishop of Seychelles.

> My dear Jimmy [he wrote] I take this opportunity to send you a few words of sympathy. I think I know how you feel after the coup you have passed through. I was indeed extremely sorry to see things going the way they were. It was very hard luck for you after all you have done to lay the foundations for a happy and prosperous Seychelles. You had worked so hard and ceaselessly to put Seychelles on the map. No-one indeed can laud themselves to have merited it better. Unfortunately you slept on your laurels too soon so others came in to reap your hard work. I feel I know your bitter disappointment.

Felix Paul, Albert René and I had gone to the same school and, although I was the youngest of the three, it could almost be said that we had grown up next to each other. Paul had been ordained Bishop of Seychelles a few years before and no-one more than he could be a better witness to what had taken place in the islands over recent years.

His letter continued:

> May this sad event in your life be but a passing cloud. Ovid's verse comes to my mind, when he was exiled by Augustus and abandoned by all his friends. 'As long as you are happy, you will number lots of friends. If clouds cover the sky you will be alone.' I am proud to say that such a verse does not apply to me. Come what may I remain your friend.

This was indeed a sincere letter from a true friend, written in good faith. I could not have expected anything more from the man who was, after all, the spiritual leader of our country. However, his last paragraph left me disarmingly sad. It was to the point:

> Seychelles radio has told us and rumours persist that you are thinking of raising mercenaries to come and help you take back the country. I doubt this could be true in your case. Knowing you as I do, I don't think that you would do such a thing, or even lend a hand to it. You have always been against bloodshed and how could you destroy what you have worked day and night constructing – our image of a peace-loving people? If ever the temptation comes, I beg you earnestly not to indulge in it. Please do not use force to dislodge those who sneaked in by force. He that uses the sword will perish by the sword. Try also to dissuade others who would be tempted to try and do things which you feel should not be done. Please continue to love and work wholeheartedly for the Seychelles and for its people who still remember you and love you.

I read this paragraph over and over again. I *had* devoted all my adult life to promoting Seychelles as islands of love, peace and laughter. How could I now use force and possibly cause bloodshed? After all, I was never hungry for power and, if we had achieved the integration I sought, I would never have become PM, let alone President. Perhaps after all those years the time had really come for me to step aside and give René a chance. I knew too at that time that having power was not exactly sleeping on a bed of roses. My innermost philosophy was also endeavouring to convince me that there is no ill wind that does not blow any good. I thought about the future in forced exile, away from the home I loved so much. Whilst feeling deeply sad, I was still able to come up with a certain smile – thinking about the books I wanted to read, the new countries I wanted to discover, the new friends I wanted to make, the new sports I wanted to learn and enjoy. Behind me I saw the hypocrisy, the duplicity and the dishonesty which had characterised my political experience. I was only thirty-seven years old. That night I made up my mind that despite everything, I had to give René a chance and I sat down and wrote an article which, two weeks later, French *Vogue* published under the title 'The Singing Philosophy'. Briefly I said that on the road of life I had discovered that there is a song somewhere to meet each and every occasion. It did not matter how well or how badly one sings, the thing is to sing because when one is singing, one has no time for envy, no time for jealousy and no time for evil conspiracy. One is left to oneself with one's own memories and with one's own dreams of what one is seeking. I ended the article with the words of Edith Piaf: 'Je ne regrette rien.'

It was only a few days later that I started receiving different offers of jobs. A Paris-based American public relations company telephoned to ask whether I would care to join them. A friend in legal practice in Brussels thought I would be useful entering into a partnership with him. Brussels was, after all, the capital of the EEC and with my French and English legal background, I could be an asset. One man was ready to finance a plush nightclub in London if I was ready to manage it. But I had some wealthy friends who could help and I had saved some money. I had done well as a lawyer and out of my father's estate. Besides, the family business and my own investments in the islands were doing well. There was the niggling worry which necessarily arises when a country enters the march towards socialism, but all indications were that René was not about to confiscate my business interests and properties – at least not just then. His apparently kind and magnanimous attitude was, of course, motivated by the human logic that there would be less to fear from a Jimmy who could keep up his standards than from a Jimmy who was starving.

Therefore I was not in a hurry to settle down behind a desk. My years in politics had been too all-embracing. Besides, I remained very peripatetic by nature. I have always felt a bit like a gypsy. To me, so long as you are running, the destination is unimportant. It is only when you stop that for every question, you can find a hundred answers and for every answer you can find a thousand questions. What I really felt like doing was lecturing. I love and will always love America. I believe that its people, on the whole, are sincere, and want peace, yet I had been troubled by the prevailing ignorance in this most important of all democracies. I felt I could play a part – and educate the American people about what was happening in the Indian Ocean; that Seychelles, Mauritius and Madagascar did exist and that the Soviets were rapidly taking control of the area.

But it takes some organisation and time to get on the US lecture circuit. Meanwhile one day I received an interesting phone call. Farhad Vladi and René Boehm, two friends in Hamburg engaged in property business and specialising in the sales of islands world-wide, had a fascinating suggestion – a coffee-table book on islands in the world which are privately owned. Needless to stress, this was attuned to my spirit and my eternal love for travel. So I found myself making plans to visit as many islands as possible – in the Atlantic, the Mediterranean, off the Scottish coast, in the Aegean Sea and the Pacific. Somehow I wanted to show that in losing home I had won the world!

Chapter Nineteen

A FEW WEEKS before the coup, René had left the Seychelles for Mauritius. The official pretext was for discussions with the Mauritius Government on the competing claims of both governments for control of the Saya de Malha bank, a rich fishing area which each country thought belonged to it under the laws of the sea that were then being debated. But if such talks with the Mauritian authorities did take place, it was not the true reason for his absence. The man quietly slipped out of Mauritius to pay a secret visit to Tanzania. He later returned home via Mauritius again and two days later personally collected some huge crates and suitcases which had arrived by air from Dar es Salaam and were alleged to contain 'personal effects'.

No customs officer would question the Prime Minister as he loaded his consignment of smuggled weapons and took them up the mountain to his home.

On the eve of the coup the Zanzibar-registered vessel *Mapinduzi* was sighted in Seychelles waters. On board was a contingent of Tanzanian soldiers – morale boosters, the back-up forces, just in case the Seychellois who had, over the months, received secret training in Tanzania and had earlier returned home did not have the courage to see the mission through.

On the morning of 4 June the young Seychellois who had received training in guerrilla warfare were quietly picked up from their homes and brought to René's house. On duty were the main conspirators – René himself, Jacques Hodoul, Ogilvy Berlouis, James Michel and Dr Ferrari. Three leading SPUP officials, Guy Sinon, Philibert Loizeau and Mathew Servina, were purposely left out because to them, the coalition was working well and René did not trust them.

Every young man who turned up was informed that tonight was going to be action night. They had two choices. Those who were ready to proceed were to receive a pep-up tablet and those who were hesitant were to receive one that would put them to sleep. On no condition was anyone to be allowed to leave the premises until after the event.

That evening Seychelles went to sleep as always. Air India had organised a cocktail party. Somebody else was hosting a dinner at Northolme Guest House. It was a normal Seychelles night. There were two or three dozen policemen on duty patrolling various parts of the islands. The police force, the only force of law and order at the time, worked unarmed in the tradition of the British police. Only thirty or so determined men with sticks would have sufficed to overpower them, but that night some eighty heavily armed and specially trained Seychellois descended on Victoria, accompanied by Tanzanian accomplices. Their targets were: the police armoury – which the British had left behind, and which held only a few outdated guns, and was located in a building which housed the Riot Control Unit; the police headquarters in downtown Victoria; Cable and Wireless Office, opposite the new port – the prime contact with the outside world; and Radio Seychelles at Union Vale on the outskirts of the town.

All four were attacked and taken over simultaneously.

In front of the Riot Control Unit premises stood one policeman, Jouanneau. He was alone on duty. The insurgents dealt with him without mercy. He was shot in cold blood. When Francis Rachel, one of the insurgents, saw this, he panicked and one of his colleagues shot him. The whole *coup d'état* was well orchestrated under the personal supervision of René himself, who was seen that night driving all over Victoria. At six in the morning, following the arrival of heavily armed Tanzanian troops, when the people woke up to prepare for Sunday Mass, the early morning news from Radio Seychelles announced that the country had been taken over. On no account was anyone to venture out of doors. Anyone who took the risk would be shot on sight. The broadcaster said that a new announcement would follow and everyone should remain tuned to the radio, which then pumped out martial music. Meanwhile cables were going out to all nations, extending the goodwill of the new regime, all in an attempt to neutralise the possibility of counter-action by those of us who were outside.

Three hours later, after Tanzanian forces had manned roadblocks and had armed selected members of the SPUP, the time had come for René to speak.

He attempted to justify the rape of the constitution by making four accusations against me – that I was an international playboy, that I had spent a lot of time outside Seychelles, that I had allowed foreigners to buy land and that I was thinking about doing away with the next elections, due in 1979, and governing as a dictator.

To you, France Albert René, man to man and lawyer to lawyer, I propose to answer these accusations.

On the question of being an international playboy, perhaps I should plead guilty. My name has been associated for years with a galaxy of beautiful women – beauty queens, models, starlets, and other ladies of various social standing. But I make no apology for that. My life has always been an open book. It was not as if one day I became President and suddenly started to spend all my time with ladies. It was a way of life, backed with a personal philosophy about which I was prepared to speak openly. There was no mediocrity nor indeed any vulgarity about this lifestyle for each and every affair I had possessed its own romantic flavour. In this respect too, I was living like all Seychellois would dearly love to live, given the choice. Anyway, people who live in glass houses should not throw stones, or, better still, the pot should not call the kettle black.

Yes, I have played, but the whole of Seychelles knows that you and your clique have likewise played. The only difference is that I played on the international stage while you were satisfied with the chicken yard.

Where I played brought so much publicity that our people forgot their insular complexes and lack of confidence so that the reaction around the islands was 'If Jimmy can do it – why not us?' Furthermore, my philosophy of life projected the image that the Seychelles was a place for beautiful people and a haven for joy, love and laughter.

On the second accusation, that I spent so much time abroad, I would be inclined to plead guilty were the charge not so childish. You know that the Seychellois compared me to a fisherman. 'We don't mind Jimmy going,' they said, 'because he always comes back with a catch.'

When I first returned to Seychelles after studying in London, the islanders were inward-looking and living at subsistence level. At the time of your coup, an airport had been built, the harbour had been widened and ocean-going liners were docking, modern hotels had been built, local housing schemes begun and the country was on the verge of a prosperous tomorrow. All these could not have happened if I had remained glued to the slopes of the islands.

But Albert, the most important point is related to your party's plan to assassinate me. Against the background of your determination to take over at all costs, had I been one of those leaders who never left home, I would have been found one morning with a bullet or two in my head.

On the third point, that I allowed foreigners to buy land, I submit that any judge would agree that there is no case to answer. Throughout our period of self-government, and later as an independent nation, it was you and nobody else, with your portfolio for Works and Land Development, who had full ministerial responsibility for land transactions, one of the most important of which was the sale of the islands of D'Arros to Prince Sharam.

On the fourth charge, about my alleged ambition to become a dictator, you know quite well that I am not guilty. You must recall the meeting we had on the eve of my departure when you were getting ready for your great rape scene. Whatever I wanted to do was to be done in consultation with you and within the framework of the law. That was why I consulted the Attorney-General. And this is why, when this allegation was repeated in democratic London by a national paper, I made it a point to seek justice and defend my political integrity. It did not take the paper long to realise that I was right and entitled to an apology and fair compensation.

Finally, let me make it quite clear that under the situation then prevailing in Seychelles, if you had any grievances, there was nothing to stop you from resigning, breaking up the coalition and causing fresh elections.

In conclusion, after answering your accusations, I have no hesitation in finding *you* – France Albert René – guilty of treason! However, as Sir John Harington epigrammatised in the seventeenth century:

> Treason doth never prosper: what's the reason?
> For if it prosper, none dare call it treason.

A great majority of the people of Seychelles knew that René had committed treason. The coup had come as a shock and a surprise to them. With the police force neutralised and the

Tanzanians in total control, there was no possible way of instigating any resistance. The new regime had imposed a total curfew and with everyone kept indoors it was impossible to determine the size of the insurgency or indeed the size of the Tanzanian occupying force. But there was one man determined to be defiant. He was Davidson Chang Him, brother of the Anglican Bishop. He assumed that no-one would dare touch him. For years a prominent SDP supporter, Davidson shouted 'Bullshit!' in his home after René had spoken and he swore to his neighbours that on no account would he recognise the regime.

Soon afterwards he was summoned to police headquarters. As he climbed the steps of the Central Police Station in Victoria, ironically only a few yards from the Anglican Cathedral, he was shot dead by one of René's staunchest supporters.

News of Chang Him's assassination reverberated throughout the community and instilled a terrible fear. President René was in firm control.

Some of his first actions smelled very much of an African military take-over. He immediately banned 'La Paloma Blanca' and made clear that it would be considered an offence to play any of the fifty songs which my brother Mickey had recorded.

At that time too a book called *Seychelles: Political Castaways*, written by Christopher Lee, now defence correspondent with the BBC, was widely read in the islands. The book was mainly concerned with recent developments in Seychelles and was highly complimentary towards me – indeed almost embarrassingly so. This was too much for René to swallow. He immediately instructed the Seychelles High Commission in London to burn all its copies. (That evening, a man who had been given the instructions turned up at my door with a gunny bag full of them.

'Sir,' he said, 'I have brought these for you. I think Mr René should know that you can't burn history.')

René knew that throughout my entire career as Chief Minister, Prime Minister and President, there had not been one drop of blood shed, nor indeed one political prisoner. From then on there was to be no mention of me over the radio. The nation had to be made to forget about me. The accusations he personally directed at me were soon forgotten as he started to speak the language of 'La Revolution'. In the eyes of the regime I had become a non-person.

In no time the man who had projected himself as a great

believer in the democratic process was behaving like a dictator, governing by issuing presidential decrees according to his mood.

The constitution was abrogated, the National Assembly was suspended, the conspirators were made ministers and the hooligans who took up the gun overnight became majors and colonels in an army which started recruitment the very next day.

The rule by fear and terror had started.

On 12 August Hassan Ali, a staunch trades unionist within the SDP, opened a letter I sent him, thanking him for the support he had given me during my years as President. I had posted a hundred or so letters to different people in the islands. Hassan Ali owned a photocopying machine and made several copies of the letter to distribute among SDP supporters in Mahé.

That afternoon he met Félix Hoareau, former superintendent of prisons (now in exile in Wales) who foresaw the consequences of Ali's action.

'Look, Hassan, you are carrying your death warrant. If I were you, I would destroy these letters immediately and collect those you have already given out.'

Hoareau was right. In the early hours of that evening, Hassan Ali left his home by car to travel the few miles to the home of relatives of his common-law wife. He never reached his destination, nor has he ever been seen since. His car was discovered abandoned on the St Louis road. Eye-witnesses told police that they had seen him being dragged by some of René's supporters into a waiting car but, as far as the authorities were concerned, that was the end of the investigation. The mysterious death of Hassan Ali's night watchman a few weeks later clouded the case further. It was widely known that he was the last person to have seen Hassan Ali alive, apart from his abductors.

Meanwhile twenty SDP supporters on the island of Praslin, who did not quite understand the true meaning of 'La Revolution', organised a political rally to protest about the arbitrary actions the regime had taken and to otherwise demonstrate that, although I was gone, the SDP was still alive. They were promptly arrested and accused of trying to overthrow the government. Although they were kept in prison for over two months, no charges were ever brought against any of them to substantiate the allegations. They were kept under appalling and degrading conditions. Psychological pressure became the order of the day, with rotten food being served and lights being kept on all night.

Soldiers were sent to cock and uncock their rifles close to the cell doors as shots were fired in the air, one bullet penetrating the cell door.

When released these people were still not free citizens. Some, like Daniel Payet, were kept under constant house arrest and others were told to report their movements to police twice a day. The message was clear. The sooner you flee the country, the better.

People quietly noted that at the time of the arrests, a Russian warship had entered Victoria harbour and more Tanzanians had flown in. Within a year René's revolution was starting to be noticed by the international press.

In a leading article, *Le Figaro* of France was already proclaiming in bold headlines: 'IN SEYCHELLES KARL MARX VERSUS TOURISM'. The paper noted that René had to find more and more money to pay for a growing army – a big unproductive body which had become an exorbitant burden on the poor country.

'It is no longer possible,' said *Le Figaro*, 'to sell a bottle of wine at a reasonable price. Taxes are regularly going up by 50 per cent.'

Under René's revolution, René became not only President of the country and Commander-in-Chief of its armed forces, but also the man who controlled all the financial transactions. Under his policy all private businesses suddenly found themselves threatened. Not by straightforward nationalisation, which would mean payment of compensation, but by a policy of slow strangulation aimed at systematically driving them into bankruptcies. In no time he created state companies covering import, export, fishing, farming, retailing, tourism and air transport, construction, hotel and catering, insurance – everything. To make it difficult for private businesses to survive he introduced a system of import licences to cover almost everything. Businessmen who made noises were subjected to punitive retroactive taxes, and some of them found their passports confiscated.

In no time the islands were losing all their professional people and intelligentsia. Either you compromised your principles or professional ethics or you were out. To replace you there was always a ready availability of Tanzanians, Guineans, Cubans and Algerians – with Russians running the National Workers Union, the only trades union allowed to exist in the one-party state.

Whilst the country was being driven to a Marxist socialism, the people, who had been cowed into silence, noted a personal lavish lifestyle for René, his wife, the family and the clique around them. The poverty-stricken country found itself buying an executive jet for presidential use. Presidential *dachas* were built on several islands and a special presidential guard was created to insulate René from public gaze.

It also became obvious that there was no difficulty for friend or family to sell any land or business at exorbitant prices, but if you did not belong to the privileged few you were likely to get less than 25 per cent of your property's worth, even though it may have been acquired for public purposes.

On Saturday 22 September 1979 several children were playing on a popular beach which the Tanzanians had used as a firing range to train René's army. They discovered an unexploded anti-tank grenade which had become exposed at low tide. One child cautioned the finder to discard it because 'it belonged to the army'. But it was too late. The monstrous bomb exploded. The result – three children blown to pieces and four maimed for life. This was bad and sad news. There was practically no mention of it in the government paper or over the radio but *Weekend Life*, the only independent paper surviving at the time, ran a splash under the headline 'Black Saturday'. This was going too far. Later, under the powers he conferred on himself, under the preservation of public security regulations which he had made, René was to declare 'all future issues of *Weekend Life* to be prohibited publications'.

A few days later René left for the sixth summit conference of heads of state of the non-aligned nations in Havana, Cuba. There he made it quite clear where he stood in the East-West conflict.

'Let me first of all state,' he said, 'that I came to Cuba despite and because of the fact that there were so many imperialist manoeuvres to prevent leaders coming to Cuba for the summit and it gives me great satisfaction to be able to express myself here in Havana only a few miles from the very heart of imperialism.

'Mr Chairman, seventeen years ago, in October 1962, at the time of the so-called missile crisis, I and thousands of others marched through the streets of London chanting, "Kennedy no, Castro si, Cuba si.' Today I am proud to state in Socialist Cuba, "Imperialism no, Castro si, Cuba si, non-alignment si." In these few words I hope I have expressed clearly what I think of the imperialist manoeuvres to degrade one of the greatest leaders of our time – a man who has given his life and his destiny to the Cuban people and to all people of the world who love individual freedom and justice – our Comrade Fidel Castro.'

After denouncing the US and the West, as well as President Sadat for his Camp David initiative, René concluded: 'Long live the non-aligned movement and down with capitalism – the revolution marches on.'

This visit did not stop at the summit hall. While there, he visited an island which sits quietly in the Caribbean sixty miles from Havana, a small peaceful-looking island named the Isle of Youth. Among the pine trees and grapefruit groves live 32,000 school children – a lot for a place with 72,000 inhabitants. It is here that Fidel Castro is busy moulding the minds of those who are destined to become tomorrow's Marxist revolutionary leaders. The target is Africa. The children have come from Ethiopia, Guinea-Bissau, Congo-Brazzaville, Angola, Mozambique – all countries with Marxist revolutionary governments.

René was impressed. He returned to Seychelles to preside over a sham election. He was to be the only candidate for President and his party, which was to supervise the election, was the only legal party. The result: 98 per cent of the vote. An article at that time in *Le Mauricien* (in Mauritius), headed 'The growth of intolerance', said that René had crossed the Rubicon. 'Who can believe,' it asked, 'that after doing away with democratic freedom and instilling a military dictatorship, a man who had previously been defeated several times would be voted in office with the support of all the population except two per cent? We find in the Seychelles situation the germination of a profound sense of intolerance, the beginning of another gulag.'

After the election he was ready to put into effect what he had seen and learnt in Cuba. On Sunday October 17 Seychelles Radio announced that compulsory national youth service, initially lasting one year, would begin in January. The programme was to provide for the conscription of boys and girls, fifteen years and over, to be instructed by Cubans and Algerians. An outer island, Coetivy, several hundred kilometres from Mahé, had been selected for that purpose. The idea was that eventually Africa's young revolutionary élite – from the eastern seaboard – would be able to acquire their Marxist indoctrination and revolutionary fervour here instead of across the Atlantic.

There was immediate widespread parental and Church resistance to the plan. The clamour and adverse reaction was such that René thought it necessary to visit the largest schools in Mahé with a view to defusing the situation. However, these visits, and the explanations which were broadcast, served only to increase the fears of parents and children alike.

The following Thursday over 5,000 children left their classrooms and converged upon State House, shouting abuse at René and calling for the downfall of his government.

It was a spontaneous act of defiance against the government's ban on demonstrations. As the majority of police felt sympathetic towards the children, they made no serious attempt to stop the march. René immediately called out the Tanzanian troops, who used tear-gas and high-handed action to quell the riots that were then starting to break out.

Meanwhile a group of young Seychellois had been meeting clandestinely to determine what could be done to overthrow the regime. Overnight a leaflet was printed and distributed freely all over the islands, calling itself *New Life*, the mouthpiece of the newly-born 'Mouvement pour la Résistance'. One of the first editorials recalled the political history of Seychelles and the fact that the rape of the constitution had taken the country several decades backwards. It accused René of imposing Marxist ideology on the people against their will:

> People realised that power, prestige, income are now distributed among those who shout, 'Hail René, hail socialism'. Seychellois who do not believe in René's socialism are now told they have no right to remain here. In this way many have lost the country which is theirs by birthright. Seychelles now belongs to René and to those who accept the perpetration of his form of slavery. We want to regain Seychelles for all Seychellois. We will return Seychelles to all Seychellois.

There were to be four issues of that leaflet. The truth hurt. René and his clique were mad with rage. The police and army were pressurised to find the culprits, but nobody would speak. The people had had enough now. They had long been praying for a return to the days when the rule of law was practised and respected. These leaflets were the first vestige of open opposition to the regime since the forced closure of *Weekend Life*. The dictator knew that he had to spread his net as wide as possible. More Tanzanians were flown in; René then declared that he had uncovered another plot to overthrow him. On that day, after the Soviet guided missile cruiser, *Marshall Vorishilov*, had entered Victoria harbour to stay for several weeks, a hundred Seychellois, all with leadership potential, were rounded up and thrown into jail that was now under military control.

Among those arrested was Bernard Verlaque, editor of *Weekend Life* who, as a stringer for Reuters, was the only representative of an international news service left on the islands. With his arrest, Seychelles was irrevocably insulated from international gaze. From then on, there would be only one news despatch to come from the islands. It would come from the newly established news agency which the regime controls.

In the aftermath of these illegal arrests, the exodus of Seychellois got bigger. All these people had one single message to tell – their island home, which was once referred to as the last, lost paradise, which was considered the pearl of the Indian Ocean and regarded as the isles of song and laughter, had suddenly become a land of fear, despair and terror.

Chapter Twenty

FOR MORE THAN two months I had been discovering the forgotten islands of Micronesia, a United States trust territory in the Pacific, as guest of Lars Eric Lindblad on his cruise ship the *Lindblad Explorer*, and in the delightful company of Catherine Olsen (a glamorous Fleet Street journalist) whose love and companionship I have shared and enjoyed ever since she came to interview me a few weeks after the coup. Kate and I had travelled to many parts of the world together but never had we found such peaceful islands. Nostalgia may not be what it used to be but I found my own mind transported back to childhood days when my country was still lost and forgotten.

We left the *Explorer* in Fiji to fly to Brisbane where we were to spend Christmas with Kate's family. One evening we were having dinner when one of the guests interrupted the conversation.

'Did you say you were from Seychelles?'

'Yes.'

'Have you heard the news?'

'What news?'

'The President has declared a state of emergency. He says that he has uncovered a plot to topple him and has imposed a strict curfew. Several people have been arrested and he has accused the former President of being behind it.'

There I was in Brisbane, thinking that in this far-off part of the Pacific I could at least be left alone to enjoy an ordinary life, but it was becoming obvious that René, who had sneaked into power by abusing the trust and confidence I put in him, now saw me behind every attempted coup, real or imaginary. Yet I had sought hard to assure the man that this was not my intention. Soon after I had made up my mind to lead my own life, I had written to *The Times* to dispel rumours that I was engaged in raising a mercenary force in order to get back to power.

In May 1978, when twenty-one Seychellois were arrested allegedly for treason, and I was once again implicated by René, I had even gone as far as writing to the British Foreign Secretary, Dr David Owen, asking him whether he would get his High Commissioner in Seychelles to inform René that I was not interested. Yet as I enjoyed the warmth of Brisbane and the democratic freedom of Australia, there were over a hundred of my friends unjustly and dictatorially locked up in René's jail.

Some had been very close associates, like Chamery Chetty, my Minister of Finance, who was in London with me at the time of the coup and had received a personal assurance from René that nothing would happen to him if he returned to the islands. Then there was Paul Chow, a business partner who had written for the *Seychelles Weekly*. There was Albert Bedier, who had been my classmate at school; and Carlette Tall, the common-law wife of Hassan Ali; Bill Mohammed, a former police inspector and my personal bodyguard; and Gerard Hoareau who too had been in London at the time of the coup and had returned to become René's Chief Immigration Officer ... All those people locked up with nobody outside to speak for them. That evening I made a point of watching the television news. The Roman Catholic and Anglican bishops in Seychelles had jointly issued a pastoral letter condemning the detentions and calling for those concerned to be either charged in court or set free. 'We ask that justice be done,' they said. 'We cannot approve of injustice or a situation totally contrary to human rights.'

I suddenly thought about Bishop Felix Paul's letter to me, that letter which had caused me to decide to give René a chance. I had given him that chance and after two and a half years all he had achieved was to turn the country into a land of tears, fear and terror.

We were only a few days away from Christmas. Again I thought about childhood days, about the spirit of Christmas, about Jesus Christ and what his life on earth meant to us. That night I went for a walk and looked at the tropical sky over Brisbane. I heard birds singing in the distant woods and I thought: this could be Seychelles. But it was not. As I walked back towards my friend's home, the words of our national anthem echoed in my mind: 'Seychellois, who are everywhere loyal, the republic *has* need of you – move together fearlessly – En avant.'

My mind was already made up. I had to do my share, to contribute my part to bring normal life back to my one and only home.

On my return to London I found a huge pile of letters from all over the world. Not one had been posted in Seychelles. The government had given itself extraordinary powers which now included the opening of private mail and, in certain cases, the total disconnection of postal services. The first I picked up was postmarked Valais, Switzerland, where many of our priests had come from. It was from a friend in Seychelles and had been brought out by a Franciscan monk who sent it on to me.

> We live in extreme fear and danger [I read] and we dare not associate with one another lest we be accused by the powers that be of organising a counter-coup. Victoria, which was once happy, its air bustling with the merriment of daily life, has now become a ghost town. How long must we endure this infamy? Our morale has been broken to note that the British whom we so much supported, the French to whom we were attached and the US with whom we collaborated have remained silent, despite the fact that they fully know the atrocities which have been committed by René's tyrannical regime.

Another letter was posted in Jersey. It was from a friend, a school classmate.

> Things are bad here. Our atheist masters are not concerned with the plight of the people. Their main concern is the army which is pampered. The masses are firmly with us but they are frightened. And let me hasten to add that by the masses, I do not mean only our old supporters, but also supporters of the SPUP, who have been disillusioned by the current government which they helped bring to power. They were promised the moon but instead, their assumed benefactors have bequeathed to them poverty, a Marxist indoctrination and the denial of basic human rights.

A third, postmarked London, was in strange handwriting. Obviously the writer had tried to change his style in case the letter was intercepted.

> Mr Mancham, what are you and your friends doing for us? Whatever the shortcomings of your elected government, which had less than a year to prove its worth, all attributes of

a civilised society disappeared overnight under the revolutionary regime. The usurpers of legality and constitution are creating a reign of terror. A large number of people, those with money, have fled. Many too have been expelled. The rule of law, civil liberties and other fundamental human freedoms have vanished. Arbitrary arrest, imprisonment without trial and confiscation of property without due compensation are regular occurrences. And you should see René in his bullet-proof car, escorted by ten military cars in front, two motor-cycles on the side and some twenty other cars behind. Nobody ever sees him. He never turns up to any cocktail party. He has never attended a funeral. It is a strange situation. René lives in fear of the people and the people live in fear of René. Please do something to help.

Reading these pleas, my conviction that something needed to be done was strengthened, but what could I do? Just making a lot of noise from comfortable London would only cause the regime to become even more repressive. I recalled the various meetings I had had and letters I had received from different mercenary groups whose interest in a possible venture had been aroused by none other than René himself. Every time the man discovered a so-called counter-coup, he shouted my name out loud and claimed I was behind it, with the financial backing of Adnan Khashoggi. Adnan, despite having lost a plot of land worth a million pounds, was not interested in getting involved, but every time René mentioned his name, a bottomless pot of gold was conjured up in the minds of the mercenaries. They all had their plans of how to topple René and were ready to go.

One summer morning a man arrived at my door. He was about fifty and stocky and spoke perfect English with an accent I could not place at first, until he told me that his organisation was based in Amsterdam. I was angry that he had arrived unannounced. I knew the British laws on mercenary activity – they had been well publicised during the Angola affair – and I did not want to have any association with these people. I was on British soil and determined to respect the country's laws.

Before he left he looked hard at me. 'Mr Mancham, I feel I should go but let me make it clear that if tomorrow I hear that you have spoken to anyone about this encounter, you will be a dead man.'

After that, I received a letter from Israel: 'If you want a repeat of the Entebbe operation, please get in touch [a box number was given]. It will cost just five million dollars.'

Then again I received a phone call from a man who said he wanted to discuss an important business deal in which I would be paid a commission. The matter was urgent and he suggested we meet in the Cunard Hotel in the London suburb of Hammersmith.

Some instinct told me that this could be phoney. On the way I told Peter Payet, my private secretary, to follow me into the bar and keep an eye on me. The man had said that he had seen my picture and would recognise me. Sure enough, as I walked in, two men stood up. They were Indians, one tall the other short. They smiled and came towards me.

The big one thanked me for coming and we sat down at a corner table. 'I hope you don't mind if I call you President Mancham,' he said. 'To me this is what you have been and this is what you will always remain. We have a plan to get you back to power, but before we tell you about it, we would like your assurance that you want to return.'

I opened my brief-case and read them one of the letters I had received.

'After this,' I said, 'how can I remain unconcerned about the plight of the Seychellois? Yes, I am interested.'

He then revealed his plan which sounded like a Hollywood film script. He showed me a letter, signed by René, agreeing to them visiting the islands to make a documentary film.

'One day,' he said, 'we will ask to film the Cabinet in progress but instead of turning the cameras, we will get all of them.' Whether he meant he was going to shoot them or capture them I did not ask. 'All we ask to do this,' he continued, 'is the exclusive right to film you on your return with all the people coming to the airport to greet you.'

The whole thing smelled. Then, to prove that he mixed in top circles, the man produced a photograph. He was standing next to Indira Gandhi who was shaking the hand of Muhammad Ali. Whether he was once Mrs Gandhi's bodyguard – or Ali's – I never found out. Finally, to prove his *bona fide*, he insisted that I join him and his friend for a drink at his house in Kew.

There was no point now in keeping Peter in a state of anxiety. I called him over, introduced him and we left the hotel. As the Indians walked towards their car, I whispered to Peter to give me ten minutes in the house then to come in and say I had to go to another appointment.

The house was well decorated. In the sitting-room hung a life-sized enlargement of the Gandhi–Ali photograph. An Indian lady turned up with a bottle of whisky, some *samoosas* and condiments and for ten minutes we talked about the plan. Then Peter arrived on cue and I left with an address in Soho where I was to meet them the next day.

I duly turned up and was escorted by the two men to an office on the third floor. Whatever their business was, it was well camouflaged behind the facade of a cinema production company.

Again it was the big man who spoke. 'As I've told you, we have the full collaboration of the Seychelles Government but tell us, Mr Mancham are you really interested in returning?'

I had already given that answer. Why ask again? I looked at him and thought I could hear a slight whirring noise. I glanced over his shoulder at the corner of the room and spotted a tape-recorder, set up to record our conversation. They had not even taken the elementary step of hiding it.

I suddenly remembered René's friendly letter. What they wanted was to find out and record my hopes and intentions. I could imagine the tape being played at the next Cabinet meeting, with everyone laughing at my expense.

'Do you have a toilet here?' I asked.

'Down the corridor,' said the little Indian. It was the first time I'd heard him speak.

'Would you excuse me?' I said, walked out and went straight to the lift.

The problem with mercenaries is that, by definition, their hearts are where the money is. The experience with the Indian was a warning to me not to respond enthusiastically in future to sinister invitations. I thought also how vulnerable I was and remembered the man who wanted me to meet his group on the outskirts of Amsterdam. I dreamt about him that night, finally getting shot in some remote country ditch.

I saw a newspaper photograph of Gurkhas arriving in London to fight for the British in some unknown future war and thought, if only I could have a hundred of them.

Meanwhile I was regularly meeting groups of Seychellois, some who were in exile, others who had settled before the coup. Each little group had its own plan and idea about how to topple the regime. Some of these were obviously jockeying for some position of importance in any new government but there was a unifying factor – the René government had to go. Their argument was consistent: 'You are the legitimate leader of the Seychelles people. Nobody since your overthrow has been allowed to project himself as an alternative leader. You have a duty to your country.'

There was no way I could dismiss such an argument. I had to spell out to them where I stood. With my family trapped in the islands, I said that I would not involve myself in any amateurish adventure and that in view of the British attitude towards mercenaries I would not involve myself with the mechanism of a mercenary endeavour. There were Seychellois living in other countries where things were easier. Seychelles did not belong to me alone. It belonged to all Seychellois. But if anyone had a serious plan, he could be assured of my blessing. Briefly, this meant that in the event of a successful counter-coup, I would be ready to assume the leadership of the government if invited to do so.

A few weeks later, a close Seychellois friend invited me for lunch at the Holiday Inn in London's Edgware Road. When I got there he said that he wanted to introduce me to someone important. I went with him up to a room on the sixth floor. He knocked on the door. It was opened by a short and dapper, well-spoken Irishman who introduced himself to me as Mike Hoare. I had read about him, a legendary figure, he had been a British Army officer in the Chindits and had led a successful campaign in the Congo. Recently he had been in the news as adviser on the film *The Wild Geese*.

He gave me a copy of a book he had written and began to talk. Immediately it became clear that he was not the usual type of mercenary. He would only fight for a cause he believed in. Money was not his prime motivation. He had friends in Washington and London and other western capitals. He knew about the strategic importance of Seychelles. The islands could be compared to a fleet of aircraft carriers in the ocean.

Finally he put the standard question: if René could be overthrown, would I respond?

I looked at him. 'Mr Hoare, my position is clear. While I've grown accustomed to life outside the islands as a common man, duty still remains duty. But as I have told my friends, I am not in a position to organise or get involved in any adventures.'

'Okay,' he said. 'This does not concern you. All I was interested in was to find out your attitude.'

With that, I left. That meeting was my one and only encounter with the mercenary leader.

After nine months in prison Gerard Hoareau and Paul Chow were released on the condition that they would leave the country on the first available opportunity. Hoareau made his way to South Africa where his parents and most of his family lived. Chow came to London. These two young men were the brains behind the Mouvement pour la Résistance and the leaflets which had been published. Colleagues who had been released earlier had told me that Gerard had been a tower of strength to all of them as they lingered suffering in René's jail. I remember him well when he returned to Seychelles after studying philosophy in Rome. He was fluent not only in English and French, but also in Italian – a real asset to the new Department of Foreign Affairs which was born at independence. Gerard was also a keen footballer and extremely popular with the youth of the country. He was with me in London at the time of the coup. Afterwards, when I had decided to give René a chance, he was also prepared to do so. After all, he was a cousin of René's wife, Geva. With Geva's brother, Ralph, being appointed High Commissioner in London soon after the coup, things seemed to augur well for the family.

Gerard was promptly made the country's Chief Immigration Officer, a highly important job, especially in the circumstances at the time. But what he saw at close quarters was too much for him to take. Corruption, bribery, favouritism, injustice, malice and vengeance were rife in every part of the administration. If you were in the good books, everything was all right. If not, you could not win.

Initially, Gerard would quietly whisper to Bernard Verlaque what was going on. Next day a frightened Verlaque would publish a few lines. It was at least some form of opposition. But when René decided to ban the paper it was obvious that something had to be done. It was then that Gerard got together with Chow to form the underground movement. Although everything was done secretly, and there was no way René could prove anything, both Gerard and Chow found themselves caught in the wide net René had thrown.

Following his illegal imprisonment, Gerard was a bitter man, committed to the overthrow of René's government by hook or by crook. He had written to me upon his arrival in South Africa and I had replied telling him that there were real leadership qualities in him and that he should not lose hope. He was still a young man, a bachelor without family ties. 'For all I know, one day you could be President,' I wrote, adding: 'When this comes about, you can always count on me as an ambassador at large for Seychelles.'

Now news had reached me that Gerard was on his way to London and badly wanted to see me.

We met at the Swiss Cottage Holiday Inn. He was accompanied by Paul Chow. When I last saw him he seemed adolescent. Now he was mature.

'Chief,' he said, 'what a pleasure to see you. We have really been through hell. I know that you have promised your moral blessing to anyone who would overthrow that bastard. That is good. We have a plan but we think that the fewer people who know, the better.'

I cut him short. 'Look Gerard,' I said. 'Since I'm not going to get involved I don't think I am entitled to more details.'

'I understand and respect your position,' he said. 'Your family are caught up on the islands, you are disenchanted with the hypocrisy of politics, your friends have let you down, but chief, you are still young and I would like to see you back on Seychelles soil again.'

That was all we spoke about the Seychelles. Afterwards we discussed friends and frivolities. When I left the boys I felt rather sad. There was a conflict within me that I could not easily resolve. On the one side was the call of patriotic duty; on the other, the promise I had given to my brother Billy not to act in any way that would bring additional pressure on to the family. This conflict also made me realise to what a low level my capacity to absorb stress had sunk over the years since the coup. Furthermore, while my barrister's background had engendered in me both respect and fear for the law, the boys had graduated from a 'university' which I, myself, had not attended – René's prison of cruelty, abuse and terror.

That autumn I had contracted for a series of lectures through a New York agency, the Keedeck Lecture Bureau, which had established a high reputation for sending speakers like the former head of the US Navy, Admiral Zumwalt, and Winston Churchill Jnr across the US to educate those who were in a position to influence policy-making. At last I was going to have my chance to tell the Americans what was happening at home in particular and in the Indian Ocean generally.

My tour was to be divided into two parts which would leave me time to return half way through to London for a business appointment. Before I left, a Seychellois friend phoned me. He wanted to see me in his office.

When I got there he told me that Gerard had asked him to arrange a taped message from me.

'It is the intention of the Movement when it is in control to invite you to resume your legal position. What we need is your response to that invitation. With you here today and gone tomorrow we think it would be a good thing for us to have the message handy.'

I said that I did not know whether I wanted to become President again. I would have to wait and see the circumstances surrounding an invitation to return. However, if my support was to constitute a legal base for them to start, then this would be forthcoming.

My friend had a tape-recorder with him and I wasted no time. It was an impromptu recording and I cannot remember exactly what I said, but, briefly, the message was that the Seychelles had become independent following a constitutional agreement, which had been formally agreed in London, under which I became President; that there was no justification for the raping and violation of that constitution in June 1977; that this constitution was the only legal basis for democracy, law and order and the respect of human rights; that the people should remain calm and disciplined, and that they would hear from me later.

Next day I left on the tour. After speaking in Minneapolis, in Minnesota, in Richmond, Virginia, and Bridgeport and New Britain in Connecticut, I flew back to London for my business appointment. It was November 1981. One evening the telephone rang.

'Chief,' said an anonymous voice, 'the Movement is on the march.'

I wanted to ask a few questions but the caller had already hung up.

It took several days for us to learn what really happened. According to the international press, at 5.40 in the afternoon of 25 November, Hoare and his men landed at Mahé airport from a Royal Swazi jet. There were forty-four of them, all carrying identical bags. Each man wore a badge depicting an overflowing tankard of beer. They were supposedly members of the Ancient Order of Froth Blowers, an ancient British organisation that did charity work for deprived children. To any onlooker they were a cheerful group, heading for a good time on the islands. They had five bags of toys for Seychelles children and there was a fair amount of laughter as they queued at the customs, each man being careful to hold on to his team's bag. Their hand luggage had gone through X-ray checks on their way from Durban by bus to Swaziland and again at Manzini Airport. But the team's bags had been stored in the hold and had not been checked. If they had, the coup would have ended prematurely. For each bag contained, concealed in a false bottom, underclothes and toiletries, an AK47 assault rifle and thirty rounds of ammunition.

Waiting for them at the terminal building was the six-man advance party who, posing as holiday-makers, had spent the past few days checking out the radio station and the barracks. Although understandably tense, these men were confident that their colleagues would get through. A number of guns had already been smuggled through on dummy runs and the bags had never been checked properly. Customs were lax at Mahé airport.

The first forty-two men, led by Hoare, passed through the nothing-to-declare zone. Some waited in the terminal while others climbed into hotel buses, throwing their bags onto the roof. Hoare met the advance party and joked that the Froth Blowers were a bunch of drunkards.

The last two – Johan Fritz and Kevin Beck, both South Africans – waited behind a Frenchman who had joined the flight in the Comoro Islands. They watched as customs officer Vincent Pillay discovered a bunch of bananas in the Frenchman's bag. Pillay was annoyed. Fruit and vegetables could not be brought into the islands in case they might infect the crop. He confiscated the bananas and was joined by his sergeant, Kerchan Esparon, who asked the two South Africans if they were carrying contraband fruit. No. Nothing to declare. But the customs men had woken up. Pillay asked Beck to open his bag. As the other Froth Blowers in the terminal watched, Esparon picked up Beck's bag and turned it upside down. The rifle fell out and the counter-coup was doomed, sabotaged by a bunch of bananas.

The plan, had there been trouble at customs, was simply to capture the customs officers and keep them quiet. But it didn't work out that way. Esparon, trying to grab Beck and rifle, was shot in the shoulder. The Froth Blowers threw toiletries and clothes out of their bags and pulled out their guns. One of them, Johan Fritz, was killed by a misdirected burst of fire.

The coup had failed. 'It was meant to be bloodless using the element of surprise, a peaceful return to constitutional normality,' Martin Dolinchek, one of the mercenaries left behind in Seychelles explained later.

Hoare tried to retrieve the situation as hostages were taken. He sent the advance party to the barracks at Pointe Larue, two kilometres away, with instructions not to let the soldiers out. Another group took over the control tower and within minutes the airport was in the hands of the mercenaries. He then followed the advance party to the barracks where a gun battle had started. One of his men had been wounded and had crawled off into the shrubs. Hoare ordered the men back to the airport and tried to get through to the Army in order to arrange a cease-fire, but the phones were out of order. An armoured car arrived from the barracks and began pounding the control tower.

In the midst of the chaos an Air India jet landed, its crew unaware of the trouble they were taxi-ing into. The two pilots were brought to the control tower while the mercenaries filled up the tanks. There was a brief discussion about the destination. Some wanted to go to Oman but eventually it was decided to head for Durban where most of the men came from.

Within a few hours of landing, the mercenaries were taking off once more, leaving behind members of the advance party and one man who had got trapped in the crossfire.

Next morning one of those who remained watched in astonishment as the Tanzanian army bombarded the empty airport for four hours before closing in for the kill. There was no-one to fight, no-one to rescue. The hostages had all slipped out before the shelling had begun.

In South Africa they were arrested and charged with hijacking. Mike Hoare was sentenced to ten years and the others got lesser terms. The day he was sentenced I had a second look at the book he had written. It ended with the following statement: 'I maintain that the mercenary soldier may yet prove to be the only effective force against the communist attack which is rapidly overwhelming Africa, at this moment, unchecked, if not actively encouraged by the West's lack of decisive counter-action.' I could not help feeling that there was a lot of truth behind those words.

Those left behind were arrested and charged with treason. They had little chance of a fair trial. The Chief Justice, Earl Seaton, a West Indian, came to Seychelles from the Bench in Tanzania – the one-party state which had brought René to power and kept him there by military force. The mercenaries were defended by Nicholas Fairbairn, former Solicitor-General for Scotland and a Member of the British Parliament, who argued that his clients could not be tried for treason since they were not citizens of Seychelles. This logic was ignored by the Chief Justice. Finally six men were sentenced to death – a strange situation in a country run by a man who, during colonial days, when he was himself so much associated with violence, had vigorously and successfully campaigned for an end to capital punishment.

After the trial Fairbairn wrote in *The Times*:

Originally they were charged with the importation of arms, but the regime insisted that they be charged with treason because that was the only crime for which they could be sentenced to death. As foreigners they could not have committed treason but the court held that that was no longer the law.

The trial was a charade; the verdicts and sentences were announced to the international press by the Attorney-General's junior before the trial began.

Of all the appalling mistakes which the British made in rejecting their empire and colonies the worst by far was to leave behind the paraphernalia of civilisation and justice so that it could be used falsely to give an impression of incorruptibility, as in this case. Originally it was proposed that the mercenaries be shot on a football field before 10,000 people who would be compelled to approve of it. But more sinister and wiser counsels prevailed and the pretence of justice proceeded.

What was not yet properly understood by the Commonwealth or the West or the United States is that the urge to be a one-party state creates a corrupt influence which no-one dares resist. Once again in the Seychelles we have seen the manifestation of a one-party state. Once again an innocent people abandoned by the British is the victim of the greed and corruption of those whom we seduced with a taste but not an understanding of western civilisation.

We have a lot to answer for. It is time we stopped pretending that those whose culture we have interfered with should be given on the one hand benefits and the assumption of equality and on the other hand should not be ever censured for activities and behaviour they would not tolerate in us.

Needless to say, the venture carried international repercussions. In no time the matter was before the United Nations which itself lost no time in affirming that the territorial integrity and political independence of the Republic of Seychelles must be respected. The Security Council condemned the aggression and decided to send a commission of inquiry to investigate the origin, background and financing of what it described as the mercenary aggression against Seychelles as well as to assess and evaluate the economic damage caused. All very well and good. But not a word about the people of Seychelles! Not a word about the fact that Tanzanian forces had been occupying the islands since the René takeover. Not a word about systematic imposition of Marxist ideology on the people. Not a word about those who have had their land confiscated without compensation, those hundreds forced into exile, those who have disappeared and those who have been brutally murdered....

For a while Seychellois like myself living abroad thought that perhaps the inquiry would provide the opportunity for the world to learn about the internal turmoil. I know that several persons wrote letters to explain just that. Among them, for example, was Carlette Tall, the common-law wife of Hassan Ali who had been made to 'disappear'. It is sad testimony to the efficiency of the UN that her letter addressed to the Chairman of the Commission, Ambassador Carlos Ozores Typaldos of Panama (the man who later made so much noise against Britain over the Falklands issue), was returned a few days later, stamped with the remark 'Addressee unknown at the UN'. Further to the letters campaign, a few thousand dollars were raised for a group to fly to New York to address the Commission but all this was in vain. When the over 100-page report came out, there was not one mention of the state of repression prevailing within the islands. The Commission had adopted the view that the plight of the Seychellois people was not within its terms of reference.

Such an attitude, of course, did not take me by surprise. I had had my own experience with that body. In fact, during my lecture tour of the US a questioner had asked what I thought of the UN, and I had answered that it was 'the Hyde Park Corner of international politics'. By listening to some of the speeches delivered there, you realised what a sadly divided world we live in; by studying the background of some of the characters who are entitled to speak there, you understand why the world is in such a mess. Even the present Secretary-General, Javier Perez de Cuellar, does not think much of the organisation he represents. In his first yearly account of his job he described the body as 'a lame duck, powerless to stop wars, defied and ignored by individual countries and internally split by super-power rivalry'. And had it not been for a US veto, left to the Third World, the Secretary-General today would not have been the Peruvian bureaucrat, but Ambassador Salim Ahmed Salim of Tanzania, who put countless pressures on the UK to grant Seychelles independence whilst the government he represents was secretly training guerrillas to wreck that very independence within less than a year after it had been granted!

Chapter Twenty-one

Over the last two years the name Diego Garcia has suddenly come on the map and is likely to remain a subject of controversy for many years to come. It is on this archipelago, which lies about 600 miles east of the Seychelles, that the US has built what, according to Admiral Zumwalt, former chief of the US Navy, constitutes the largest and costliest naval theatre since Pearl Harbor. The archipelago has been turned into a vital US strategic base, capable of accommodating B52 strategic bombers, in an eleventh hour attempt to counter-balance the rapid penetration and presence of the Soviet Union in the zone. The point is that today in the sea of this area runs the world's most important oil route. Thirty per cent of the oil consumed by the United States, 60 per cent of that of Europe and 90 per cent of that of Japan is carried through here by super-tankers every day.

Once upon a time this whole area was a 'western' lake, under the control and influence of the British and the French, who had bases in Aden (now South Yemen), in Mombasa (Kenya), on the island of Gan in the Maldives, in Trincomalee in Ceylon (now Sri Lanka), Djibouti in the Horn of Africa and in Madagascar, astride the Mozambique Channel. However, through the process of decolonisation and the ludicrous British decision to pull out East of Suez, it soon became obvious that the Soviet Union would lose no time to fill the vacuum. Until 1967 there were no Soviet naval vessels in the Indian Ocean, but by the end of 1968 a small permanent presence had been established. Today they have untold numbers of warships operating the naval bases in South Yemen, in the Dahlak archipelago in Ethiopia, as well as anchorage facilities in Mozambique, Madagascar, Mauritius and Seychelles.

Yet if US military strategists had their choice, the US naval base would have been situated in the Seychelles, which is spread over 200,000 square miles of ocean. These islands, although small, are solid specks, most of which have the potential of being turned into stationary 'aircraft carriers'. The original idea was for a base on the island of Aldabra, which is considered the most strategically placed in the zone, closer to the Horn of Africa. However, the British and the Americans had to shift further eastwards to Diego Garcia following intense pressure from the conservationists in Britain and the USA, who wanted at all costs to preserve the quality of life of the booby birds and the giant tortoises, who are the sole inhabitants of this forgotten atoll.

So where the birds and tortoises have won, men, women and children have been made to suffer. One thousand two hundred Creole labourers lived in Diego Garcia in the Chagos archipelago. While many in Europe and elsewhere would have regarded them as 'poor', enlightened minds would have envied the quality of life which prevailed. The weather was good, the atmosphere free of pollution and, with an abundance of sea food, there was certainly no-one dying of hunger. Today if you want to see them you have to travel more than a thousand miles further south to Mauritius. For it is there that they were dumped in 1971, and it is from there that the problems and controversy starts.

Diego Garcia could have very well been another island in the Seychelles archipelago. Geographically it is much nearer to the Seychelles than to Mauritius and, as an archipelago, its physical features represent a natural extension of the other coral islands of the Seychelles group. However, for some unknown reason, when the Seychelles was made a crown colony separate from Mauritius in 1903, Diego Garcia was left arbitrarily linked to Mauritius. But the Chagos-Agalega Company, which had secured a long lease for the commercial exploitation of the islands, was headquartered and managed from Seychelles. There were no original inhabitants on the Chagos and ironically the labourers who went to work there were more identical to the sea-faring Creoles of Seychelles than the Indians which predominate in Mauritius. For these reasons, the government of Sir Seewoosagur Ramgoolam did not have much hesitation, on the eve of Mauritius' independence, to sell the island's sovereignty to the British for £3 million. Sadly, though, the British and American administrations were more interested in the acquisition of a piece of 'strategic territory' than in the welfare of the people who lived there. Instead of being given an alternative home somewhere in the United Kingdom or in the USA, they were sent to an overcrowded Mauritius, where nearly one million people have to survive on a sugar economy which is devastated every three or four years by vicious cyclones. True, the British Government, in association with the US, paid £1 million for the settlement of these people, but the Mauritius Government had more pressing priorities for the money. The outcome was, of course, a godsend for the propaganda machinery of the pro-Soviet Marxist Mouvement Militant Mauricien (MMM), Paul Berenger.

Berenger had been trying for years to win power in Mauritius. Backed by finances from the Soviet bloc and from Colonel Gaddafi of Libya, the MMM had a similar beginning to René's SPUP. There was no way the MMM could stage a coup in Mauritius for there politics run on a communal basis and the MMM was identified with the minority Creoles, whereas the majority in Mauritius were Hindu-Indians. However, the Diego Garcia controversy was to provide him with a base for an appeal which transcended the communal divisions. With Indira Gandhi's India taking a pro-Soviet leaning, Berenger's MMM won sympathy when it came forward with the concept of Indian Ocean – zone of peace, which finally grouped together the communist parties of the Seychelles, Madagascar, Mauritius, Réunion and Comoros, under the label of 'Progressive Movements of the Indian Ocean'.

Whilst on the surface the concept of 'zone of peace' was explained as a necessity to avoid a super-power confrontation, in practice it became obvious that the group's main purpose was to denounce the US presence in Diego Garcia and to demand the dismantling of the base. Since the coup in Seychelles which overthrew me, René has hosted two conferences of the group, in 1978 and 1979, to which were also invited participants from Libya, Algeria, Angola, Benin, Cape Verde, Congo, Guinea, Guinea-Bissau, Mali, Mozambique, São Tomé and Príncipe and Tanzania. At both meetings US 'imperialism' was constantly attacked. There was no criticism of the Russian build-up in the area, no support for the idea of a balanced presence. It was obvious that the group is a Soviet front organisation, dedicated to bring this strategic area under total Soviet control and influence.

For the West things could not have developed in a worse way. Soon the Shah, who had been encouraged by Washington to build a large navy, to help counter-balance the growing Soviet power in the zone, was to fall, leaving an Iran in internal turmoil.

And, as if this was not enough of an advantage in the geopolitical chess game in the region, the Soviets had the ruthless audacity to invade Afganistan and establish another military presence only a few months later. Subsequently, making use of the plight of the Diego Garcia people, who had become destitute and poverty-stricken in the overcrowded slums of Mauritius, Berenger launched a vitriolic campaign against the United States, when posters like 'American Imperialists – Even your machine guns don't make us afraid' were prominently displayed all over the island. Uncle Sam was again portrayed as the villain among the two big powers. Meanwhile, Washington rushed to the assistance of the ageing Ramgoolam and, together with the British, offered another £4 million to help the displaced islanders. It was a case of too much too late. The damage had already been done. Berenger had convinced the people of the evils of 'American imperialism'. 'Diego Garcia was bought under duress. Diego Garcia must be returned to Mauritius,' he shouted. And on this policy he was swept to power.

The allegation that Diego Garcia was bought 'under duress' raises an interesting point in international relationships. Microstates cannot have their cake and eat it. If a tiny country accepts the privilege of sitting alongside the big powers at the UN with a vote which is as potent as any, then that country must be presumed equal enough to enter into a formal agreement with a bigger power. It would be all too easy to shout 'duress' ten years after the contract.

The problem with the western democracies is that they are all too ready to sacrifice what they preach as 'sacred principles' for what they describe as 'the national interest'. This is clearly shown by the Seychelles experience. Although the British Government was a vital party to our constitutional agreement, just over a year after René had raped our constitution, Prime Minister James Callaghan was welcoming and feasting him in London – thereby compounding his treachery and condoning his treason.

And this attitude carried on when the Conservative Party got into office. Although it was then clear that René was ruling like a dictator – and with the help of Tanzanian soldiers suppressing our people – the Government kept providing British taxpayers' money to help him consolidate his position. Not one iota of the Falkland-Island-stand-on-principle approach for the unfortunate Seychellois people.

When Sir Frederic Bennett, MP, questioned what was happening, Richard Luce, MP, Parliamentary Under-Secretary of State in the Foreign and Commonwealth Office, wrote back to him on 6 March 1980:

> The Seychelles Government has been critical of the West and unhelpful to Britain on various matters ... I have no doubt that the Soviet Union would like to acquire naval facilities on the Seychelles; ...
> It is not clear how much René is prepared to respond to influence from ourselves or from the West in general. Meanwhile, we are very much aware of the strategic importance of the Seychelles in the Indian Ocean context. I hope to include a visit to Seychelles ... which would give me an opportunity to consider what more we might do to keep the Seychelles Government in line.

In line with whom? In line with the interests of the West – but not in line with the Seychelles people!

Similar attitudes have, of course, been adopted by France and the United States.

French President Valéry Giscard d'Estaing always wanted to become the 'man of Africa'. However, soon after assuming the presidency, he dismantled the Secretariat for African and Malagasy affairs which had proved an effective body during de Gaulle's time and beyond, under the competent management of Jacques Foccart. By appointing a single adviser to replace the Secretariat, Giscard demonstrated how much he personally wanted to administer this particular area of external affairs. His first appointment, René Journiac, was the official he sent to meet me in Paris when I went there with a request for help after the coup. Journiac lost his life in an aeroplane accident in February 1980 whilst on a diplomatic shuttle between Chad and Gabon.

Giscard's African policy to extend French influence and culture with all regimes in Africa, irrespective of political colour, saw him distancing himself from such traditional allies and men of principle like Houphouët-Boigny and Senghor. His term of office was characterised by military interventions in Chad, Zaire and Central Africa, by his meeting with Sekou Touré who had, over the years, forced millions of Guineans into exile and, finally, by the mistakes he made about Seychelles.

It was impossible to think that we were in the twentieth century and in the age of European unity, when France rushed to Seychelles, just after the coup, a load of technicians and advisers to replace the British officials whom René had arrested and kicked out of the country. As if this was not enough, France provided substantial aid to boost the illegal regime, including the gift of a patrol ship, *Topaz*. However, the French individuals who went to the islands were soon to realise that the Seychellois were unhappy, that human rights were being violated every day and that there was in fact no popular support for the regime. When they spoke their minds they were themselves arrested and kicked out of the country, accused by René of planning to overthrow him. From that moment there was a coolness in Franco-Seychelles relationships. But come the election of President Mitterand and the formation of a socialist-communist government, René was soon in Paris to conclude an agreement for assistance in the fields of defence and security, which meant the arrival in Seychelles of French military advisers to serve alongside the Tanzanians in the supreme task of keeping the Seychellois in bondage. In return for French military assistance, René allowed more regular visits of French warships in Port Victoria. When Mme May Moine, the Seychelles Chargé d'Affaires in Paris, who had resigned from her post following a revealing fact-finding mission to René's Seychelles, protested at this French intervention in the internal affairs of her country in favour of a regime with no respect for human rights, her French husband, Jacques Moine, an official at the Ministry of Defence in Paris, found himself arbitrarily suspended. His duty was deemed incompatible with the attitude of his Seychellois spouse. A similar attitude was also adopted in the case of a young Seychellois student who had been studying law in France for over two years as beneficiary of a French scholarship. One morning he was informed that his scholarship had been terminated at the request of the Seychelles Government because of his antipathy to René's politics. Strange as it may sound, it looked as if Port Victoria was now in the position of dictating to Paris.

While so vigorously denouncing developments in Poland, the United States have kept quiet about what is happening in Seychelles. The point is that, in Seychelles, the US tracking station is still very much in operation. The moral of our experience is that any dictator will be allowed to get away with the most blatant abuse of human rights if he is fortunate enough to have a US tracking station in his country and provided he is clever enough not to interfere with it. The hypocrisy and double standards behind Washington's silence finds its greatest manifestation in the noise the American Government recently made about developments in the island of Grenada where Prime Minister Bishop has imitated René almost point by point. The difference, of course, is that Grenada is close to Cuba, in an area which President Reagan described as 'our hemisphere'. It does not occur to the American leader that burdened with a sophisticated American tracking station and the huge naval base that is being built next-door, the Seychelles have become as much a part of the 'American hemisphere' as any other country.

The readiness of western leaders to sell their souls in order to gain temporary political advantages is most disturbing. Thus the vital questions of freedom, justice and human decency, on which depend the peace of the world and the consequent survival of the human race, are virtually being subordinated to a narrow interpretation of the 'national interest'. The truth, however, is that, in the long run, honesty remains the best policy. Enduring friendship between nations must include the people of these nations. And the people hate and seldom forgive the friends and accomplices of their oppressors.

Furthermore, the prevailing attitude is, in the long run, certainly not in the 'national interest' because it confuses the nation, diminishes the respect for the values the people were brought up to believe in and, in consequence, weakens the national resolve to remain great.

Those who are engaged in the Indian Ocean in promoting Soviet design must be recognised for who they are. It is no mere accident or coincidence that on 15 February 1980 a maritime agreement between the Soviet Union and the Seychelles was signed. It is no mere accident or coincidence that Seychelles twice hosted the anti-US 'zone of peace' conference. It is not just mere accident that a Marxist ideology is being imposed on the Seychellois people. It is no mere coincidence or accident that Tanzanian soldiers have been in Seychelles since 1977. It is no mere accident or coincidence that the Soviet Union has a larger diplomatic mission in Seychelles than in the UK. It is no mere accident or coincidence that the Soviets have a warship in Port Victoria harbour whenever René imposes a state of emergency to crack down on opposition. It is no mere accident or coincidence that the Seychelles team was one of the first to arrive in Moscow for the 1980 Olympics, but it made a point of boycotting the 1982 Commonwealth Games in Brisbane. It is no mere accident or coincidence that René flew all the way to Havana to cry, alongside Castro, 'Cuba si, Imperialism no!' Yet despite the West's systematic outcry about events in Poland and Afghanistan, there is not a word said about the anguish and terror under which the Seychellois people, who are friends of the West, are living today.

But time and tide waits for no man – and every dog has his day. Meanwhile, as this adaptation of Sir Walter Scott's verses on patriotism so emphatically puts it:

> Breathes there the man, with soul so dead
> Who never to himself hath said,
> This is my own, my native land!
> My own dear land where my footsteps wandered,
> Even to thee my heart still turns again.
> For thee my love grows ever fonder,
> Till in its might it is akin to pain,
> Ever to thee I'm bound by love and duty,
> No dearer land in all the earth
> By all sweet ties of home and love and beauty
> To thee I cleave, dear land that gave me birth.

Epilogue

Andraitz, Majorca: 17 August 1982

Catherine Olsen's house in this small town in a quiet part of Majorca was an ideal spot to work on this book. It has no telephone and no radio and for two weeks I had been putting the finishing touches to the manuscript. That day I had just finished lunch when the husband of the housekeeper ran up the garden path. He was very excited and told me in a mixture of Spanish and sign language that someone was on the telephone for me.

As I followed him through the town to his house, I was worried. I had left his number with my staff in London with strict instructions that it should be used only in emergencies. My brother Billy had been very ill and I prayed that the news would not be bad. I picked up the telephone. It was a reporter from a South African radio station telling me over a crackling line that sections of the Army were mutinying in Seychelles. The insurgents had taken over key installations and there were reports of heavy fighting. René, it seemed, was stuck on an outlying island and powerless to intervene.

No longer could I concentrate on the book. I went back to the house, feeling exhilarated, wanting to know all the details. Catherine's neighbours, the film director Dougie Hiscock and his wife Annabel, kept coming round every few minutes to tell me that reporters from Fleet Street and South Africa – from the press and television – had got hold of their number and wanted to talk to me. The peace was shattered and Annabel kindly invited me to work on her patio table, rather than run back and forward from villa to villa.

Throughout the day I learnt from the reporters more of what was happening. The attempted coup was the work of one of the four garrisons on the island. The first garrison is located in the mountains of Sans Souci where René lives. It is under Tanzanian control and its main objective is to guard the President. The second, on a hill overlooking Victoria, controls traffic and population movements between Victoria and René's home. The third is based at Union Vale in Victoria and controls the radio station, Cable and Wireless, the electricity power house and the harbour of Victoria, the only harbour on the island. The fourth garrison is based at Pointe Larue next to the airport and contains most of the Tanzanians.

It was the third garrison which had mutinied. Led by a group of sergeants and NCOs, the soldiers had taken over the key installations. Once they had been secured, one of the first actions taken was to play 'La Paloma Blanca' over Radio Seychelles – the first time my favourite song had been heard since René had banned it.

Each reporter had the same questions: what was behind the mutiny and was I involved? Throughout the day and night and all through the following day I gave the same answer. Such a mutiny had been on the cards for a long time. After the 1977 coup René had promoted the hooligans who had taken part to Army officers. Despite the fact that their only military background was a few weeks of guerrilla training in the Tanzanian bush, they held the ranks of major and colonel. In René's new society, these men had become the capitalists with privileges beyond those enjoyed by the ancient feudal lords of Europe. Meanwhile, with no other source of employment, the young Seychellois had been drafted into the Army and soon saw that the sergeants and NCOs were better educated and disciplined than the senior officers. The young men were idealists and they soon realised that René's promises could not be kept and that his society was corrupt. The result was inevitable. René was reaping what he had sown.

To the second part of the question, whether I was involved, the answer was no. The telephone call to my Spanish friend was the first I had heard of it.

Would I support the insurgents?

'I would give my blessing to any movement that would restore liberty to my country.' The question and answer were repeated time and again. No sooner did one call finish than the telephone rang again. Poor Dougie and Annabel got no peace and with each call it became obvious that the initial optimism was proving false. The insurgents were not experienced enough in the ways of the world nor ruthless enough to succeed. Instead of shooting their so-called superior officers, they locked them up in the prison which is situated near the radio station. One of the officers escaped and alerted the Tanzanians at Pointe Larue so that by the time the insurgents reached the airport, the Tanzanians were prepared. Instead of quietly repeating their peaceful take-over of the installations, they found themselves coming under heavy fire. From that moment they realised that they had little chance. Without control of the airport they were marooned.

However, they did not give way. Their spokesman announced on the radio that they were mutinying against their officers and demanded the resignation of the Defence Minister. It was obviously a ploy to entice René back to Mahé. In Mahé the people were restricted by a curfew by the insurgents but on the outlying islands there was jubilation. René's flag was lowered and burnt and the people sang 'La Paloma Blanca' with its defiant words: 'No one will take my freedom away'.

However, it was to be only a taste of freedom. René was calling for Tanzanian reinforcements to fly in and in desperation the insurgents sought help over the radio from Mrs Thatcher. Obviously they were impressed by the Iron Lady's role in the Falklands War, but in their case there was no response. They then turned to Kenya, little realising that that country had only the previous week put down an attempt by the Air Force to overthrow the government.

Again there was no response and, as a last resort, they called for South Africa to get rid of the Tanzanians. But even as they were doing so, the reinforcements were flying in. Before dawn on 18 August several hundred Tanzanians marched, heavily armed, towards Victoria for a savage and brutal confrontation with the Seychellois insurgents.

Whilst René spoke in terms of twelve people killed – the exact number will perhaps never be known – eye-witnesses spoke of the collection of over 100 bodies. Overnight Seychelles acquired its own collection of true martyrs. These people were not insurgents – they were liberators.

The task of all Seychellois living today must be to see to it that they did not die in vain and that some day a monument be erected in the heart of Victoria to their memory. When that day comes along we will all together again sing our cherished freedom song, 'La Paloma Blanca' without let or hindrance.

> When the sun shines on the mountains
> And the night is on the run
> It's a new day, it's a new way
> And I fly up to the sun
>
> Una paloma blanca
> I'm just a bird in the sky
> Una paloma blanca
> Over the mountains I fly
> No-one can take my freedom away

P.S. London, November, 1982

Sometimes I feel that my address and phone number have become too well known. People are constantly calling, phoning or writing, and always the subject is the same – home, Seychelles, my native land and the growing Russian interest – and what the West is doing about it.

I was packing my bags for a break in America where I feel more removed from the unhappiness. There at least the people I meet don't automatically jump on me to ask me what is going on, although at parties, when my identity becomes known, the same old story must be told if people are not to consider me rude.

As I packed, there was yet another call.

'Mr Mancham, I have got a painting for you. Are you going to be at home so that I can deliver it?'

I didn't know what the man was talking about. What painting? It turned out he was a picture framer and that some young Englishman had brought in a painting, asking him to frame it and send it to me. He did not remember the man's name but there was a letter with it.

An hour later Peter collected it – a water-colour of a Seychelles scene painted in 1937. The note was addressed in Lancashire and I recognised the name Tony Duckworth as a young man I had met on the islands who ran a boat hire business until he joined the other hundreds René had kicked out.

The note was short and to the point: 'This picture by Emile Hugon reminds me of Seychelles in happier times. My heart bleeds. Can nothing be done?'

A few days later I learnt about the death of a young Seychellois on an isolated beach in Mahé. According to the Seychelles

Government version he and a friend, who was said to have been a foreigner, were killed while trying to assemble a bomb. Scattered around their bodies were MPR leaflets.

A spokesman for the Movement in London, whilst agreeing that the two men were supporters of the MPR, stated that they were tortured and killed by Tanzanian troops before their bodies were burned. The young Seychellois was later identified as 24-year-old Simon Desnousse, well educated, from a good family background, who had played a prominent role in the anti-government demonstration when René had wanted to send children to an outlying island for political indoctrination.

So more tears for Seychelles as her drama continues and as another winter approaches for the sad victims of the raped paradise.

Index

Abdul Aziz, King, 189
Abse, Leo, 57
Agnelli, Giano, 11
Aleman, Karin and Miguel, 188
Ali, Hassan, 213, 220, 232
Ali, Muhammad, 223, 224
Allan, Sir Colin, 112-13, 117, 157
Allied Circle Education Trust, 36
American Society of Travel Agents, 123, 150
Amin, Idi, 13, 159-62, 167, 169, 200
Amoro Libero, 120
Amra, SS, 27
Angelin, the Revd, 57-8
Anguilla, 115
Annigoni, Pietro, 76
Ark Royal, HMS, 54
Armah, Kwasi, 33, 34
Aronda, SS, 24
Arteh, Foreign Affairs Minister, 184
Ashraf, Princess, 148
Asquith, Herbert, 64, 112
Associated Press, 56

Badrut, Andrea and Cappi, 183
Bandaranaike, Mrs Sirimavo, 181, 182
Bante, Taferi, 13, 191-2
Bassey, Shirley, 182, 183-4
Beatrix, Queen of the Netherlands, 94
Beck, Kevin, 229, 230
Bedier, Albert, 220
Behren, Baron von, 149, 203
Belafonte, Harry, 27, 55
Bennett, Sir Frederic, 238
Bentley, John, 185
Bentley, Sheherazade, 185

Berenger, Paul, 236, 237
Berlouis, Ogilvy, 208
Bernhard, Prince of the Netherlands, 94
Bhutto, President Ali, 182-3, 193
Biancolini, Countess Lamia, 128
Bischoff, Dr Heinrich, 196
Bisera, Olga, 120-1, 158
Bishop, Maurice, 240
Boehm, René, 207
Boissier, Gerard, 125-6
Bokassa, Jean-Bedel, 162-4, 165, 167
Bonaparte, Napoleon, 38
Bond, Karl i, 164-5
Bonnetard, Chief Justice Sir Nicholas Patrick France, QC, 43
Bossy, Chief Magistrate Eric, MBE, 75
Boumédienne, Colonel Houari, 81, 82, 84, 181-2
Boutlefika, Abdelaziz, 181
Braemar Castle, MV, 28, 30, 36
Britannia, HM Yacht, 105
Broot, Cassen, 94
Brugère, Alain, 201
Brynner, Yul, 94
Bunche, Ralph, 54
Butler, R. A., 60

Caillé, Robert, 178
Callaghan, James, 9, 14, 198, 237
Calypso, 26
Camille, Edi, 31, 125
Carter, Jimmy, 191, 192, 193, 194, 203
Castro, Fidel, 59, 215, 216, 240
Cath, Nancy, 140, 146
Catholic Relief Service Agency, 62

Central Intelligence Agency, 66, 151, 152, 190, 191, 192, 193, 203
Chagos-Agalega Company, 235
Chang Him, Davidson, 212
Chaplin, Charles, 96, 183
Charles, Prince of Wales, 146
Chassagne, Yvette, 201
Chetty, Chamery, 117, 118, 195, 220
Chiang Kai-shek, 165, 193
Chow, Paul, 220, 226, 227
Church, Senator, 190
Churchill, Winston Jnr, 227
Churchill, Winston S., 55, 105, 138
CIA, see Central Intelligence Agency
Commarmond, Gustave de, 48
Commonwealth Heads of Government Conference, 9, 10, 202
Cooke, Alistair, 158
Co-ordinating Committee for the Liberation of Africa, 167
Cousteau, Jacques Yves, 26, 93
Coward, Noël, 94, 183
Crawford, Robin, 26
Crawford, Sir Frederick, 26
Crossroads of Our Influence, The, 85

Dagama, Mr, 26
Daily Express, 121, 146, 158, 185
Daily Nation, 58
Daily Telegraph, 75
Dale, David, 199
Dawson, Major Geoffrey, 116
Delhomme, André, 57-8
Delhomme, Dr Hilda Stevenson, 74
Desnousse, Simon, 246
Deverell, Sir Colville Montgomery, 72, 73, 74
Dharboven, Adi, 196
Diouf, Abdou, 166, 167
D'Offay, Tony, 47, 48, 49, 50
Dolinchek, Martin, 230
Dorin, Bernard, 201
Douglas-Home, Sir Alec, 59, 60
Duckworth, Tony, 245
Dunn & Bradstreet, 86

Edinburgh, Prince Philip, Duke of, 36, 54, 55, 104, 105
Ekland, Britt, 95, 98, 104-5

Elizabeth II, Queen, 9, 54, 81, 98, 135, 137, 158, 202
Elliott, Captain, 109
Eskimo, HMS, 54
Esparon, Kerchan, 229-30
European Economic Community, 107-8, 206
Eustace, Father, 24-5
Evans, Heather, *see* Mancham, Heather
Evening Standard, 35

Fairbairn, Nicholas, 231-2
Fairbanks, Douglas Jnr, 158
Fallaci, Oriana, 121
Farah, Empress of Iran, 148
Far East Scientific Centre, 180
Farrow, Mia, 96
Felly, Roger, 202-3
Ferrari, Dr Maxime, 196-7, 201, 208
Figaro, Le, 214
Foccart, Jacques, 238
Fonda, Henry, 183
Ford, Gerald, 190
Fraser, Malcolm, 151
Frederick, Lynne, 96
French, W. & C. (now French Kier Ltd), 86
Frichot, Robert, 133
Fritz, Johan, 229, 230
Furness Withy, 86

Gadaffi, Colonel, 121, 164, 182, 185, 236
Gandhi, Mrs Indira, 54, 141-2, 144, 183, 223, 224, 236
Garba, Brigadier Joe, 202-3
Gaulle, General Charles de, 14, 37, 84, 85, 200, 238
Gaulle, Madame de, 85
Giscard d'Estaing, Valéry, 178, 182, 199, 200, 201, 238
Gloucester, Duke and Duchess of, 158
Gokal, Abbas K., 195, 196
Goldwater, Barry, 66
Goodbye Emanuelle, 178
Gowan, General, 159
Grandcourt, Frankie, 78
Granville, Keith, 104

250

Greatbatch, Sir Bruce, 87, 90, 94, 97, 98, 103, 104, 106, 107, 112
Greenam, Dennis, 14, 114-15, 116, 117, 131, 132, 135-6, 198, 199, 202
Greenwood, Anthony, 70, 72

H., Miss (teacher), 23, 24
Haase, Joachim, 106, 142
Hambros (merchant bankers), 106
Hardy, Thomas, 178
Harington, Sir John, 211
Harrison, George, 11, 95
Hart, Dame Judith, 138, 151
Hass, Hans, 93
Hassan, Sir Joshua, 76
Hefford, Colonel E. A., 152
Heintz, Carl and Eleanor, 46, 66
Heintz, Carl Jnr, 66
Hemmings, David, 94
High Wind in Jamaica, A, 185
Hiscock, Dougie and Annabel, 242, 243
Hoare, Mike, 225-6, 228, 229, 230
Hoareau, Félix, 213
Hoareau, Gerard, 220, 226-7, 228
Hoareau, Michel, 25-6
Hodoul, Jacques, 208
Honey, Sir De S. M. G., 23
Hook, Chief Police Officer, 63, 70
Hoover, Herbert, 46
Hope, Bob, 66
Houlder, John, 86
Houlder Brothers, 86
Houphouët-Boigny, Felix, 165-6, 167, 238
Hoveyda, Amir Abbas, 149
Hubbard, Ron, 146
Hughes, Thomas, 75
Hugon, Emile, 245
Hunnicutt, Gayle, 94
Hussein, King of Jordan, 121, 185, 193

International Labour Organisation, 78, 106
International Planned Parenthood Federation, 57
Iran, Shah of, 148, 203, 236
Isabelle, 68-70

Isola, Peter, 76

Janet, 187
Jawara, President Sir Dauda, 166
Johns, Vera, 172
Johnson, Lyndon, 39, 126
Joseph, Mr, 45
Jouanneau, Police Officer, 209
Joubert, David, 53, 55-6, 59, 63, 70, 72, 80, 81, 82, 83, 84, 99, 105, 133
Journiac, René, 200-1, 238

Kallisto, 180
Kambona, Oscar, 168-9
Kampala, SS, 41, 76
Kane, Falilou, 111-12
Karanja, SS, 54, 76
Katzin, Kitt, 176, 177
Keedeck Lecture Bureau, 227
Kennedy, Edward, 145-7, 191
Kennedy, Jacqueline, 101
Kennedy, Joan, 145
Kennedy, John, 39, 40, 56, 67, 185, 191, 215
Kennedy, Robert, 145, 185
Kenyatta, Jomo, 12, 53, 99, 193
Kerr, Sir John, 135, 150
Kershaw, Anthony, 108
Kevan, David, 154
Khalid, King of Saudi Arabia, 128, 189
Khalidia (Khashoggi's yacht), 10, 128, 130
Khashoggi, Adnan, 9-10, 11, 125-30, 183, 189, 196, 199-200, 222
Khashoggi, Dr Mohamed M., 129
Khashoggi, Essam, 129
Khashoggi, Soraya, 183-4
Kilief, Peter, 28-9
King, Martin Luther, 185
King, Rex, 77
Kinski, Klaus, 179
Kinski, Natasha, 178-9
Koester, Dr Heintz, 196
Komlosy, Denis, 87
Kopechne, Mary Jo, 145-6
Korkorian, Kirk, 11
Kristel, Sylvia, 178

Lachman, Charles, 189

Laker, Sir Freddie, 123
Lee, Christopher, 212
Lee Kuan Yew, 142-3, 202
Legum, Colin, 85
Leighton, Sara, 76-7
Lerner, Alan Jay, 100
Lestor, Joan, 131-2, 133, 136
Lichfield, Patrick, Earl of, 105
'Lifestyle' (BBC documentary), 123, 125
Lindblad, Lars Eric, 87, 94, 219
Lindblad Explorer, 87, 219
Lipkowski, Jean de, 178
Llewellyn, Roddy, 98
Loizeau, Philibert, 58-9, 75, 208
Loren, Sophia, 96
Lousteau-Lalanne, Bernard, 196
Lousteau-Lalanne, Debby, 196-7
Luce, Richard, 238
Luyt, Louis, 176

Machel, Samora, 82
McKenzie, Bruce, 12, 13, 196
MacLeish, Archibald, 67
Macmillan, Harold, 34-5
Makarios, Archbishop, 26-7, 56, 96
Malan, Daniel, 170
Malatesta, Peter, 66
Mancham, Anne-Marie (sister), 20
Mancham, Caroline (daughter), 122
Mancham, Evelyn (mother), 19-20, 25, 46, 158
Mancham, Francis ('Babi'; brother), 20
Mancham, Frank (brother), 20, 171
Mancham, Heather (née Evans: wife), 36, 45-6, 53, 54, 55, 96, 100, 119, 120, 120-1
Mancham, James R.
 birth, 19
 childhood, 19-27
 education: primary, 22-5; secondary, 26-7; in law, 27-39; political, 33-6
 as lawyer, 43-7
 marriage, 46, 121-2; see also Mancham, Heather
 meetings: with African leaders, 159-69, 173-8; with celebrities, 94-9, 101-2; with de Gaulle, 84-5;
 with Mrs Gandhi, 141; with Pope Paul V I, 78-9; with Queen, 104-5; with Trudeau, 124-5
 parents, *see* Mancham, Evelyn; Mancham, Richard
 as playboy, 68-9, 76-7, 96-100, 101-2, 119-22, 140-1, 144-6, 178-9, 182-5, 187-9, 210
 politics, entry into, 34-6, 47-8
 and Seychelles: airport project, 86-7, 88-9, 92-3; conservation, 94; creation of Democratic Party (SDP), 53, 55; creation of News Service, 56; election campaigns, 73-4, 90, 117-18; as Chief Minister, 90-134; as exile, 198-246; Independence, 157-9 (moves towards, 88-157); joins UN, 182, 186; made KBE, 158; as President, 158-97; as Prime Minister, 134-58; publishes *Weekly*, 53; and René's coup, 198-246; and Hoare's counter-coup attempt, 222-33; *see also* René, Albert; and SPUP, *see* Seychelles People's United Party; strikes, 105-7; tourism development, 93, 103-4; views on Seychelles' present and future, 234-46
Mancham, Michael (brother), 20, 73, 171, 212
Mancham, Philip (half-brother), 20
Mancham, Richard (father), 19, 22, 25, 27, 34, 37, 40, 41, 50, 56, 57-8, 80-1, 170-1
Mancham, Richard Jnr (son), 122, 194
Mancham, Thomas ('Billy'; brother), 20, 25, 32, 227, 242
Manchester, University of, 33, 36
Mao Tse-tung, 186
Mapinduzi, 208
Maradan, Monseigneur Oliver, 34
Marcos, Ferdinand, 144
Margaret, Princess, 97-8
Marine Nature Park Commission, 93
Marshall Vorishilov, 218
Marx, Karl, 214
Mather, Carol, 203-4
Matson, Greg, 12
Maugham, Somerset, 183

Mauricien, Le, 216
Mauritius Marxist Movement (MMM), 236
Mazerieux, Major Ernest de Coulhac, 48
Mengistu, Haile Mariam, 192
Messmer, Pierre, 108
Meurer, Stephanie, 150
Michel, James, 208
Middle Temple, 27, 31, 32, 35, 59, 67
Millionairess, The, 96
Minnelli, Liza, 96
Minoufe, Princess, 149
Mitterand, François, 239
Mobutu Sésé Séko, President, 164-5
Mohammed, Bill, 220
Moine, Jacques, 239
Moine, May, 201-2, 239
Mondon, Philip, 121
Montini, Giovanni Battista, *see* Paul VI, Pope
Moreau, Vicomte de Séchelles, 22
Morgan, Gilbert, 193
Mott, Duogy, 116
Mouvement pour la Résistance, 226, 245
Moye, Guy Ali, 36
Mozambique Liberation Movement, 82
Mulder, Dr Connie, 173-4, 175
Mungai, Dr, 98-9
Myth and Reality of Operation Bokassa, The, 163

Nassau Bay, 92
Nasser, G. A., 30
Nation, 152
Needham, Jack, 146
Negritude (Senghor), 166
Nehru, Jawaharlal, 54, 141
New Life, 217
Newsweek, 123, 140, 145
Nixon, Richard, 153, 159
Nkomo, Joshua, 82
Nkrumah, Kwame, 33, 34
Norbert, Rev. Brother, 23
Norman-Walker, Sir Hugh, 84-5, 112
Numeiry, President of Sudan, 162
Nyerere, Julius, 12, 80, 99, 159, 160, 167-9, 199

OAU, *see* Organisation of African Unity
Oberfeld, Vicky and Oscar, 188
Obote, Dr A. Milton, 55, 161
Obote, Mrs Milton, 55
O'Brien, Dennis, 95
Observer, the, 85
OCAM, *see* Organisation Commune Africaine et Mauritian
O'Donnell, Brother Austin, 27
Ojukwu, General, 165
Olsen, Catherine, 219, 242
OPEC, *see* Organisation of Petroleum Exporting Countries
Organisation of African Unity, 11, 55, 80, 82, 83, 91, 98-9, 110, 159, 165, 166, 167, 170, 173, 174, 175, 181, 184
Organisation Commune Africaine et Mauritian (OCAM), 111-12, 163, 192
Organisation of Petroleum Exporting Countries, 201
Osman, Governor (of Mauritius), 141
Oxford and Asquith, Earl of, 46, 47, 53, 57, 60, 61, 64-5, 84, 112
Owen, Dr David, 220

Paglia, Bruno and Kika, 188
Pan Am, 61
Paris, University of, 37
Park Chung Hee, President, 143-4
Parkinson, Norman, 96
Paul, Bishop Felix, 204-6, 220
Paul VI, Pope, 78-9
Payet, Daniel, 214
Payet, Harry, 63
Payet, Peter, 223, 224, 245
People, the, 62, 103, 152, 174, 193
Perez de Cuellar, Javier, 233
Pertini, President of Italy, 121
Peterson, Dr Roger Tory, 94
Philco Ford Corporation, 61
Phillips, Davina, 119-20
Phillips, Leonard, 119-20
Piaf, Edith, 206
Pillay, Vincent, 229
Pirate, The (Robbins), 9
Planters Association, 35, 36, 48
Polanski, Roman, 178-9

Pompidou, Georges, 199
Pool, Guy, 103-4
Portenova, Baron Enrico and Sandra di, 188
Pothin, Serge, 63
Praslin, the Marquis de Choiseul, 201, 202
Progressive Movements of the Indian Ocean, 236

Quant, Mary, 123
Quarry, Miranda, 96
Quinn, Anthony, 185

Rachel, Francis, 209
Radio Seychelles, 106, 209, 216
Radziwill, Prince Stanislaw, 100
Radziwill, Princess Lee, 100
Ralph (Geva René's brother), 226
Ramgoolam, Sir Seewoosagur, 80, 141, 202, 235, 237
Ramphal, Shridath, 202
Rankin Kuhn (travel company), 154
Rassool, George, 31, 125, 204
Ravenstein, Plonja Van, 96-7
Rawlings, Flt Lt Jerry, 202-3
Raymond, Paul, 123
Rea, David, 107
Reagan, Ronald, 240
Reflections and Echoes from Seychelles (Mancham), 124
René, France Albert, 11-13, 15, 58-9, 60, 62, 63, 64, 68, 70, 72, 73-4, 75, 79, 80, 82, 87, 90, 91, 92, 97, 103-4, 105-6, 110, 111, 116, 118, 131, 132, 133, 134, 135, 137, 139, 140, 148, 152, 157, 158, 159, 166, 169, 174, 175, 176, 187, 190, 194, 196, 197, 198, 200, 201, 203-18 *passim*, 219-27 *passim*, 231, 236-40, 242-6; open letter to, 210-11
René, Francis, 194
René, Geva, 176, 190, 194, 196, 197, 201, 215, 226
René, Margaret, 175
Reuters, 56, 218
Rhee, Syngman, 143, 193
Rhoodie, Dr Eschel, 173, 174-7
Rhoodie, Mrs Eschel, 176

Richmond, Fiona, 158
Rippon, Geoffrey, 108
Robbins, Harold, 9, 128
Rochambeau, la Comtesse Jacqueline de, 189
Roistsch, Ursula, 125, 126, 128
Roselie, Finley, 74-5
Rossi, Count Theo, 183
Rousset-Rouard, Yves, 178
Rowan, Charles, 39
Rowlands, Ted, 136-7
Royal Navy, 157
Rusk, Dean, 67

Sachs, Gunther, 11
Sadat, President Anwar, 121, 161, 216
St Ange, Karl, 110
St Kitts-Nevis, 115
Salim, Salim Ahmed, 91, 233
Sandys, Duncan, 54, 55
Sandys, Miss, 55
Sartre, Jean-Paul, 37, 38
Scott, Sir Peter, 94
Scott, Sir Walter, 241
SDP, *see* Seychelles Democratic Party
Seaton, Earl, 231
Selassie, Haile, 13, 159, 191
Sellers, Peter, 11, 95-6
Selwyn-Clarke, Sir Selwyn, 23, 35
Senghor, Leopold Sedar, 166, 167, 238
Servina, Mathew, 208
Seychelles, Bishop of, 78, 79
Seychelles Club, 70
Seychelles College, 22
Seychelles Democratic Party, 53, 55, 60, 63, 64, 65, 70, 72, 75, 80, 81, 90, 103, 109, 110, 117, 118, 133, 135, 137, 167, 175, 212, 213
Seychelles Development Corporation, 77
Seychelles Liberation Movement, 81, 100, 110, 117
Seychelles News Service, 56
Seychelles People's United Party, 58, 63, 64, 70, 72-3, 74-5, 80, 82, 87, 90, 91-2, 98, 103, 105, 110, 117, 118, 120, 133, 137, 152, 175, 193, 208, 209, 221, 236
Seychelles: Political Castaways (Christopher Lee), 212

Seychelles Radio, 106, 209, 216
Seychelles Taxpayers and Producers Association, 47, 48
Seychelles Weekly, the, 53, 55, 56, 63, 70, 75, 76, 79, 152, 174, 175, 220
Seychellois, the, 35, 36, 48, 53
Shaheen, Bob, 126
Sharam Pahlavi Ria, Prince, 148, 149, 203, 211
Shell Oil, 57
Shepherd, Lord, 89-90, 158
Silent World, The, 26
Sinatra, Frank, 66
Sinon, Guy, 175, 208
Smith, Ian, 26, 48, 80, 110, 111
Smith, Stephen, 146
Smuts, General Jan, 170
Snowdon, Lord, 97-8
Sorensen, Theodore, 191
Southwark, Bishop of, 35
SPUP, *see* Seychelles People's United Party
SSU Calling, 36
Stern, 92
Stevenson, Adlai, 67
Stonik, Dr Valentin, 180
Stravens, Joseph, 53
Sukarno, Dewi, 183
Summit Conferences of Non-aligned Countries, 181-2, 215-16
Sunday Express (Johannesburg), 176, 177
Sweet-Escott, Sir Bickham, 23

Talal, Prince of Saudi Arabia, 11, 180-90, 193
Tall, Carlette, 220
Telli, Diallo, 82
Tess (Polanski), 178
Tess of the D'Urbevilles (Hardy), 178
Thatcher, Margaret, 185, 244
Thorpe, Sir John, 34, 56
Time, 145
Times, The, 204, 219, 231
Tito, Josip Broz, 121, 182
Tolbert, Fox, 115-17
Topaz, 239
To the Point International, 170
Touré, Sekou, 238
Touze, Raphael, 107-8

Tower, Senator John, 66
Triad Corporation, 125, 126, 128, 129 Centre, 128-30
Trinacra Films, 178
Trudeau, Justin, 124, 125
Trudeau, Margaret, 124-5
Trudeau, Pierre, 124-5, 202
Tshombe, Moise, 84
Turner, Admiral Stanville, 192
Twistleton-Fiennes, Lt Col. the Hon. Sir E. E., 23
Twistleton-Fiennes, Sir Ranulph, 23
Typaldos, Carlos Ozores, 232

Underwood, Harold, 63
United Nations
    Educational, Scientific and Cultural Organisation (UNESCO), 188
    Organisation, 54, 58, 91, 109, 110, 111, 113, 143, 182, 185, 186, 187, 188, 193, 232-3, 237; Centre for Economic and Social Information, 93

Ventura, Vivianne, 182, 184-5
Veranjo, Carlos, 149
Verlaque, Bernard, 218, 226
Villiers, Mr and Mrs Les de, 176
Vladi, Farhad, 207
Vogel, Robert, 196
Vogue (British), 96
Vogue (French), 128, 178, 179, 206
Vorster, Balthazar Johannes, 177

Wachtmeister, Titi, 95-6
Wagner, Helga von Mayerhoff, 140-1, 142, 143, 144, 145-7, 158
Wagner, Robert, 145
Wanderlure, 66
Wand-Tetley, Peter, 87
Washington Post, 193
Watson, Paul, 125, 127
Waugh, Evelyn, 47
Webb, Mr and Mrs Derrick, 67
Weekend Life, 215, 218
Whitlam, Gough, 135, 150-1
Whitlock, William, 89
Wild Geese, The, 225
William Hickey column (*Daily Express*), 121, 146, 185

Williams, Mennen, 67-8
Wilson, Harold, 119
Wilson's College, 31
Wontner, Sir Hugh, 37
Wordsworth, William, 5
World Travel Conference, 188
World Wildlife Fund, 94
Wright, M. D. J., 201

Yang, H. K., 153
Ying, Ho, 54, 55
Young, Andrew, 193

Zanzibar, Sultan of, 54, 55
Zimbabwe African People's Union, 82
Zumwalt, Admiral, 227, 234

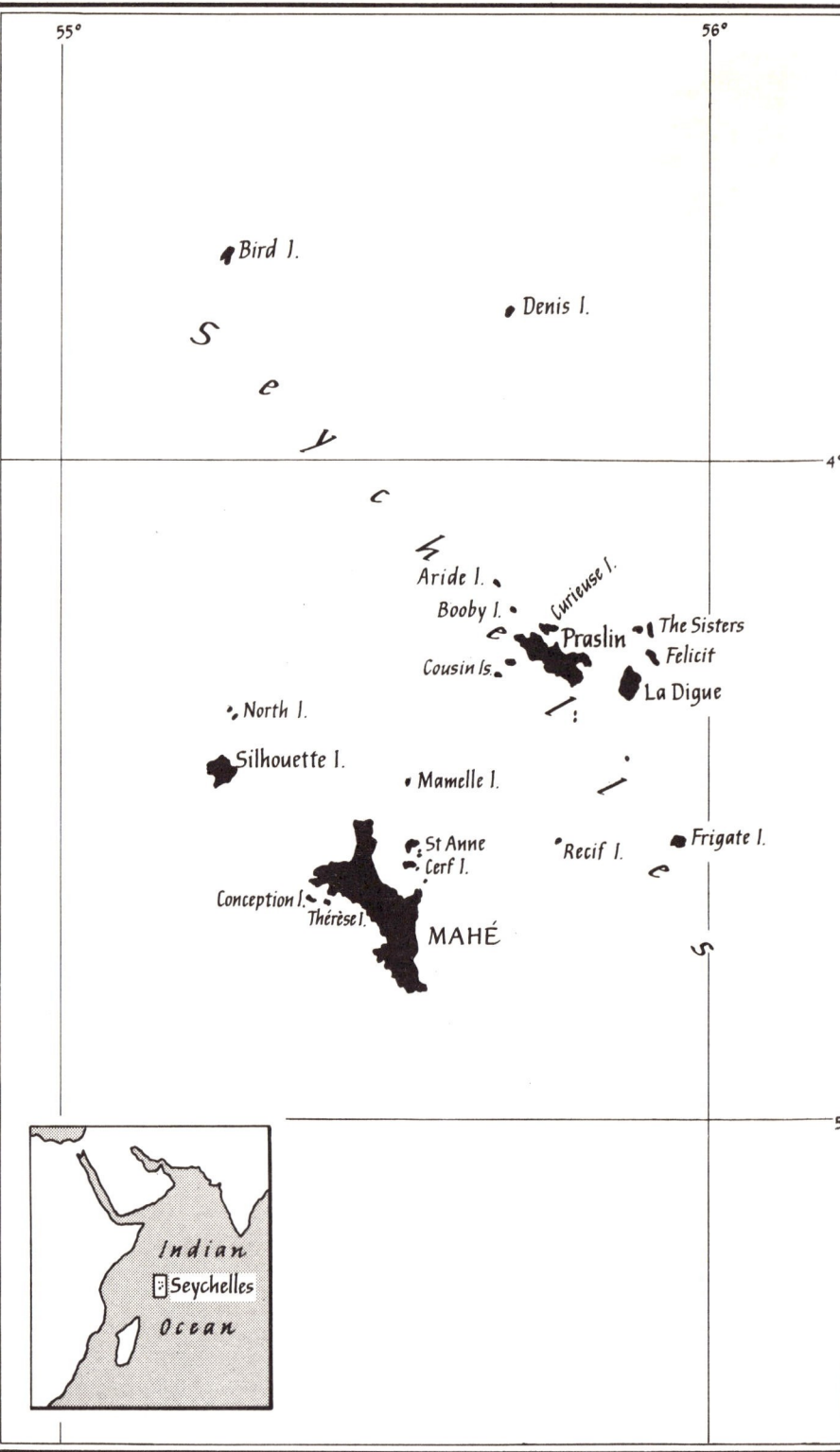